# Mastering XenApp®

Master the skills required to implement Citrix XenApp® 7.6 to deploy a complete Citrix®-hosted application from scratch

**Sunny Jha**

BIRMINGHAM - MUMBAI

# Mastering XenApp®



First published: December 2015

Production reference: 1041215

Published by Packt Publishing Ltd.
Livery Place
35 Livery Street
Birmingham B3 2PB, UK.

ISBN 978-1-78528-486-1

www.packtpub.com

# Notice



Some of the images in the chapters are taken from the Citrix® website and documentation.

# Credits

**Author**
Sunny Jha

**Reviewer**
Akshay Poddar

**Commissioning Editor**
Veena Pagare

**Acquisition Editor**
Kevin Colaco

**Content Development Editor**
Adrian Raposo

**Technical Editor**
Jayesh Sonawane

**Copy Editor**
Swati Priya

**Project Coordinator**
Sanchita Mandal

**Proofreader**
Safis Editing

**Indexer**
Hemangini Bari

**Graphics**
Jason Monteiro

**Production Coordinator**
Conidon Miranda

**Cover Work**
Conidon Miranda

# About the Author

**Sunny Jha** is a subject matter expert who specializes in Citrix® and virtualization with an experience of 5 years. He has a passion for learning and exploring new technologies, with Citrix® being his favorite. He started with supporting and then implementing solutions for enterprises using Citrix® and Windows.

He worked as a consultant and subject matter expert in medium-to-large Citrix® projects remotely from India with the projects' locations being the U.S., UK, and Australia. He currently lives in Delhi.

Special thanks goes to my mom and dad for supporting me during the writing of this book. Also, I'd like to thank my colleagues for helping me understand the Citrix XenApp® concepts.

# About the Reviewer

**Akshay Poddar** has been working in the field of IT infrastructure for quite a long time, developing expertise in Citrix®, VMware, Windows, Linux, and web hosting. He has earned certifications and completed training in CCA-V, CCA-N, VCP 5, VCP-Cloud 5, MSCA, and CCNA, and is an expert in many technologies, whether it be IBM X series, HP, or Dell; Blade Centers, servers, or enterprise storage such as IBM v3700 or v70000; HP MSA series; Huawei Oceanstore Series. He is an expert in Citrix XenApp®, XenDesktop®, VMware ESX/ESXi, vCenter, Windows Server 2008/2012, Microsoft Active Directory, DNS, DHCP, and so on. He is also well-versed in backup solutions, such as Symantec Backup EXEC, VEEAM, and others.

After completing his BTech at the Rajasthan Technical University, Kota, he worked as a VMware and cloud computing trainer in Mumbai. He later moved to a core IT company, where he worked as a project engineer on many complex projects, including VMware SRM, DC-DR setup, Microsoft SCVMM, Citrix XenApp®, Citrix XenDesktop®, Citrix NetScaler®, networking, storage, SAN switch zoning, and others. He is currently working as a pre-sales and solution architect for one of the companies in Mumbai, India.

He has spent a lot of his time training people on Citrix®, VMware, and cloud computing (OpenStack), sharing his valuable experience with fresh talents in the field. He has also been a technical blogger (`http://www.v4virtual.com`) for many years.

---

I would like to thank my parents, family, and friends who have been a great encouragement. You have always supported me in every curve of life, and I just can't imagine what would I have done without you all.

---

# www.PacktPub.com

## Support files, eBooks, discount offers, and more

For support files and downloads related to your book, please visit `www.PacktPub.com`.

Did you know that Packt offers eBook versions of every book published, with PDF and ePub files available? You can upgrade to the eBook version at `www.PacktPub.com` and as a print book customer, you are entitled to a discount on the eBook copy. Get in touch with us at `service@packtpub.com` for more details.

At `www.PacktPub.com`, you can also read a collection of free technical articles, sign up for a range of free newsletters and receive exclusive discounts and offers on Packt books and eBooks.

`https://www2.packtpub.com/books/subscription/packtlib`

Do you need instant solutions to your IT questions? PacktLib is Packt's online digital book library. Here, you can search, access, and read Packt's entire library of books.

## Why subscribe?

- Fully searchable across every book published by Packt
- Copy and paste, print, and bookmark content
- On demand and accessible via a web browser

## Free access for Packt account holders

If you have an account with Packt at `www.PacktPub.com`, you can use this to access PacktLib today and view 9 entirely free books. Simply use your login credentials for immediate access.

## Instant updates on new Packt books

Get notified! Find out when new books are published by following `@PacktEnterprise` on Twitter or the *Packt Enterprise* Facebook page.

# Table of Contents

# Preface

Citrix XenApp® need no introduction as it is one of the leading software application virtualization solutions these days. The advantage of using Citrix XenApp® as a preferred virtualization solution has its own benefits; it enables users to connect to the enterprise application from anywhere and from any device, giving the look and feel of a locally installed application.

While it allows remote access to the users and workers, XenApp®, at the same time, also makes the connection, which is established, secure so that there is no risk to enterprise applications or enterprise data. This means it doesn't compromise corporate security.

We have drafted this book for administrators who want to upgrade their skills, right from administering Citrix XenApp® to implementing Citrix XenApp®. This book contains eight chapters that focuses on the step-by-step installation of the infrastructure components and Citrix® components, and explains how to make the infrastructure and the Citrix® components work together to deliver the effective solution for the application virtualization for Citrix®.

## What this book covers

*Chapter 1, Understanding the XenDesktop® and XenApp® Architecture*, contains an introduction to the FMA architecture. It explains the strength and uniqueness of the new architecture and the latest version, 7.6. It also deals with the types of edition available for Citrix XenApp® and XenDesktop®. It also covers the use cases of Citrix XenApp®.

*Chapter 2, Initiating the Hypervisor*, covers the step-by-step installation of Citrix XenServer®, which acts as a hypervisor solution for Citrix XenApp®. It also contains the steps for creating the storage solution for the POC lab, and explains how to create a virtual machine on Citrix XenServer®.

*Chapter 3, Setting Up the Infrastructure Components*, covers the step-by-step installation of the four different infrastructure components—domain controller, DHCP, certificate authority, and SQL database—which work with Citrix XenApp® to support the Citrix XenApp® features and functionality.

*Chapter 4, Setting Up the Citrix® Components*, is one of the very important chapters of this book. In this chapter, you will actually start preparing and installing the Citrix® infrastructure. It covers the step-by-step installation of the components, such as License Server, Delivery Controller, StoreFront™, and also other Citrix® components.

*Chapter 5, Setting Up the XenApp® Resources*, contains the steps to configure the components. It explains how to prepare the master virtual machine and the master image for the virtual machine. It also lets you create Machine Catalog and delivery groups.

*Chapter 6, Configuring Policies*, explains the policies that can be implemented in the Citrix XenApp® infrastructure. As an administrator, you must be aware of how useful and complex can group policies for Citrix XenApp® be.

*Chapter 7, Setting Up Citrix Provisioning Services™*, covers the step-by-step installation of Citrix Provisioning Services™. It also contains the steps to configure the provisioning with which you can stream the OS images to physical or virtual machines, making life easy for the administrator when it comes to managing the operating system with software and system updates.

*Chapter 8, Setting Up NetScaler®*, covers the steps to use NetScaler®, also known as Swiss Army knife by Citrix®. Except the gateway and load balancing solution, it can do lots of stuff. It also covers the method of importing and configuring VPX and setting the gateway for StoreFront™.

# What you need for this book

In order to make the most from this book, you need to have a POC lab system with hardware that has an 8 core processor (the processor should support virtualization), 32 GB memory, and 1 TB HDD.

When it comes to software, you need the following:

- VM Workstation 10
- Citrix XenServer® ISO Image
- Microsoft Windows 2012 R2 ISO Image
- Citrix XenApp® 7.6 ISO Image
- Citrix® Provisioning 7.6 ISO Image
- Citrix NetSclaer® 11.0 for XenServer®

# Who this book is for

This book is for those administrators who are currently managing an implemented environment, and want to learn how to deploy a Citrix-hosted virtualization solution for the application in a Windows Server 2012 R2 environment. A reasonable knowledge and understanding of the core XenApp elements and concepts used during the virtualization of the applications are assumed.

# Conventions

In this book, you will find a number of text styles that distinguish between different kinds of information. Here are some examples of these styles and an explanation of their meaning.

Code words in text, database table names, folder names, filenames, file extensions, pathnames, dummy URLs, user input, and Twitter handles are shown as follows: "You can name it `Mirror`"

**New terms** and **important words** are shown in bold. Words that you see on the screen, for example, in menus or dialog boxes, appear in the text like this: "Clicking the **Next** button moves you to the next screen."

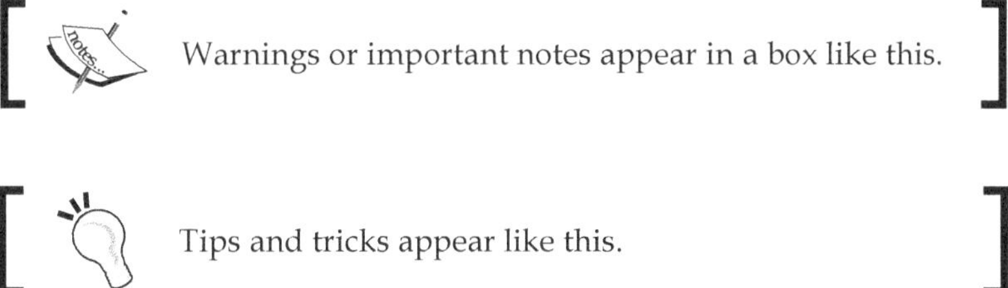

Warnings or important notes appear in a box like this.

Tips and tricks appear like this.

# Reader feedback

Feedback from our readers is always welcome. Let us know what you think about this book—what you liked or disliked. Reader feedback is important for us as it helps us develop titles that you will really get the most out of.

To send us general feedback, simply e-mail `feedback@packtpub.com`, and mention the book's title in the subject of your message.

If there is a topic that you have expertise in and you are interested in either writing or contributing to a book, see our author guide at `www.packtpub.com/authors`.

# Customer support

Now that you are the proud owner of a Packt book, we have a number of things to help you to get the most from your purchase.

## Downloading the color images of this book

We also provide you with a PDF file that has color images of the screenshots/diagrams used in this book. The color images will help you better understand the changes in the output. You can download this file from `http://www.packtpub.com/sites/default/files/downloads/MasteringXenApp_ColorImages.pdf`.

## Errata

Although we have taken every care to ensure the accuracy of our content, mistakes do happen. If you find a mistake in one of our books—maybe a mistake in the text or the code—we would be grateful if you could report this to us. By doing so, you can save other readers from frustration and help us improve subsequent versions of this book. If you find any errata, please report them by visiting `http://www.packtpub.com/submit-errata`, selecting your book, clicking on the **Errata Submission Form** link, and entering the details of your errata. Once your errata are verified, your submission will be accepted and the errata will be uploaded to our website or added to any list of existing errata under the Errata section of that title.

To view the previously submitted errata, go to `https://www.packtpub.com/books/content/support` and enter the name of the book in the search field. The required information will appear under the **Errata** section.

# Piracy

Piracy of copyrighted material on the Internet is an ongoing problem across all media. At Packt, we take the protection of our copyright and licenses very seriously. If you come across any illegal copies of our works in any form on the Internet, please provide us with the location address or website name immediately so that we can pursue a remedy.

Please contact us at `copyright@packtpub.com` with a link to the suspected pirated material.

We appreciate your help in protecting our authors and our ability to bring you valuable content.

# Questions

If you have a problem with any aspect of this book, you can contact us at `questions@packtpub.com`, and we will do our best to address the problem.

# 1

# Understanding the XenDesktop® and XenApp® Architecture

Citrix XenApp and XenDesktop is a unified solution for application and desktop virtualization that delivers the Windows-based application and desktop to any user, working from anywhere and any device. This unified technology is for any type of users, for example, task workers, knowledge workers, and mobile workers. This unified technology can deliver the application and desktop securely to individual while providing high-definition end user experience.

In this chapter, you will learn:

- The strength and uniqueness of XenApp and XenDesktop 7.6
- To identify the edition of XenApp and XenDesktop 7.6
- To explain the architecture of FlexCast
- To identify the use cases of XenApp and XenDesktop 7.6
- To identify the component required for implementation
- The high-level concepts of planning the deployment

# Core strength of XenApp® and XenDesktop® 7.6

The latest version of XenApp and XenDesktop 7.6 works on the FlexCast management architecture, which gives you the flexibility to deliver the virtualized solution of Windows application and desktop in a cost-effective way, enabling the organization for BYOD (Bring Your Own Device). With this version, organization can deliver highly available windows applications and desktop solutions, which are highly secure and can be accessed from anywhere. This version of XenApp and XenDesktop has the capability to meet the needs of today's modern workforce.

## Going mobile

Nowadays, use of tablet is increasing really fast, and tablet users expect to have the ability to be productive on their tablets when they are travelling or away from office. XenApp and XenDesktop 7.6 can deliver this seamlessly and in a secure way.

With the release of HTML5 support, users can use their applications on devices such as Chromebook and at the same time, Citrix Receiver is available for leading mobile OS such as Android and iOS, enabling them to work on the go.

## HDX™ user experience

HDX technologies enable the high-definition experience for users on any device, over any network using almost 90 percent less bandwidth than other competing solutions. HDX experience gives strong completion to the local PC experience, even when working on the multimedia apps, removable devices and 3D graphics. With the help of HDX, administrators can have high graphics-intensive applications such as Autodesk Maya, Adobe Photoshop, and others on server using the server-level graphics card such as NVIDIA GRID K1 and GRID K2.

## Cloud-ready

XenApp and XenDesktop 7.6, based on Citrix third generation FlexCast management architecture, is the only hybrid cloud-ready solution platform. With the help of this, we can publish the apps and share desktops on cloud solutions such as Apache CloudStack-based Citrix CloudPlatform or Amazon Web Services (AWS). With this, it makes life easier for the administrator to easily handle the XenApp environment expansion plan.

## Any Windows, web, or SaaS application

With this version, you can provide your workforce with any type of application they need, including Windows, web, and SaaS application. It delivers on demand application or desktop delivery solution that enables Windows application and desktop to be virtualized, centralized and managed in the datacenter and be instantly delivered as a service to users anywhere on any device. For web and SaaS application, the receiver seamlessly integrates them to a single interface, so end users only need to log on once for secure access to all their applications.

## Open, scalable, and proven

Based on number of use cases, industry validated that scalability of XenApp and other 10,000 Citrix-ready products, this version powerful unified application and desktop computing infrastructure that is easier than ever to manage. The open architecture works with your existing hypervisor, storage, operating system, application, directory, and system management infrastructure with complete integration and automation through comprehensive SDK.

# Different editions of XenApp® and XenDesktop®

Let's go through the types of edition, which are available with the latest version of Citrix XenApp and XenDesktop.

| XenApp 7.6 Edition | XenDesktop Edition |
|---|---|
| Citrix XenApp 7.6, Platinum Edition: Comprehensive enterprise-class, cloud-ready app virtualization solution with HDX technology, advanced management, monitoring, and security. | Citrix XenDesktop 7.6, Platinum Edition: Comprehensive enterprise-class, cloud-ready desktop virtualization solution with HDX technology, FlexCast delivery technology, advanced management, monitoring, and security. |
| Citrix XenApp 7.6, Enterprise Edition: Enterprise-class app virtualization solution with HDX technology that delivers a range of virtual app and remote access models for any device. | Citrix XenDesktop 7.6, Enterprise Edition: Enterprise-class desktop virtualization solution with HDX technology and FlexCast delivery technology that delivers a range of virtual app and desktop delivery models for any use case. |
| Citrix XenApp 7.6, Advanced Edition: High-performance app virtualization solution with Citrix HDX technology. | Citrix XenDesktop 7.6, VDI Edition: High-performance VDI solution for delivering virtual desktops with Citrix HDX technology. |

In addition, Citrix also offers the evaluation license—a simple, free download for up to 99 users for 90 days to enable organizations to test the concepts and get started easily.

# Licensing of XenApp®

Like the previous version of XenApp, this version also utilizes a concurrent licensing model. With the concurrent model, each concurrent user consumes a single license while accessing one or more application and/or XenApp published desktops. A licensed concurrent user is only licensed for the period during which the access to the Citrix environment is required. Once access is terminated by the user, the license returns to the license pool and becomes available for other users to consume.

# Licensing of XenDesktop®

XenDesktop licensing offers a flexible user/device license model that aligns with enterprise-wide desktop usage and underlying Microsoft desktop virtualization licensing and concurrent licensing for customers, with users needing only occasional access to virtual desktops and apps.

User licensing gives users access to their virtual application and desktop from unlimited devices, and device licenses gives an unlimited number of user access to their virtual desktop and apps from a single device.

# FlexCast® architecture

Citrix unified the application virtualization and desktop virtualization with the help of FlexCast architecture (FMA). With this architecture, XenApp and XenDesktop can meet all the requirement of application and desktop virtualization with its unique Citrix FlexCast delivery. With this delivery, technology IT organizations can deliver apps and desktops to any user on any device. They can also do a number of customizations to meet the performance, security, and flexibility requirements for best user experience.

# Use cases

With the unified architecture, we can now deliver server-based computing with the help of XenApp and virtual desktop integration with XenDesktop.

| | Hosted on Server | Hosted on Desktop |
|---|---|---|
| Delivered as Desktop | x | x |
| Delivered as Application | x | x |

Now we can deliver the application and desktop on the preceding use cases, and with this, IT can provide each type of user with the virtual computing environment suited to their need while optimizing the security, performance, personalization, and cost.

In the modern world, we have different kinds of users.

# Task worker

Task workers perform a set of well-defined tasks. They access a set of applications and have limited requirements of their PCs. However, since these workers are interacting with your clients, partners, and employees, they have their critical data. FlexCast architecture enables IT to provide shared desktop and application hosted on the server or desktop to task workers while keeping their data secure.

# Knowledge workers

While traditional office workers perform their duties in office only, today's knowledge workers don't just work in the office; all day, they attend meetings and visit different branch offices, and they also work from home. These workers expect access to all of their corporate applications and data wherever they are. FlexCast enables these users to work seamlessly, moving among their various physical environments.

# Mobile worker

Mobile workers need access to their virtual desktop from anywhere, regardless of their ability to connect to a network. In addition, these workers expect the ability to personalize their PCs by installing their own application and storing their own data. FlexCast allows the users to retain control over their personal computing environment while allowing IT to control the corporate computing environment.

## Shared workstation

Maintaining even the most state of the art university and business computer lab, conference room, or training centers has its own challenges. The primary challenge is the constant requirement of re-provision of desktops with the latest operating systems and applications as the needs of your organization change. FlexCast provides the tools for the provision of a new environment from a single, easily-managed image.

For detailed feature and use cases, you may visit `https://www.citrix.com/go/products/xendesktop/feature-matrix.html` XenDesktop 7.6 and XenApp 7.6 Features and Entitlements.

## Standard deployment Citrix® Component

In the standard XenApp and XenDesktop infrastructure, Citrix components are positioned as shown in the following image:

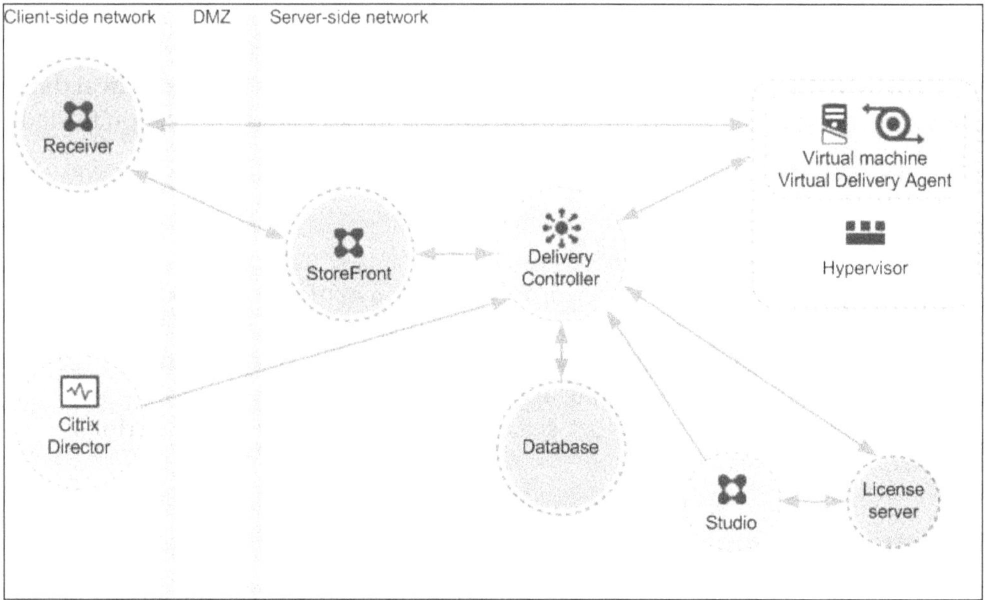

# Citrix® components

The following are the components of Citrix:

- Citrix Receiver
- Citrix Director
- StoreFront
- Citrix Delivery Controller
- Citrix Studio

## Citrix Receiver™

Citrix Receiver is an easy-to-install client software that provides access to your XenDesktop and XenApp installations. This is a mandatory client which has to be installed on the user's device to establish the connection with the XenApp environment. Citrix also releases support for the user device on which users don't have permission to install the Citrix Receiver; in those cases, user can access the resources from the HTML5-supported browser.

## Citrix® Director

Citrix Director provides a detailed and intuitive overview of XenDesktop environments. It enables support and helpdesk teams to quickly and seamlessly perform crucial support tasks for their end users while, at the same time, monitoring and troubleshooting system issues before they become system-critical.

## StoreFront™

StoreFront provides a unified interface for XenApp, XenDesktop, and VDI-in-a-Box to deliver the resource, either via web or receiver to the users. It also allows users to connect from anywhere and any device.

Most of you are already aware that Citrix announced the end of life for the Citrix web interface on August 24, 2016, but you can still use the web interface. If you have the software maintenance or subscription advantage programs, then the EOL date is June 30, 2018. The reason behind the end of life was that the web interface was written in J# code, and Microsoft had announced the end of life of this technology. As a result, Citrix developed StoreFront from scratch to provide the next generation features.

Just like web interface, StoreFront also authenticates users and enumerates desktops and applications into the stores that users can access through the receiver, but it goes beyond web interface to simplify the management of XenApp and XenDesktop deployments. StoreFront has the ability to enumerate the resource and authenticate multiple XenApp Farms or XenDesktop sites, which improves the performance.

It also has some other attractive features:

- StoreFront has the ability of intelligent resource filtering technology, which enables IT administrators to deliver different sets of applications and desktops to the users while they are getting enumerated from different sites or farms. This feature is handy during the upgrade or migration as it helps in easy transition from the older version to the newer.
- It also has the ability to allow users to access the apps and desktops from any device. Also, the devices on which the receiver cannot be installed, application and desktops can be accessed via an HTML5-compatible browser. It also supports single sign in where users have to login once; post this, it gives instant access to critical apps and desktop and this improves productivity.
- It supports simplified account provisioning via which users can log on to their assigned resources by just entering their e-mail address or server address or by using the StoreFront provisioning file for the receiver.
- StoreFront also supports the most advanced authentication and protection for the XenApp and XenDesktop resources.

## Delivery Controller

Installed on servers in the data center, the controller authenticates users and manages the assembly of users' virtual desktops and application environments and brokers connections between users and their virtual desktops and applications. It controls the state of the desktops, starting and stopping them, based on demand and administrative configuration.

Also, from the Delivery Controller server, you manage the complete XenApp infrastructure, starting from managing the administrator to optimizing the user experience. This is the first server that you install to create the XenApp environment. When installing this, you configure most of the parts starting from naming your site, configuring the database, specifying your License Server, and other tasks.

## Citrix® Studio

Citrix Studio is a high-level admin console to configure and manage the XenApp and XenDesktop components. Admin can do the following tasks with the help of Citrix Studio:

- Configure sites
- Create and manage Machine Catalog
- Create and manage delivery groups
- Create Citrix policies for users and computers
- Set up configuration logging
- Configure the task for administrator, licensing, StoreFront, and others

# High-level concepts of designing the infrastructure

While designing the infrastructure, we are going to consider the five layer model, which will help us implement unified and standardized solutions for every use of XenApp and XenDesktop 7.6.

- **User layer**: In this layer, we identify and define the unique user groups, the endpoints they will be using to connect, and their location
- **Access layer**: In this layer, we define how a user group will gain access to their resources, focusing on access policies and desktop/application stores
- **Resource layer**: This layer defines the application and data provided to each user group
- **Control layer**: This layer defines the underlying infrastructure required to support the user accessing their resources
- **Hardware layer**: This layer defines the physical implementation of the overall solution

This model gives us the ability to create an extremely flexible model with which user groups can have their own set of access policies and resources, which can be shared. Regardless of how the user accesses and the resource layer are defined, they all are managed by a single, integrated control layer.

# Summary

In this chapter, you learned about the architecture and different components of XenApp and XenDesktop.

Specifically, you learned about the core strength of XenApp and XenDesktop. You also learned the different editions available for XenApp and XenDesktop, the concept of licensing, and its components. In the end, you learned the high-level concept of designing XenApp and XenDesktop.

In the next chapter, we will initiate the deployment of XenApp and XenDesktop by initiating the bare metal with the help of Hypervisor OS.

# 2

# Initiating the Hypervisor

In this chapter, we will be setting up the hypervisor for our application and desktop delivery via XenApp and XenDesktop 7.6.

Before we start, let's try to understand what can be done with the help of virtualization.

With the help of virtualization, we get the ability to virtualize multiple virtual machines, and at the same time, run on a single physical host. Virtual machines (VMs) running on a host are completely independent from other machines and separated from the host by a software operating system known as hypervisor.

XenApp and XenDesktop have the architecture that is designed to allow the management of a virtual desktop and application hosting server to run on multiple hypervisors. In this module, we will go through step by step on how to configure the hypervisor for application and desktop delivery via XenApp and XenDesktop 7.6.

Once done with this chapter, you will be able to:

- Install the hypervisor
- Install the hypervisor management console
- Configure the storage repository
- Create a virtual machine

# Virtualization

Virtualization gives us the ability to create the virtual environment, which support a multiple guest operating systems. Hypervisor OS is used to divide the physical host into multiple virtual machines, wherein each machine has its own operating system. In this, we can virtualize:

- Server operating system
- Desktop operating system
- Virtual appliances, which can be used as network/security devices

# Components

We need three things in order to utilize the host (physical machine) resources such as CPU, HDD, and Network cards so that the guest operating system can run on the host and this combination is also known as platform virtualization, which will let us create the emulated environment:

- **Hypervisor**: This is software which will be installed on the bare metal and will then enable the physical host to run multiple virtual machines on it with their own dedicated virtual hardware
- **Guest operating system**: This is software which will be installed on the virtual hardware
- **Virtual machines**: This is a separate computer which will be represented to users with their own network identity, operating system, configured applications, and data

# Hypervisor for XenApp® and XenDesktop® 7.6

The XenApp and XenDesktop 7.6 architectures support the following hypervisor:

- Citrix XenServer
- Microsoft Hyper-V
- VMware vSphere

In this book we will use the XenServer to virtualize the virtual machine which will be required for application and desktop delivery.

# Why XenServer®

According to Citrix and other lab tests, XenServer is the most effective hypervisor that can be used to deliver the best-in-class application and desktop delivery. GPU virtualization increases graphic performance; new 64-bit kernel, which improves networking and storage performance; and workload geo-tagging to restrict the work load to run in the particular location for security reasons.

# Installing the XenServer® host

In this book, we will be using XenServer 6.2. If you want to know more about this feature, you can go to `http://www.citrix.com/products/xenserver/overview.html`, and download the media files from `www.citrix.com/xenserver`.

Before we begin to install XenServer, let's take a look at some of the system requirements:

- The hardware must support HVM (Intel-VT or AMD-V enabled)
- Minimum 4 GB memory required
- At least 36 GB hard disk
- At least one network card

Once the preceding requirements are met, perform the following steps to install XenServer:

1. Insert the XenServer installation disc in the computer, or you can also use the PXE boot option from TFTP server, if applicable to your environment.
2. On powering on the machine, the computer will boot from the installation disc, and you will get the welcome screen from XenServer:

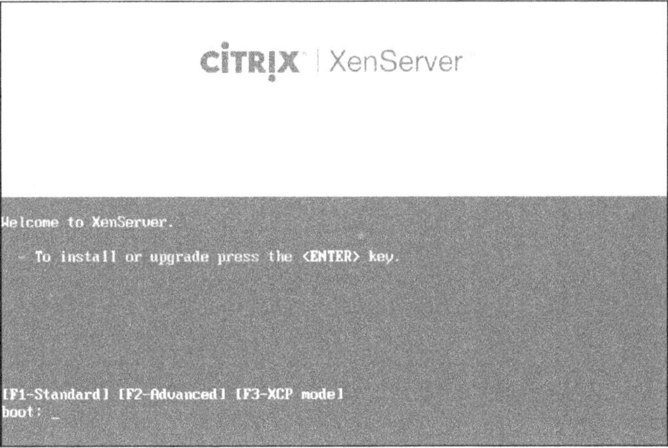

> If a system hardware warning screen is displayed and you suspect that hardware virtualization assist support is available on your system, check the support site of your hardware manufacturer for BIOS upgrades.

3. Post welcome screen, it will automatically advance to the installation of the modern server hardware drivers, which comes with XenServer itself. However, if you want to install any supplementary packs, which contain additional drivers, press *F9*. T installer will take you through the wizard to install all necessary drivers.
4. Once you have installed all of the required drivers, click on **Ok** to proceed.
5. You are prompted to choose the required keymap as per your computer. You can use the arrow keys to choose the **keymap**:

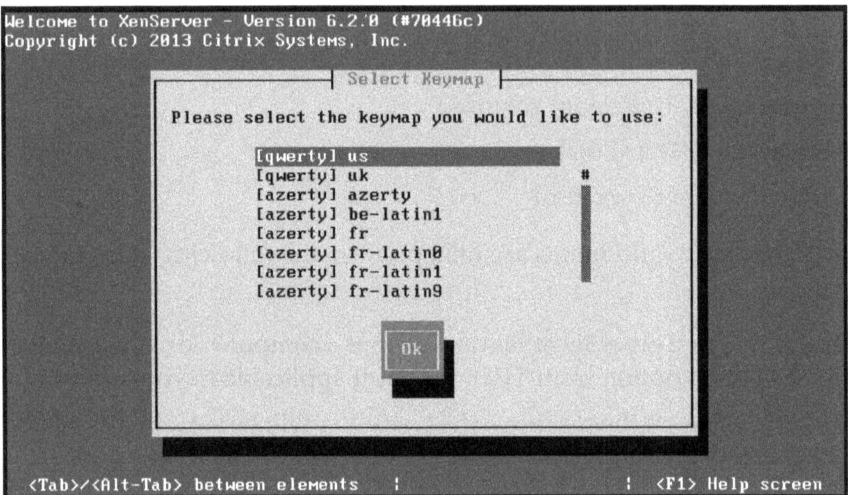


6. The XenServer **End User License Agreement** (EULA) will be displayed. Use the *Page Up* and *Page Down* keys to scroll through and read the agreement. Choose **Accept EULA** to proceed:

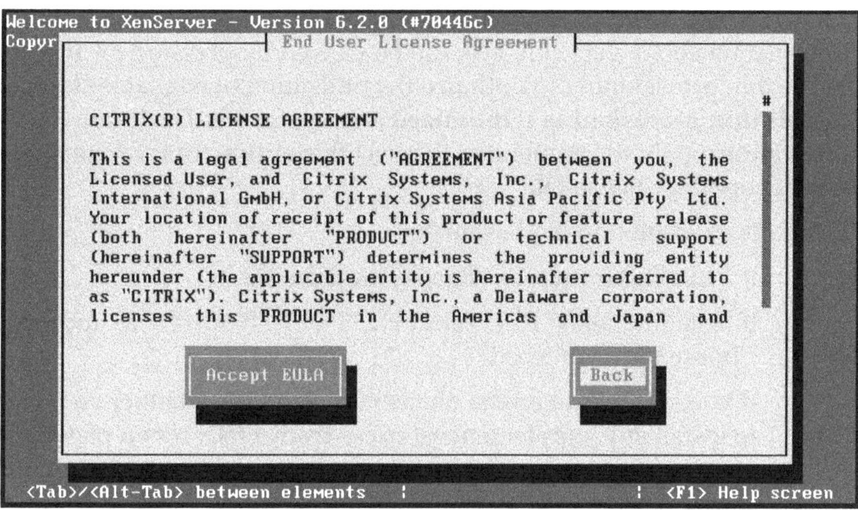


7. After accepting the XenServer **End User License Agreement**, the installation wizard will prompt you to choose the **Virtual Machine Storage**. In this scenario, we will use the local storage; we can choose thin provisioning if available. Select an installation action as appropriate. You may see any of the following options:

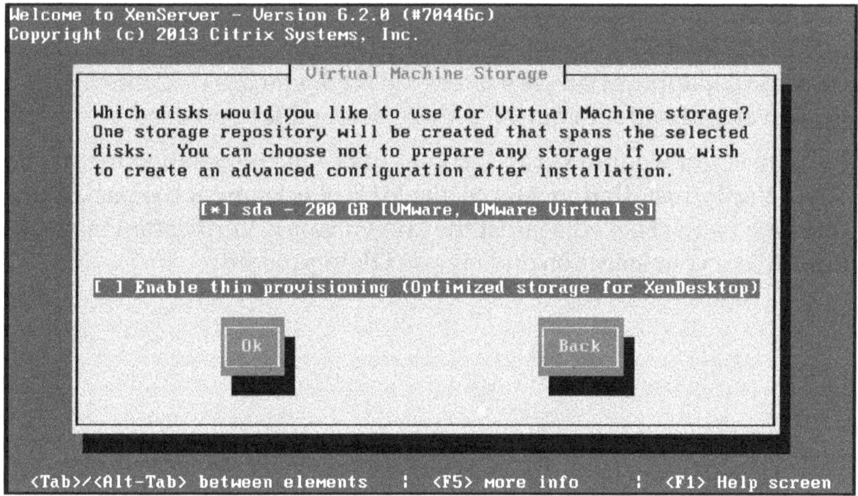


8. Perform a clean installation. Make your selection, and choose **Ok** to proceed

9. Choose which disk(s) you would like to use for virtual machine storage. Information about a specific disk can be viewed by pressing *F5*. If you want to use thin provisioning to optimize the utilization of available storage, select **Enable thin provisioning (Optimized storage for XenDesktop)**. XenDesktop users are strongly recommended to select this option for local caching to work properly. Choose **Ok**.
10. Select your installation media source:
    - If installing from a CD, choose **local media**.
    - If installing using PXE, select HTTP or FTP or NFS, as appropriate. Choose **Ok** to proceed.
    - If you select local media, the next screen asks whether you want to install any supplementary packs from a CD. If you plan to install any supplementary packs provided by your hardware supplier, choose **Yes**.
11. If you select HTTP, FTP, or NFS, set up networking so that the installer can connect to the XenServer installation media files. If the computer has multiple NICs, select one of them to be used to access the XenServer installation media files, and then choose **Ok** to proceed. Choose **Automatic configuration (DHCP)** to configure the NIC using DHCP, or Static configuration to configure the NIC manually. If you choose **Static configuration**, enter details as appropriate. If you choose **HTTP** or **FTP**, you are then prompted to provide the URL for your HTTP or FTP repository, and a username and password, if appropriate. If you choose **NFS**, you are prompted to provide the server and path of your NFS share. Select **Ok** to proceed.
12. Indicate if you want to verify the integrity of the installation media. If you select **Verify installation source**, the MD5 checksum of the packages is calculated and checked against the known value. Verification may take some time. Make your selection and choose **Ok** to proceed:

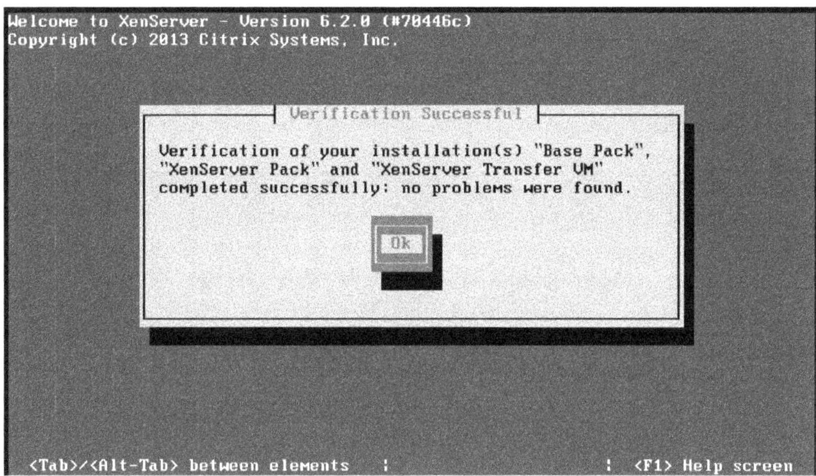


13. On the next screen, you will be prompted to set the root password, which you can use later to connect your XenServer via XenCenter management console. You will also use this password (with the username root) to log in to xsconsole, the system configuration console:

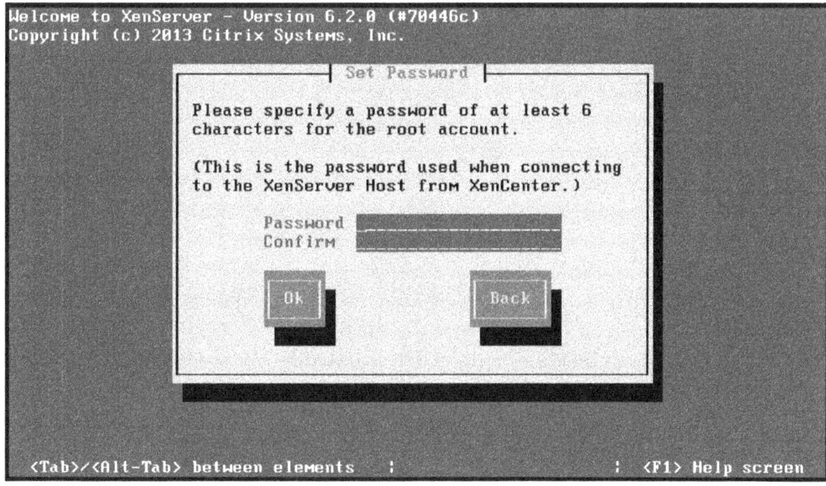

14. Next screen will be the screen where you need to configure your networking part. This screen will have two options—**Automatic configuration (DHCP)** and **Static configuration** for XenServer Management interface. I will choose **Static configuration**:

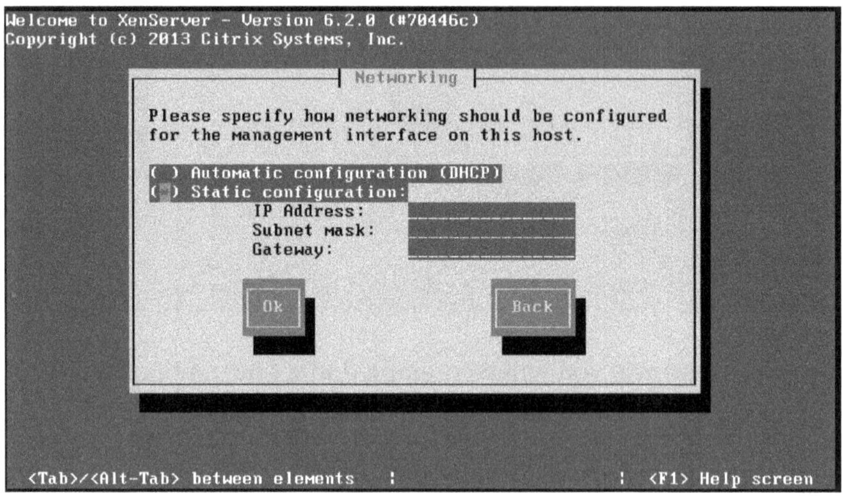

To be part of a pool, XenServer hosts must have static IP addresses or be DNS addressable. When using DHCP, ensure that a static DHCP reservation policy is in place.

15. Specify the hostname and the DNS configuration, manually or automatically, via DHCP.

    In the **Hostname Configuration** section, select automatically set via DHCP to have the DHCP server provide the hostname along with the IP address. If you select manually specify, enter the desired hostname for the server in the field provided.

If manually specifying the hostname, enter a short hostname and not the fully qualified domain name (FQDN). Entering an FQDN may cause external authentication to fail.

In the **DNS Configuration** section, choose automatically set via DHCP to get name service configuration using DHCP. If you select manually specify, enter the IP address(es) of your primary (required), secondary (optional), and tertiary (optional) DNS servers in the fields provided. Select **Ok** to proceed:

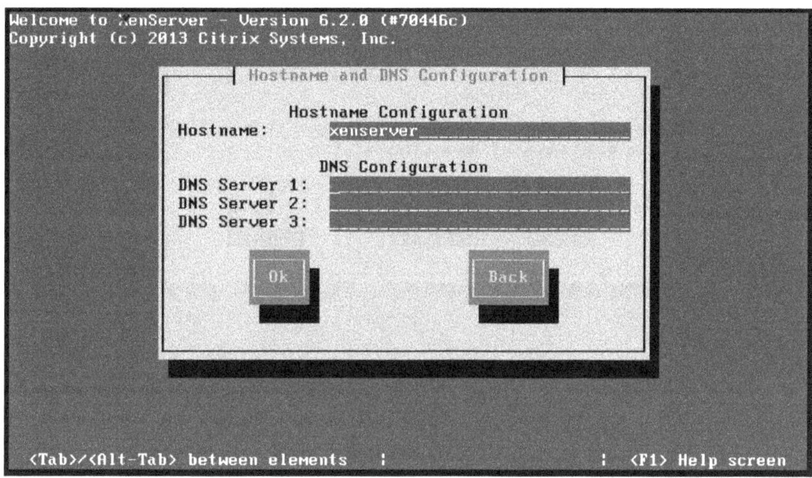


16. On proceeding to next screen, you will be asked to choose the time zone, geographical area, and city. You can type the first letter of the desired locale to jump to the first entry that begins with this letter. Choose **Ok** to proceed.
17. Next, XenServer gives you the ability to choose how you would like XenServer to determine the time: using NTP or manual time entry. Make your selection and choose **Ok** to proceed.

    If using NTP, either select NTP is configured by my DHCP server to have DHCP set the time server or enter at least one NTP server name or IP address in the fields below. Choose **Ok**.

XenServer assumes that the time set in the BIOS of the server is the current time in UTC.

18. After performing all the required prerequisite configuration, the installation wizard will take you to the following screen. Select **Install XenServer**:

If you selected to set the date and time manually, you will be prompted to do so during the installation. Once set, choose **Ok** to proceed.

19. If you are installing from a CD and selected to include supplementary packs, you will be prompted to insert them. Eject the XenServer installation CD and insert the supplementary pack CD. Choose **Ok**.
20. Select **Use media** to proceed with the installation and repeat for each pack to be installed.
21. Post installation completion, you will be asked to eject the installation CD (if installing from CD). Select **Ok** to reboot the server:

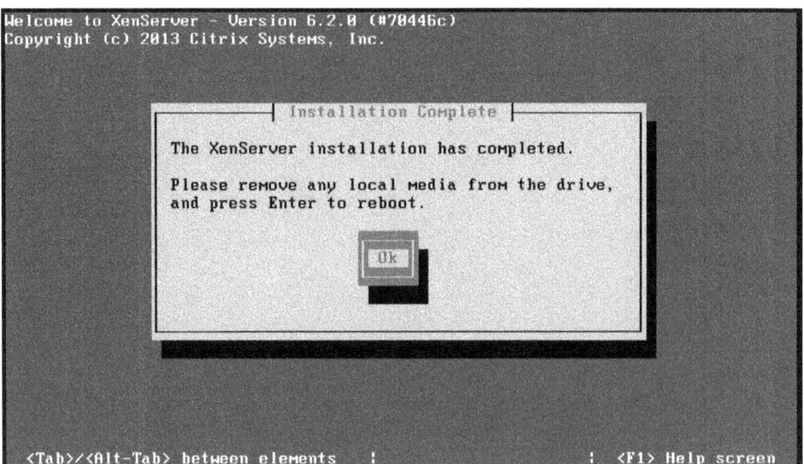

After the server reboots, XenServer displays xsconsole, a system configuration console. To access a local shell from xsconsole, press *Alt* + *F3*; to return to xsconsole, press *Alt* + *F1*.

Make a note of the IP address displayed. You will use this when you connect XenCenter to the XenServer host.

# Installing XenCenter®

XenCenter must be installed on a remote Windows machine that can connect to the XenServer host through your network. The .NET framework version 3.5 must also be installed on this workstation.

The XenCenter installation media is bundled with the XenServer installation media. You can also download the latest version of XenCenter from `www.citrix.com/xenserver`.

Before installing XenCenter, be sure to uninstall any previous version. Follow these steps to install XenCenter:

1. Launch the installer.
2. If installing from a XenServer installation CD then insert the CD into the DVD drive of the computer on which you want to run XenCenter.
3. Open the `client_install` folder on the CD. Double-click on `XenCenter.msi` to begin the installation.
4. Follow the Setup wizard, which allows you to modify the default destination folder and then install XenCenter.

# Connecting XenCenter® to the XenServer® host

To connect XenCenter to the XenServer host, follow these steps:

1. Launch XenCenter.
2. The program opens to the **Home** tab.

3. Click on **Add New Server** as shown in the following screenshot:

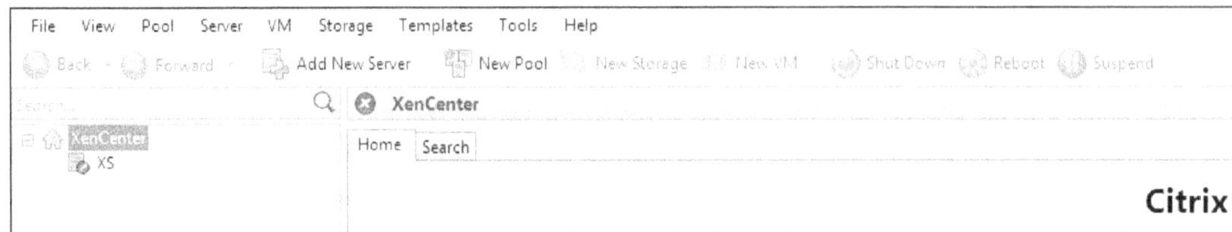


4. Enter the IP address of the XenServer host in the **Server** field. Type the root username and password that you set during XenServer installation. Click on **Add**.
5. The first time you add a new host, the **Save and Restore Connection State** dialog box appears. This enables you to set your preferences for storing your host connection information and automatically restoring host connections.

If you later need to change your preferences, you can do so using XenCenter or the Windows Registry Editor.

To do so in XenCenter, select **Tools** and then **Options**. The **Options** dialog box opens. Select the **Save and Restore** tab and set your preferences. Click on **Ok** to save your changes.

To do so using the Windows Registry Editor, navigate to the `HKEY_LOCAL_MACHINE\Software \Citrix\XenCenter` key (if you installed XenServer for use by all users) and add a key named `AllowCredentialSave` with the string value `true` or `false`.

# Configuration of storage repository

A pool is comprised of multiple XenServer host installations, bound together as a single managed entity. When combined with shared storage, a pool enables VMs to be started on any XenServer host in the pool that has sufficient memory and then dynamically move between hosts while running (XenMotion), with minimal downtime. If an individual XenServer host suffers a hardware failure, you can restart the failed VM(s) on another host in the same pool.

If the High Availability (HA) feature is enabled, protected VMs are automatically moved in the event of a host failure.

To set up shared storage between hosts in a pool, you need to create a storage repository. A XenServer storage repository (SR) is a storage container in which virtual disks are stored. SRs, like virtual disks, are persistent, ondisk objects that exist independently of XenServer. SRs can exist on different types of physical storage devices, both internal and external, including local disk devices and shared network storage. A number of different types of storage are available when you create a new SR, including:

- NFS VHD storage
- Software iSCSI storage
- Hardware HBA storage

The following sections walk you through setting up common shared storage solutions — NFS — for a pool of XenServer hosts. Before you create a new SR, you need to configure your NFS or iSCSI storage. The setup differs depending on the type of storage solution that you use, so it is best to refer to your vendor documentation for details. In all cases, to be part of a pool, the servers providing shared storage must have static IP addresses or be DNS-addressable. For further information on setting up shared storage, see the XenServer Administrator's Guide.

It is recommended that you create a pool before you add shared storage. For pool requirements and setup procedures, see the XenCenter Help or the XenServer Administrator's Guide.

# XenServer® hosts with shared NFS storage

The basic hardware requirements are as follows:

- Two or more 64-bit x86 servers with local storage
- One or more Windows workstation(s), on the same network as the XenServer hosts
- A server exporting a shared directory over NFS

Follow this high-level procedure:

1. Install the XenServer host software on the servers.
2. Install XenCenter on the workstation(s).
3. Connect XenCenter to the XenServer hosts.
4. Create your pool of XenServer hosts.
5. Configure the NFS server.
6. Create an SR on the NFS share at the pool level.

# Configuring NFS storage

Before you create an SR, you need to configure the NFS storage. To be part of a pool, the NFS share must have a static IP address or be DNS-addressable. You must also configure the NFS server to have one or more target(s) that can be mounted by NFS clients (for example, XenServer hosts in a pool). The setup differs depending on your storage solution, so it is best to see your vendor documentation for details.

To create an SR on the NFS share at the pool level in XenCenter, follow these steps:

1. On the **Resources** pane, select the **pool**.
2. On the toolbar, click on the **New Storage** button. The **New Storage Repository** wizard opens.
3. Under **Virtual disk storage**, choose **NFS VHD** as the storage type. Choose **Next** to continue.
4. Enter a name for the new SR and the name of the share where it is located. Click on **Scan** to have the wizard scan for the existing NFS SRs in the specified location.

The NFS server must be configured to export the specified path to all the XenServer hosts in the pool.

5. Click on **Finish**.

The new SR appears in the **Resources** pane, at the pool level. For more information, refer to `http://support.citrix.com/article/CTX141501`.

# Creating a virtual machine

The first thing that we need to have before we start creating the virtual machine is the CIFS, also known as Common Internet File System library where we can keep our installation ISO media, and this will be known as an ISO library.

To configure the ISO library, follow these steps:

1. On the **Resources** pane, select the pool. On the toolbar, click on the **New Storage** button. The **New Storage Repository** wizard opens.
2. Under the **ISO library**, chose **windows file sharing**. Chose **Next** to continue.
3. Enter the name of the new SR.
4. Enter the location information of the share and enter the service account details if you want to use a different user to connect to the share.
5. Click on **Finish**. The new SR will appear in the resource pane at the storage level.

# Creating a virtual machine from a CD, ISO image

In this section, we will be creating virtual machine from a CD, ISO Image. The following procedure provides an example of creating Windows 7 (32-bit) VM. The default values may vary depending on the operating system that you choose.

To create a Windows 7 (32-bit) VM, follow these steps:

1. On the XenCenter toolbar, click on the **New VM** button to open the **New VM** wizard.

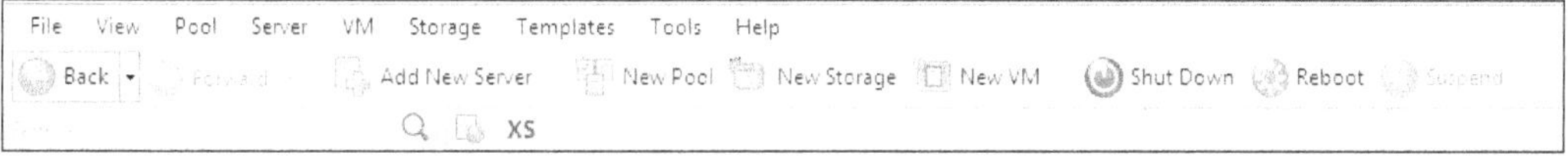


2. The New VM wizard allows you to configure the new VM, adjusting various parameters for CPU, storage, and networking resources.
3. Select a VM template and click on **Next**.
4. Each template contains the setup information needed to create a new VM with a specific guest operating system, and with optimum storage. This list reflects the templates that XenServer currently supports.

> If the OS that you intend to install on your new VM is compatible only with the original hardware (for example, an OS installation CD that was packaged with a specific computer), check the copy host BIOS strings to VM box.

5. Enter a name and an optional description for the new VM.
6. Choose the source of the OS media to install on the new VM.

Installing from a CD/DVD is the simplest option for getting started. To do so, choose the default installation source option (DVD drive), insert the disk into the DVD drive of the XenServer host, and choose **Next** to proceed.

XenServer also allows you to pull OS installation media from a range of sources, including a pre-existing ISO library. An ISO image is a file that contains all the information that an optical disc (CD, DVD, and so on) would contain. In this case, an ISO image would contain the same OS data as a Windows installation CD.

To attach a pre-existing ISO library, click on the **New ISO library** and indicate the location and type of ISO library. You can then choose the specific operating system ISO media from the drop-down list. Following are the steps for virtual machine installation on XenServer host:

1. The VM will run on the installed host. Choose **Next** to proceed.
2. For a Windows 7 VM, the default is one virtual CPU and 2,048 MB of RAM. You may also choose to modify the defaults. Select **Next** to continue.
3. Allocate and configure storage for the new VM.
4. Click on **Next** to select the default allocation (24 GB) and configuration, or you may wish to:

   Change the name, description, or size of your virtual disk by clicking on **Properties** and add a new virtual disk by selecting **Add**

5. Configure networking on the new VM. Click on **Next** to select the default network interface card (NIC) and configurations, including an automatically-created unique MAC address for each NIC, or you may wish to:

   Change the physical network, MAC address, or quality-of-service (QoS) priority of the virtual disk by clicking on **Properties** and add a new virtual NIC by selecting **Add**

6. Review settings and then click on **Finish** to create the new VM and return to the **Search** tab. An icon for your new VM appears under the host in the **Resources** pane. On the **Resources** pane, select the VM and then click on the **Console** tab to see the VM console.

7. Follow the OS installation screens and make your selections.
8. Once the OS installation completes and the VM reboots, install the XenServer Tools.

XenServer Tools provide high-speed I/O for enhanced disk and network performance. XenServer Tools must be installed on each VM in order for the VM to have a fully-supported configuration. A VM will function without them, but performance will be significantly hampered. XenServer Tools also enable certain functions and features, including cleanly shutting down, rebooting, suspending, and live migrating VMs.

> You must install XenServer Tools for each VM. Running VMs without XenServer Tools is not supported.
>
> To install XenServer Tools on a Windows VM, the VM must be running the Microsoft .NET Framework Version 4.0 or later. If a VM is running Windows 2003, you need to install the Windows Imaging Component (see your vendor documentation for details) before installing.

# XenServer® Tools

To install XenServer Tools, follow these steps:

1. On the **Resources** pane, select the **XenServer** host and then the **Search** tab.
2. The XenServer Tools not installed blue status text appears next to the new VM.
3. Click on the text to open the XenServer Tools setup wizard on the VM console.
4. Click on the **Install XenServer Tools** button, and then run `Xensetup.exe`.
5. When prompted, click on **Yes** to allow the program to make changes to the computer.
6. Accept the License Agreement, and click **Next** to continue.
7. Choose a destination folder and click on **Install**.
8. Select **Reboot now** and then **Finish** to complete the installation.

For more information on this, refer to: `http://support.citrix.com/article/CTX141502`.

# Summary

In this chapter, you learned about how to setup the hypervisor for XenApp and XenDesktop 7.6. Specifically, you learned how to install the XenServer 6.5 and the XenCenter Management console to manage XenServer host. We also saw how to configure the storage repository by using NFS VHD storage, and created a Windows 7 32 bit Virtual Machine.

In the next chapter, we will discuss how to set up the infrastructure component, which will be required to run XenApp and XenDesktop 7.6.

# 3

# Setting Up the Infrastructure Components

In this chapter, we are going to work on setting up the base of our Citrix XenApp infrastructure, which is the prerequisite and a very important part of the Citrix XenApp desktop infrastructure.

## Overview

We will be setting up four different infrastructure components listed here:

- **Domain controller**: As per Citrix, at least one domain controller is required for the XenApp 7.6 deployments, and that should have the active directory domain services role installed on it.
- **Dynamic Host Configuration Protocol** (**DHCP**): The DHCP plays an important role when we configure Citrix Provisioning Services, which is the software streaming technology by Citrix. With Citrix Provisioning Services, one can provision or re-provision computers in real time from the single shared disk image. We will discuss Citrix Provisioning Services in detail later in this book.
- **Setting up a certificate authority**: We will be setting up this Microsoft component to generate a certificate, which can be used for various components such as StoreFront and Delivery Controller to secure the connection.
- **Setting up SQL server 2012**: This is a very important part of the XenApp 7.6 infrastructure because the SQL server database will store all the static information of the XenApp site configuration.

Once you complete this chapter, you will be able to install and manage the non-Citrix infrastructure, which plays a very important role in the XenApp site deployment and working as well.

# Setting up the domain controller

In this section of this chapter, I will take you through the step-by-step configuration of the active directory domain service. We will do this configuration on one of the preinstalled Microsoft Windows 2012 R2 servers.

We will use this role of Microsoft for authenticating the XenApp 7.6 users to apply group policy and manage computer accounts.

We already have the preinstalled Microsoft Windows server 2012 R2, so now we will set up the active directory domain service on it. Before we start doing the configuration, there are a few points that you should be aware of:

In earlier versions of Microsoft Windows, we used to have the DCPROMO command to install the ADDS, but in Microsoft Windows 2012, it is not supported.

It is recommended that the server on which you will be installing ADDS should have a static IP address assigned to it.

Let's begin the configuration by following these steps:

1. To start the configuration, click on **ADD roles and features** on the server manager dashboard:

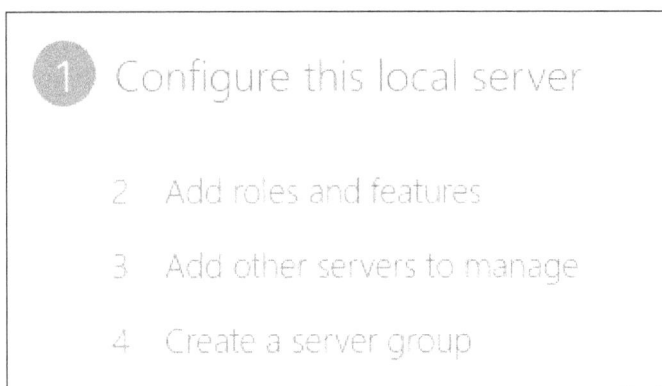

2. It will pop up the very first screen with the tittle **Before you begin**, which basically give the overview of the wizard. We will click on **Next** to move forward:

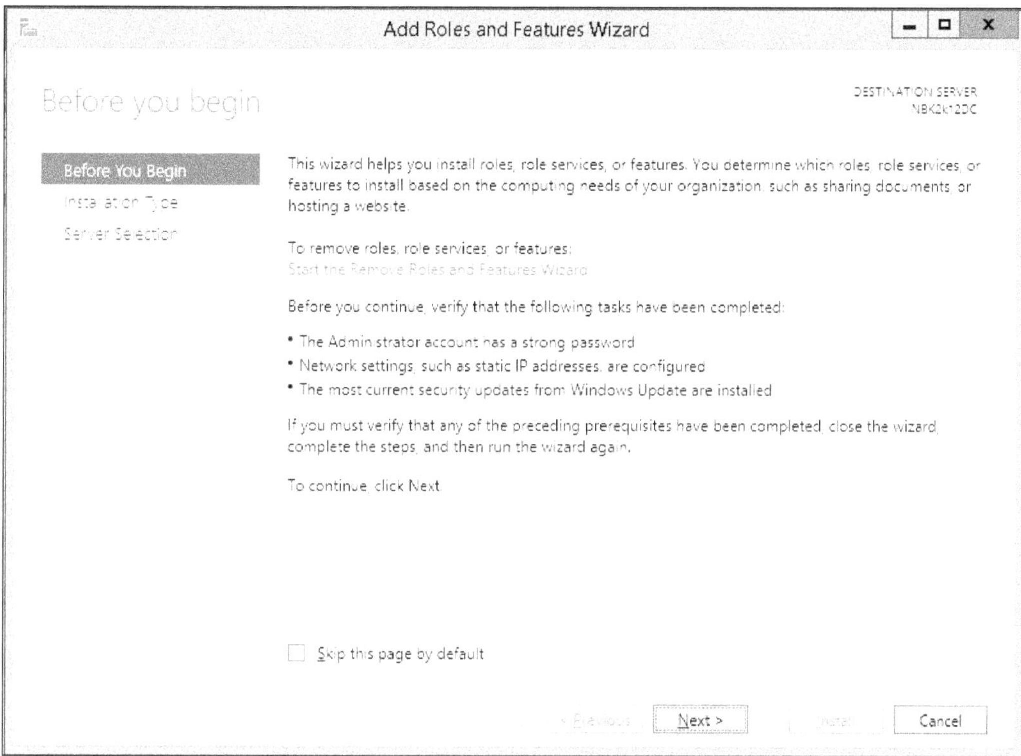


3. In Windows 2012, installation has been divided into two parts:
    - Role-based or feature-based installation
    - Remote desktop services installation

4. Earlier, remote desktop services used to be the part of the role-based installation. Here, we will select **Role-based or feature-based installation** and click on **Next** to move forward:

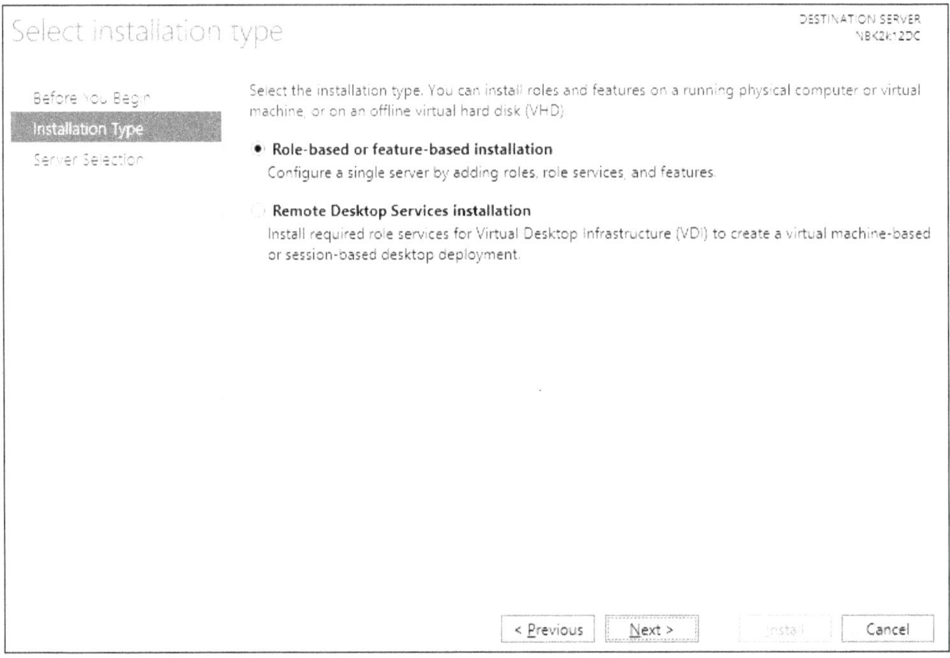


5. The next window will show you the list of roles that you can add to your Microsoft Windows 2012 R2 server, but here, we will select the **Active Directory Domain Services**:

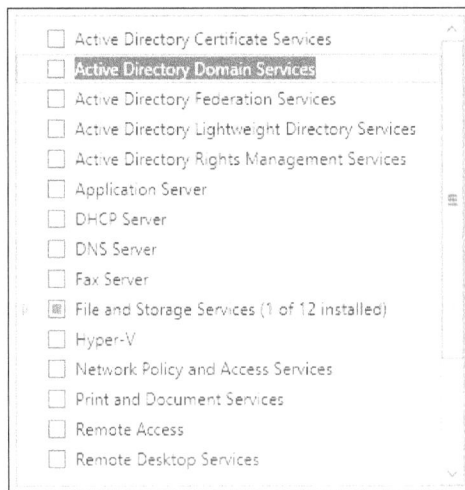

Active Directory Certificate Services
Active Directory Domain Services
Active Directory Federation Services
Active Directory Lightweight Directory Services
Active Directory Rights Management Services
Application Server
DHCP Server
DNS Server
Fax Server
File and Storage Services (1 of 12 installed)
Hyper-V
Network Policy and Access Services
Print and Document Services
Remote Access
Remote Desktop Services

6. The moment you will choose the ADDS, it will pop up another window that will show you the list of services, which is prerequisite to install active directory domain services:

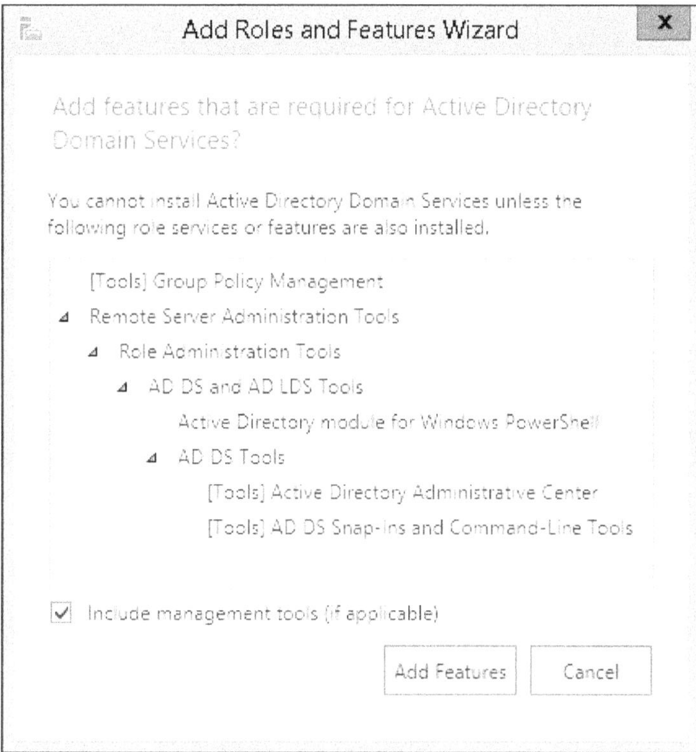


7. Click on **Add Features** to proceed.
8. The next window will show you the list of features that can be added. We will just skip this section as all the roles and features were selected in the last window.
9. The next window will contain the information about the roles that you are going to install.

10. Click on **Next** to proceed:

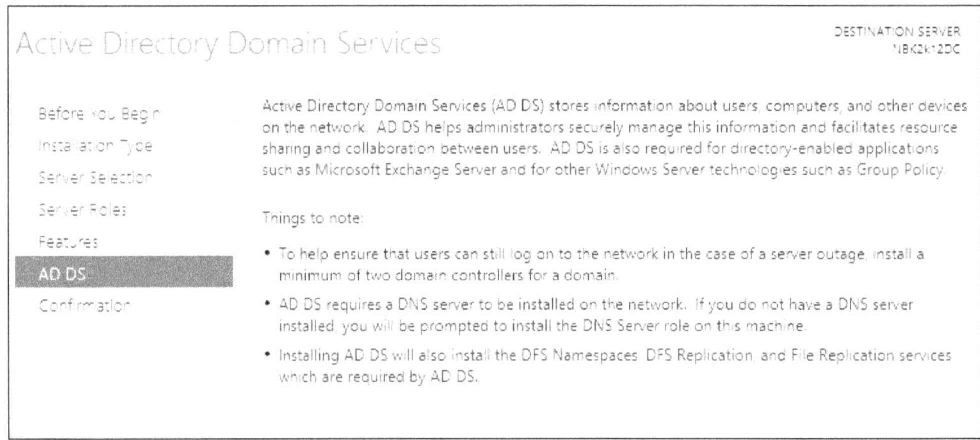


11. Now, the next window will show you the summary of roles and features that will be installed to convert the Windows 2012 server into the domain controller role. It also has the checkbox to restart the server automatically post installation without administrator intervention; you can check the box as per your convenience. Click on **Next** to proceed with the installation:

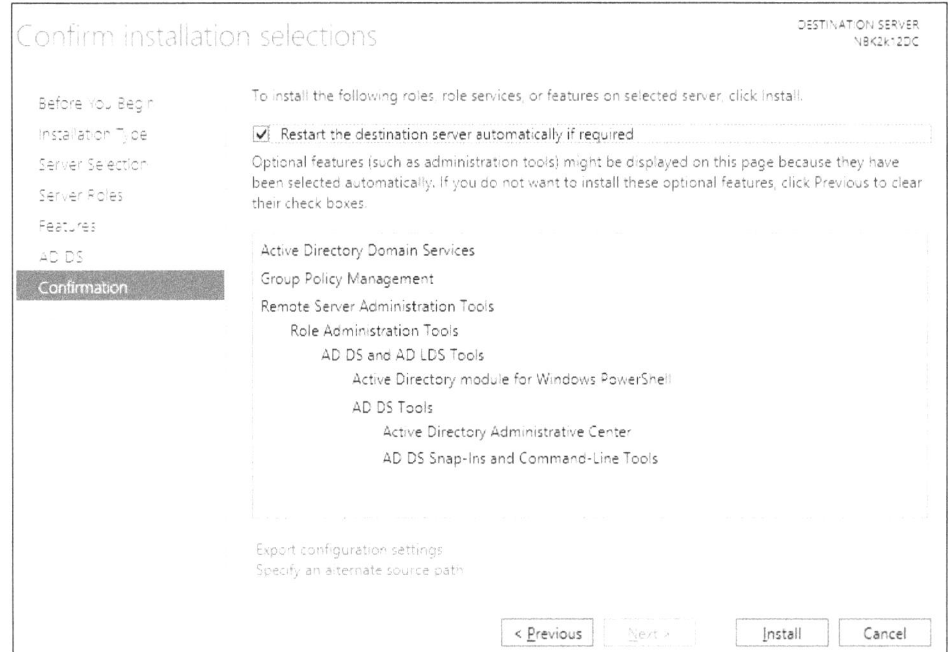

12. You will get the status bar, which will show you the progress of installation. It will take a while to install the roles and features on the server. Once the installation is complete, you can click on the **Close** button:

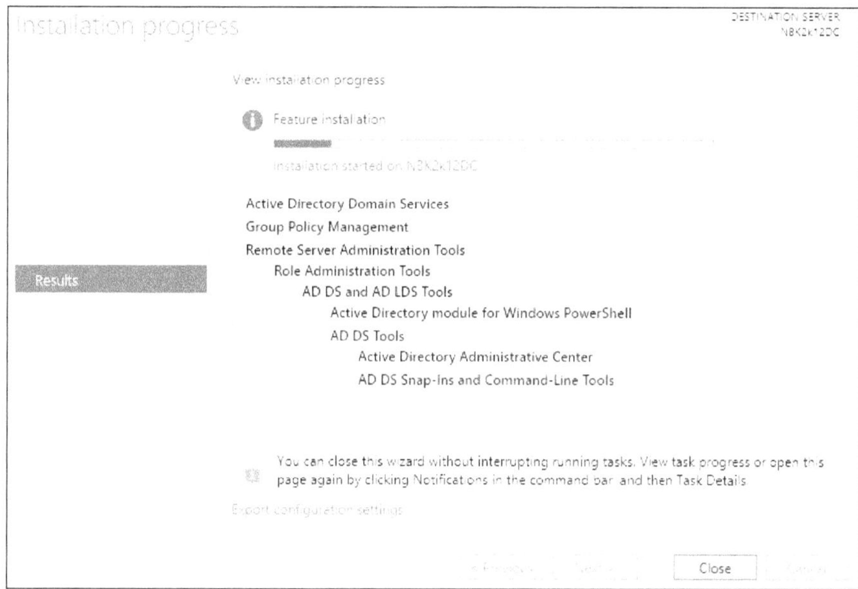


13. We are done with the installation of active directory domain services:

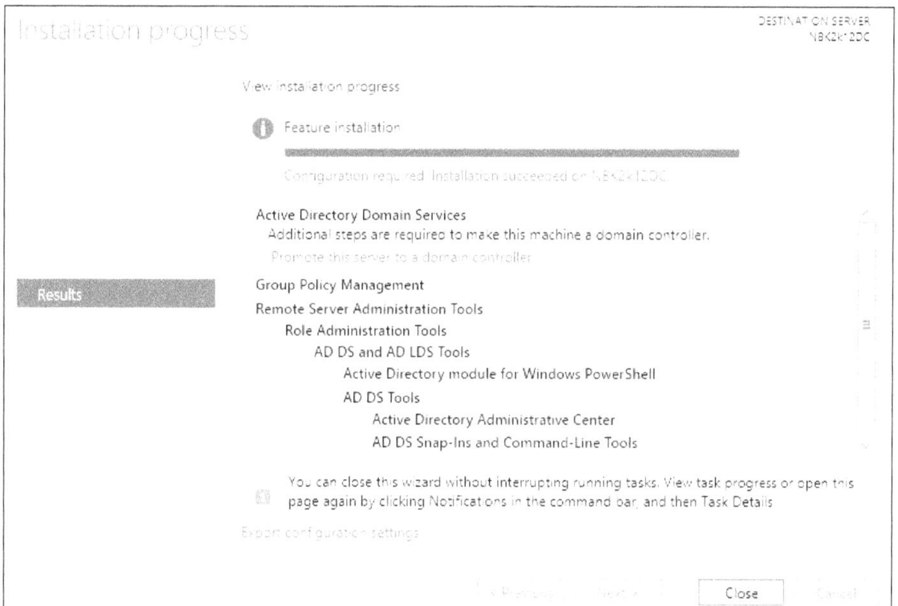

# Configuring the domain controller

In this section, we will configure the installed active directory domain services on the server. In this process, we will promote the server to a domain controller. Follow these steps:

1. In the server manager window at the top, you will be able to see the exclamation mark flag. Click on the exclamation mark flag, and it will show you **Post-deployment configuration** and the **Promote this server to a domain controller** option. Click on this **option**:

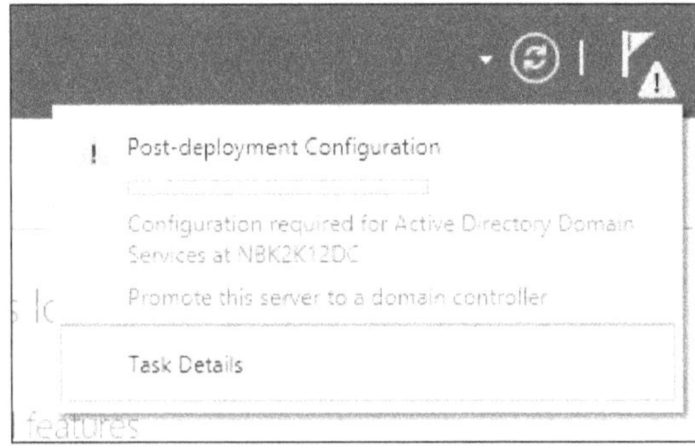


2. The next screen will pop up giving you three options to choose from— **Add a domain controller to an existing domain**, **Add a new domain to an existing forest**, or **Add a new forest**. Here, we will select the last one.
3. Post selection, we have to choose the domain name as well. After providing the name, you can click on **Next**:

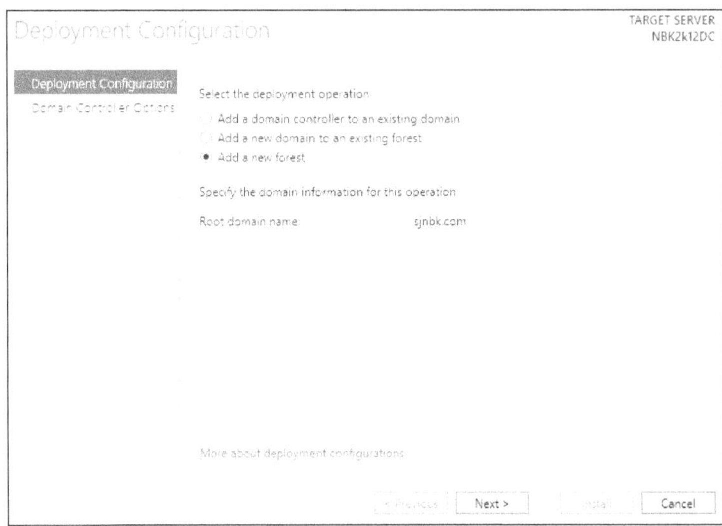

4. In the next window, you will have the option to choose the forest and functional level on which your domain controller will operate. Also, you can choose the capabilities that you want to add to the newly-built domain controller:

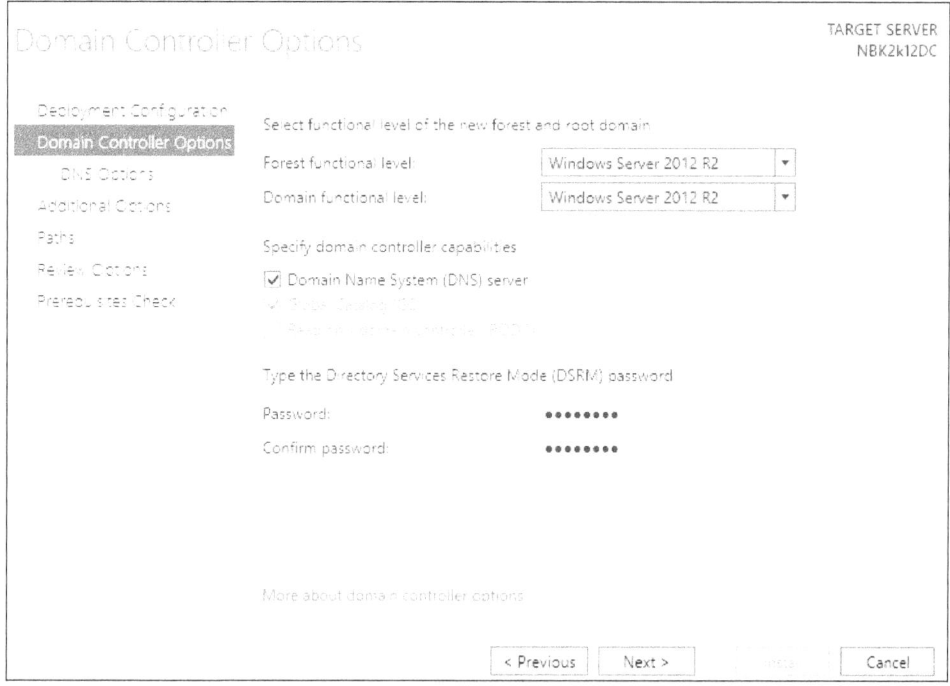


5. It will also ask for the directory services restore mode password. Click on **Next** to continue.

6. The next screen configuration wizard will validate the NetBIOS domain name; make sure that it is not a duplicate:

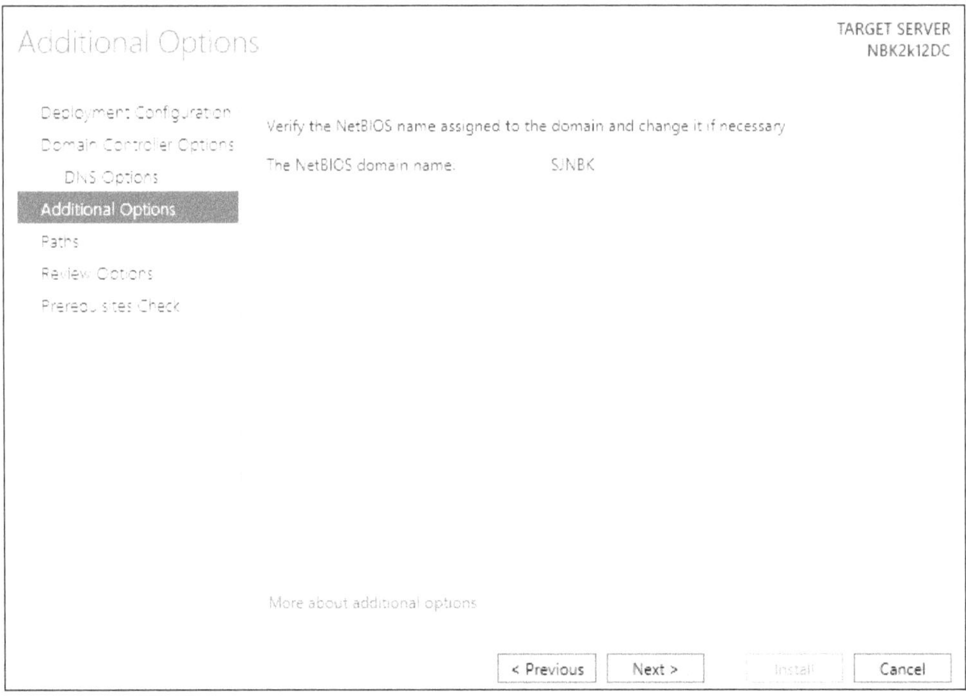


7. Post verification, you can click on **Next** to proceed further.
8. The next screen will show you the location where active directory domain services will store its database, log, and sysvol files. You can change the location as per your convenience.
9. Click on **Next** to proceed:

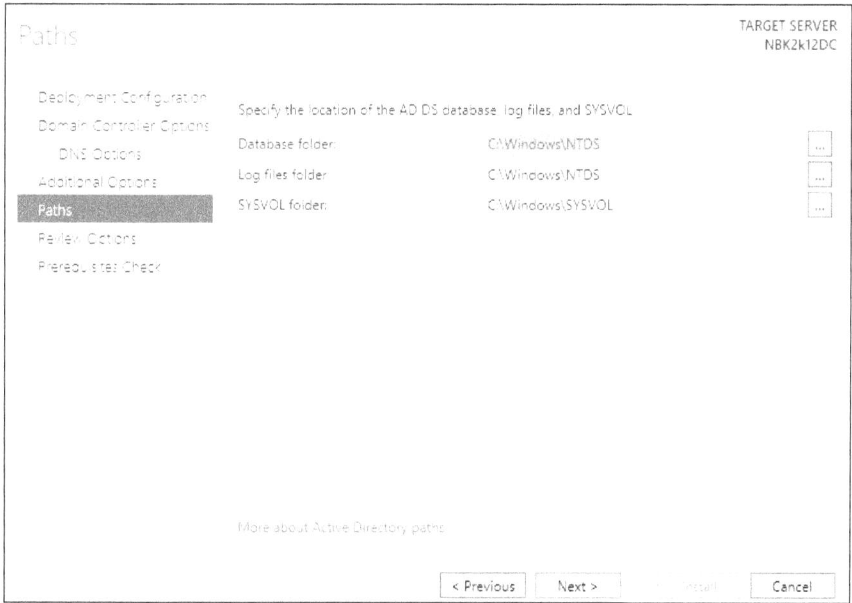


10. The next screen will be the review screen where you can review all the configuration instructions you have given so far. If you want to make any changes, you can go back and update from here. Click on **Next** to proceed:

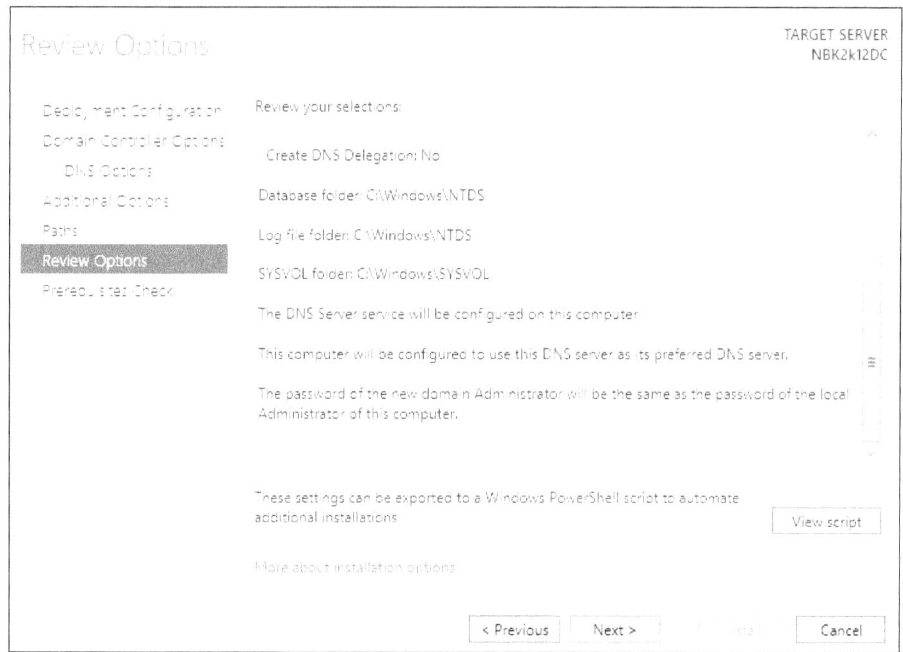

11. You can also generate the PowerShell script for the future deployments from the same window.
12. On the next screen it will validate the configuration information provided so far and make sure that it meets the prerequisite check. If the configuration will pass the test, it will show the following screen:

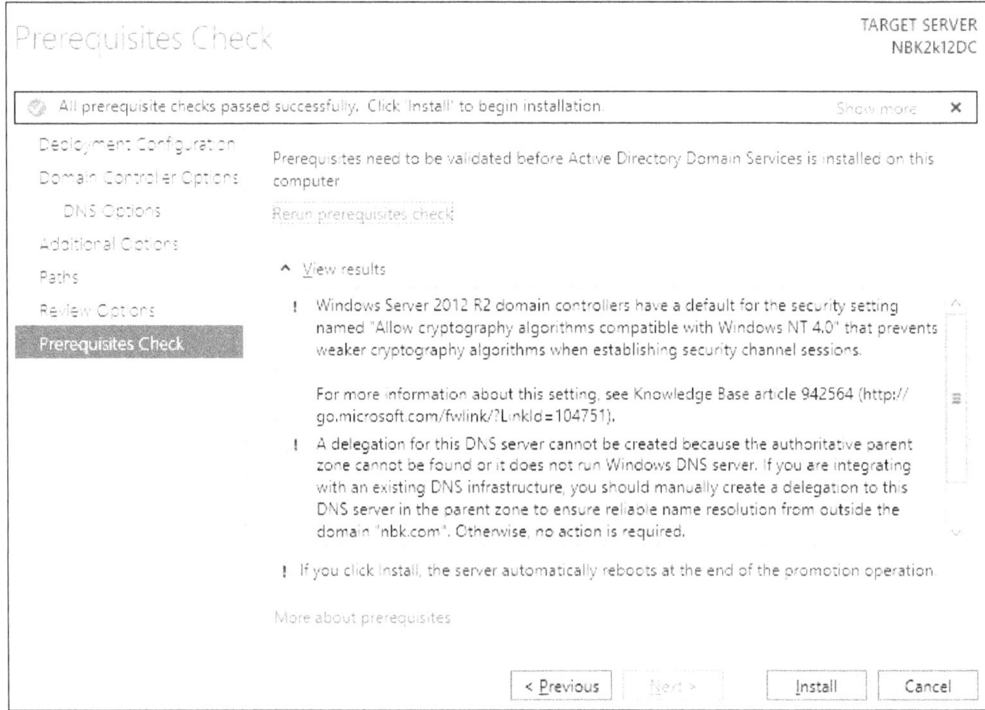


13. Click on **Install** to start the installation process.

Track the progress of installation as the process will take time to complete the configuration and promote the server to domain controller. Post completion, it will reboot the server, and once the server will be back up, it will be the domain controller and a part of the domain you created.

# Setting up the Dynamic Host Configuration Protocol

The role of the Dynamic Host Configuration Protocol is to assign the IP configuration to the clients automatically, which means this server role can help us in avoiding the manual task of assigning the IP configuration to the clients manually.

I have included this topic here because this Windows server role will play a critical role when we will implement the Citrix Provisioning Services to create and manage the disk images, and with the help of DHCP, we will boot the machines/virtual machines and configure the IP details as well.

We will install this server role on the Microsoft Windows 2012 R2 server. Let's take a look at the step-by-step configuration of DHCP:

1. To start the configuration, open the server manager and then click on **Add roles and features**:

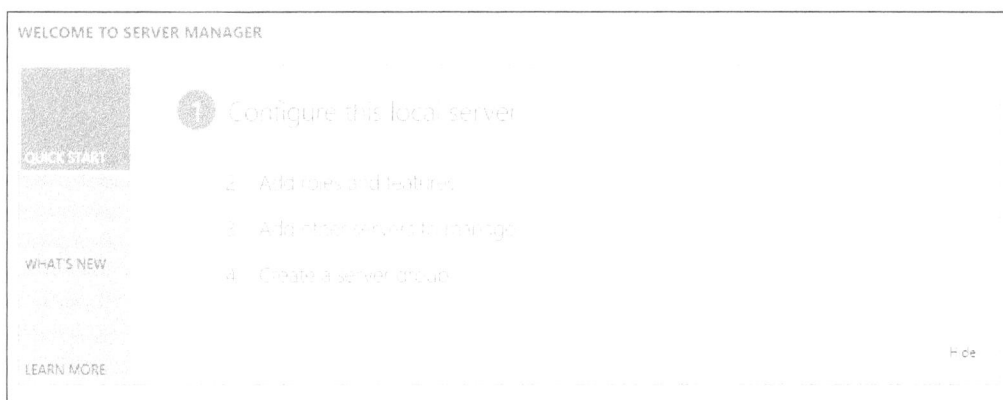

2. It will open a wizard that will take you through the steps of installation required to install DHCP role to the server. Click on **Next**:

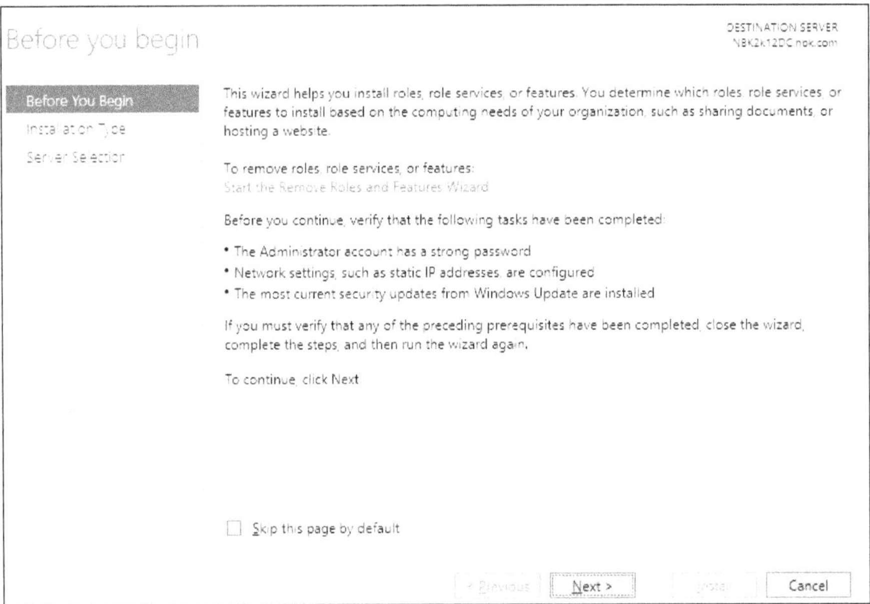


3. In the **Select installation** type window, we will choose **Role-based or feature-based installation** as DHCP is a Windows server role. Click on **Next**:

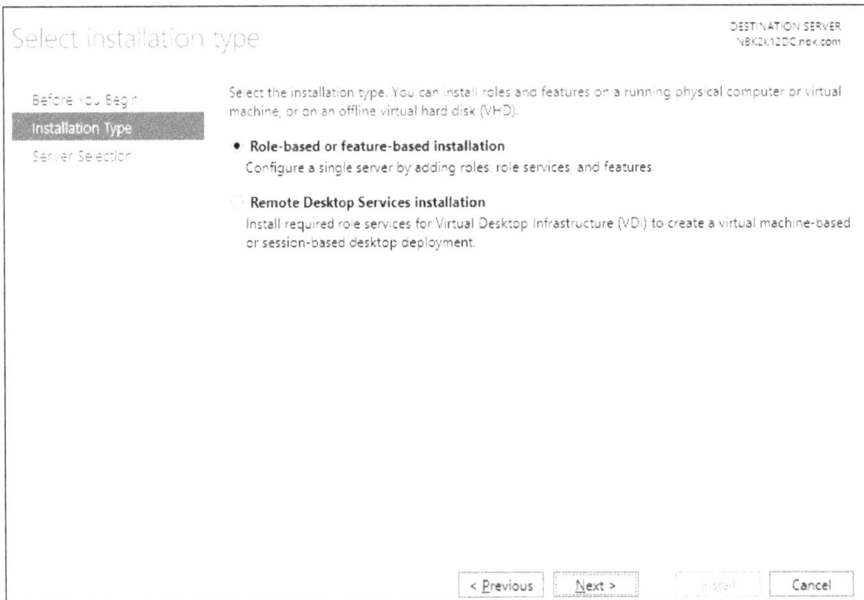

4. The next screen will appear, which will have the list of roles that can be installed on the Windows server. Choose **DHCP Server**:

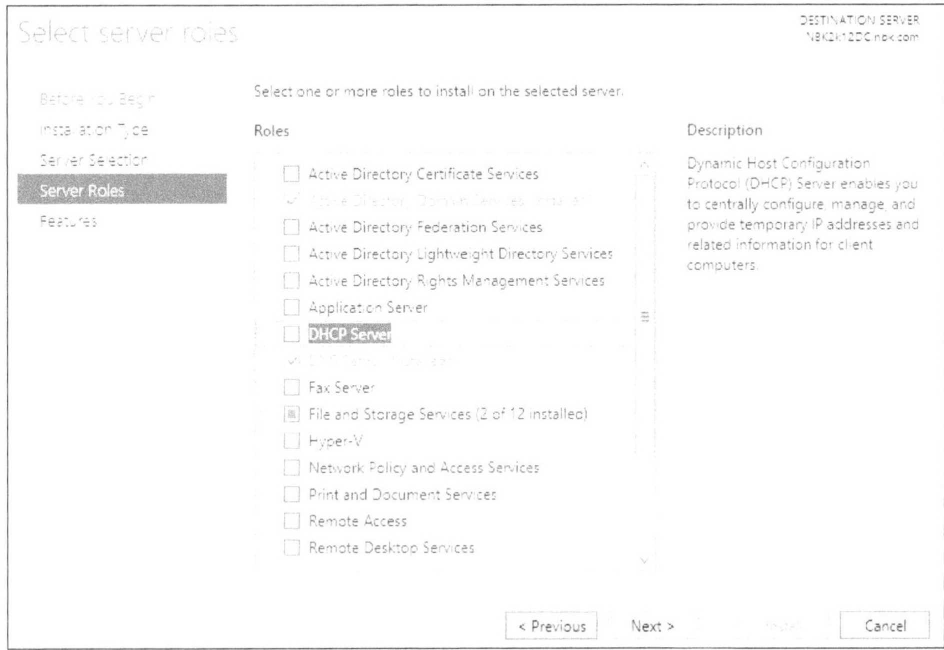

5. The moment you choose **DHCP Server**, it will pop up the list feature that will be required to manage the DHCP role. Click on **Add Features** and then on **Next** to proceed:

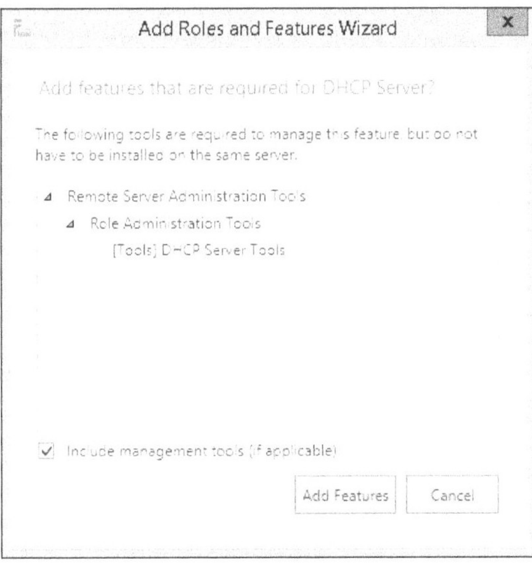

6. The next screen will appear to choose the features. We have already made our selection, so click on **Next** to proceed:

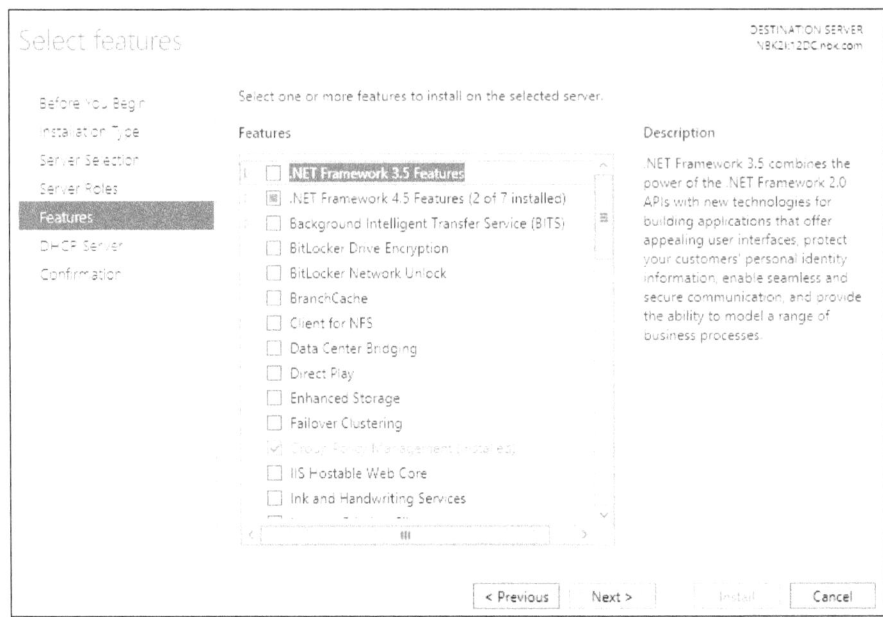

7. The next screen will give a brief description about the DHCP role and tips to go through. Click on **Next**:

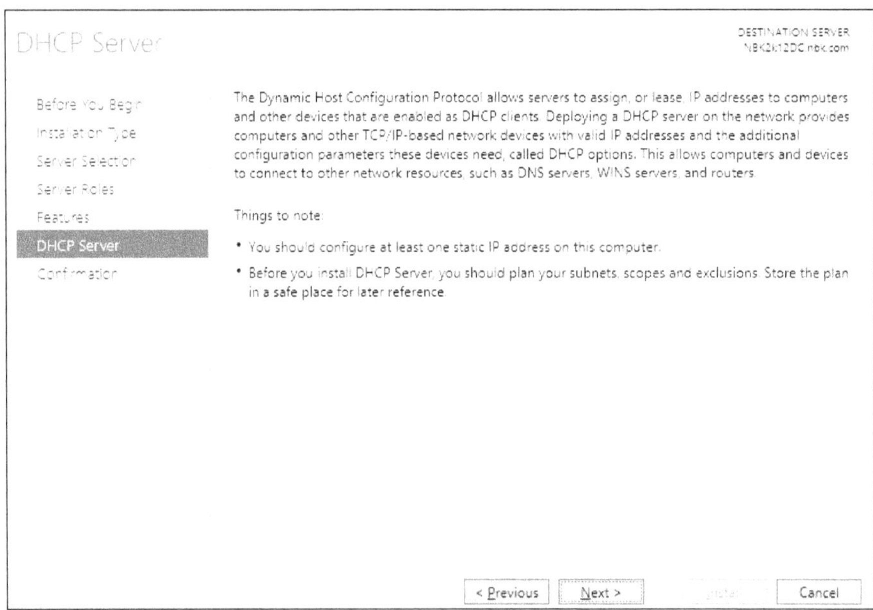

8. The next screen will show you the list of roles and features, which have been selected to install on the server. To confirm, click on **Install**:

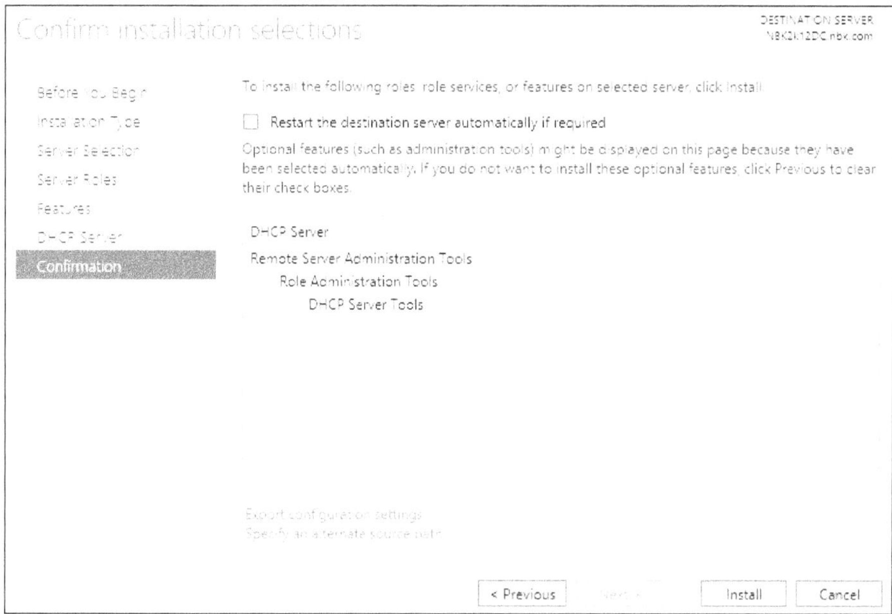


9. The next window will show you the progress on the installation status. Once the installation is complete, click on **Close**:

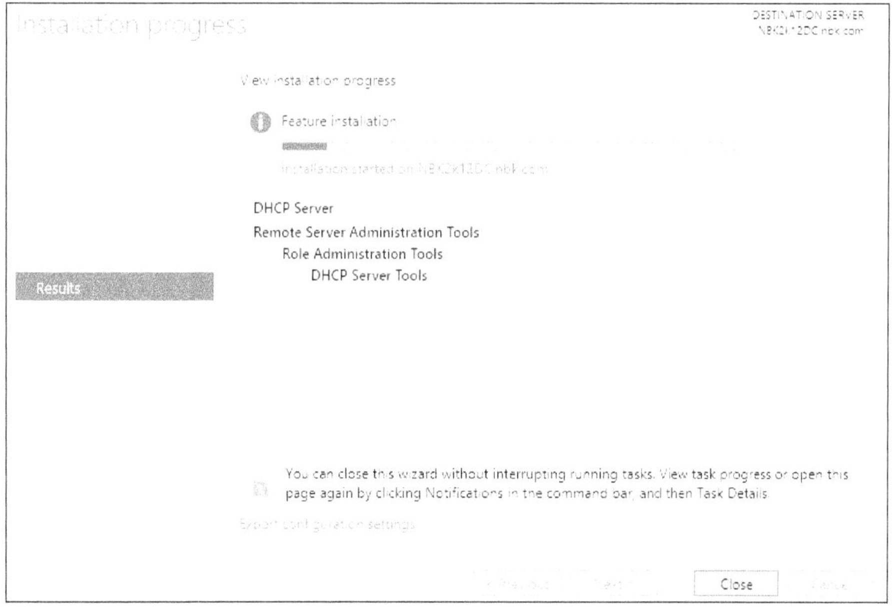

10. Once the installation is complete, the next step is to authorize the DHCP server. The reason behind authorizing the DHCP server is to make sure that DHCP is configured properly and also register the DHCP server in the active directory database that gives the authority to serve the network clients.

Only an enterprise administrator can authorize the DHCP server.

11. Click on **Commit** to authorize:

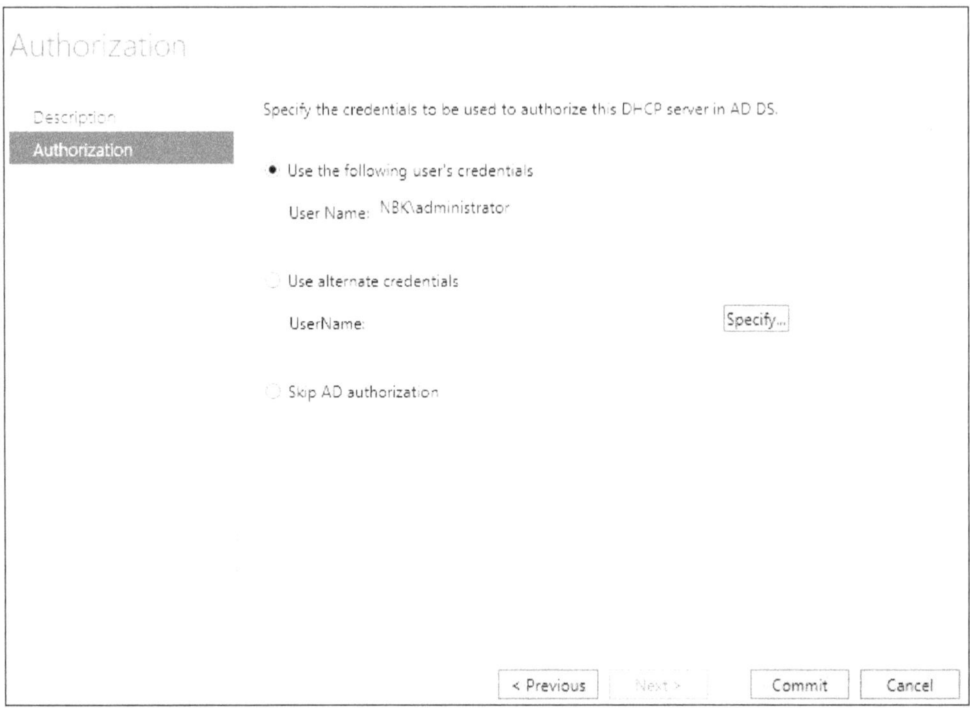

12. It will show you the following state. Click on **Close** to complete the process of authorization:

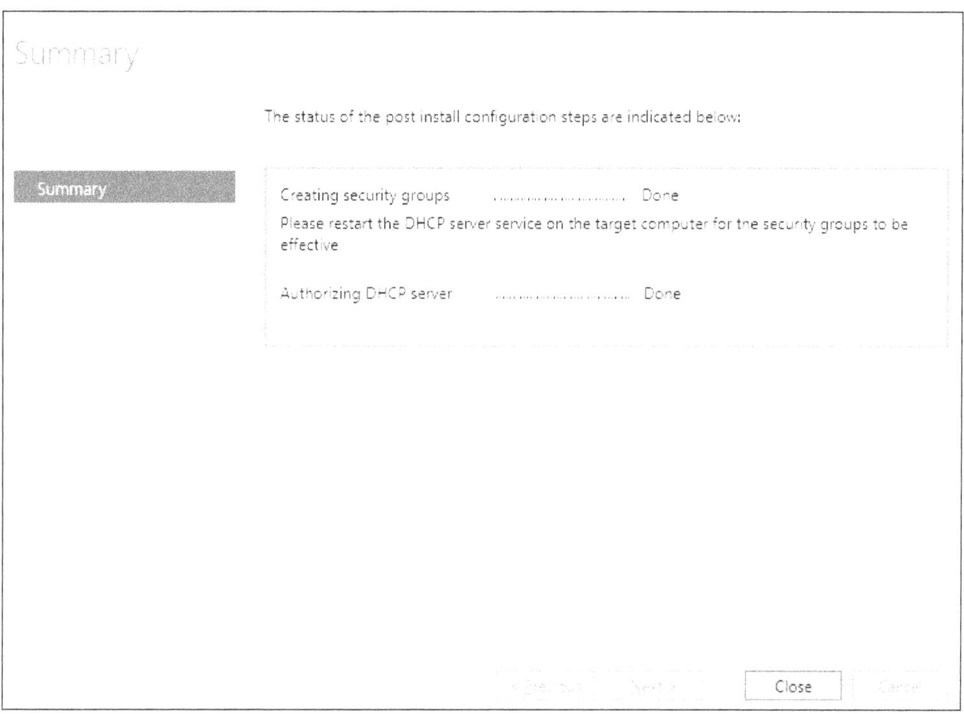


We will not configure the scope as of now; it will be done later in this book when we will implement the Citrix Provisioning Services. At that time, we will also configure the PXE boot inside DHCP.

# Setting up a certificate authority

The certificate authority is responsible for verifying the identity of organization components such as users and computers. The certificate authority verifies entity and vouches for the identity by generating the digitally signed certificate.

In this section, we will install the certificate authority role active directory certificate services on Windows server 2012 R2, and post installation, it will act as a certificate authority of the domain.

Let's go through the step-by-step installation of role active directory certificate services:

1. To start, click on **Add roles and Features** in the server manager:

2. On the installation type screen, we will choose **Role-based or feature-based installation** as active directory certificate services is the role of the Windows server:

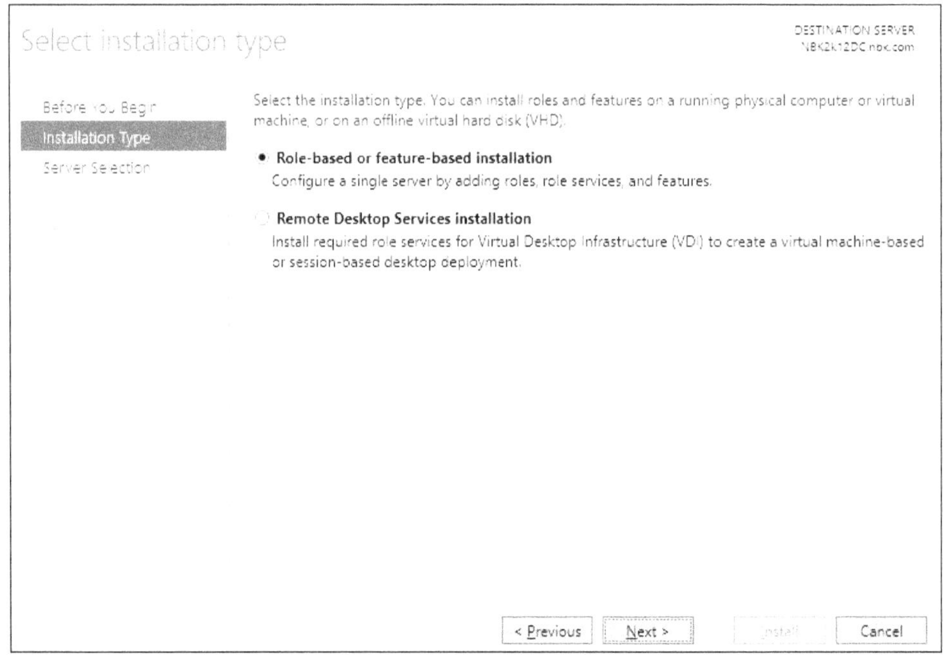

3. The next screen will show you the list of roles that can be installed on the Windows server. Choose **Active Directory Certificate Services**:

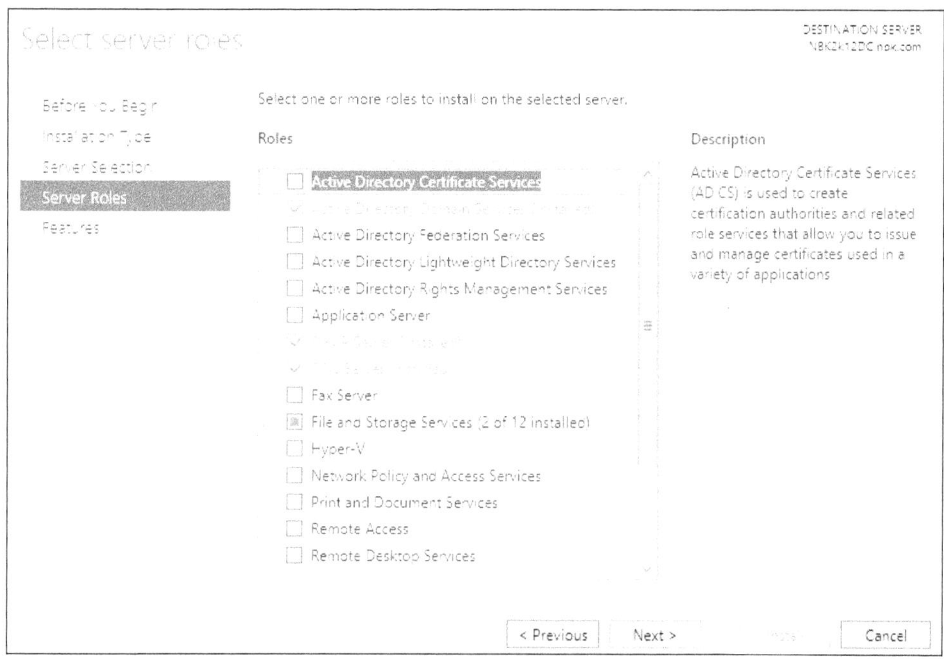


4. Post selection, it will pop up the list of features that will be required to manage this role. Click on **Add Features** and then click on **Next** to proceed:

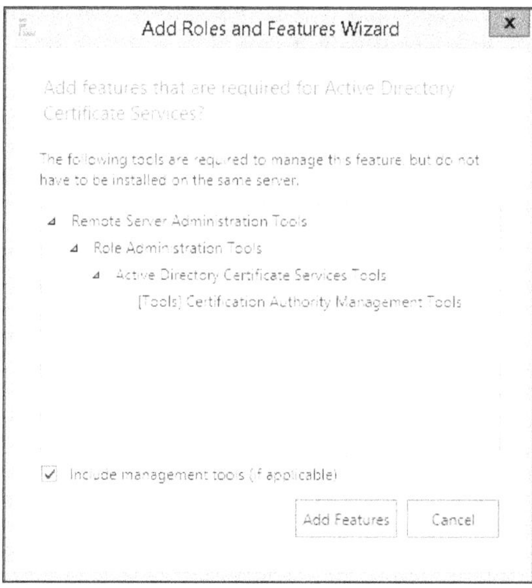

5. The next screen will show you a brief description of active directory certificate services and things to consider. Click on **Next** to proceed:

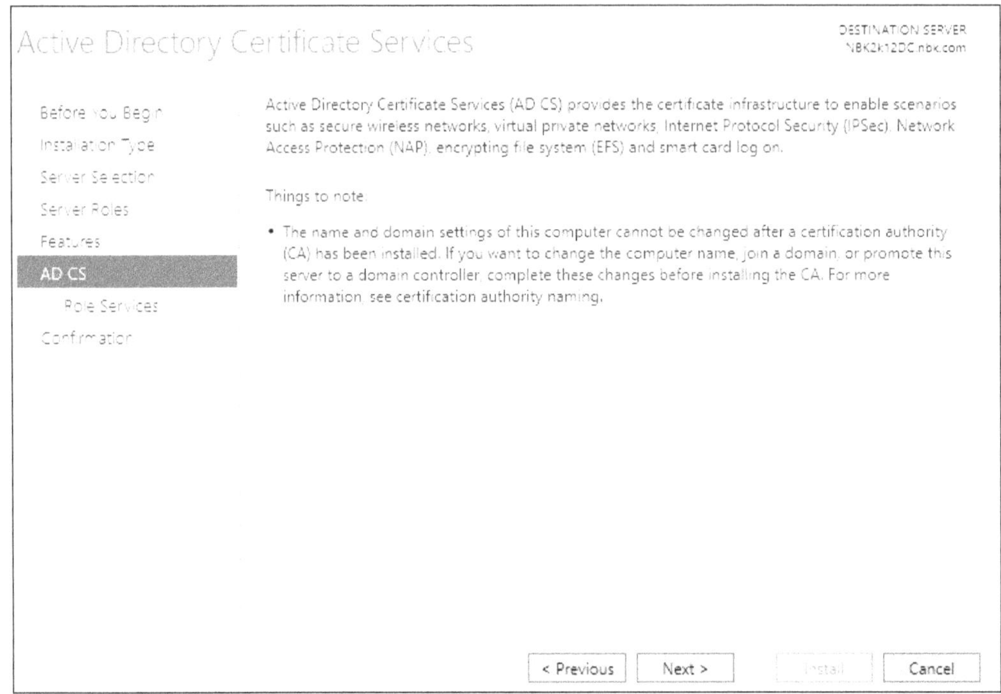

Active Directory Certificate Services
DESTINATION SERVER
NBK2k12DC.nbx.com
Before You Begin
Installation Type
Server Selection
Server Roles
Features
AD CS
Role Services
Confirmation
Active Directory Certificate Services (AD CS) provides the certificate infrastructure to enable scenarios such as secure wireless networks, virtual private networks, Internet Protocol Security (IPSec), Network Access Protection (NAP), encrypting file system (EFS) and smart card log on.
Things to note:
• The name and domain settings of this computer cannot be changed after a certification authority (CA) has been installed. If you want to change the computer name, join a domain, or promote this server to a domain controller, complete these changes before installing the CA. For more information, see certification authority naming.
< Previous
Next >
Install
Cancel


6. The next screen will give you the list of role services that you may want to add to your certificate authority. In this section, we will only choose **Certification Authority** and click on **Next**:

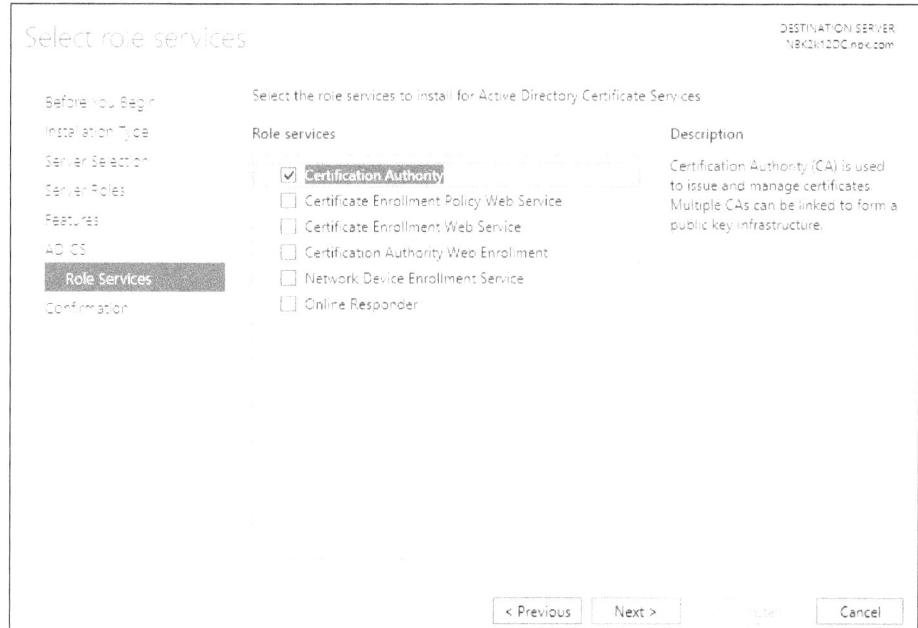


7. The next screen will show you the selection that you have made during the installation wizard and it will require your confirmation to proceed. To confirm, click on **Install**:

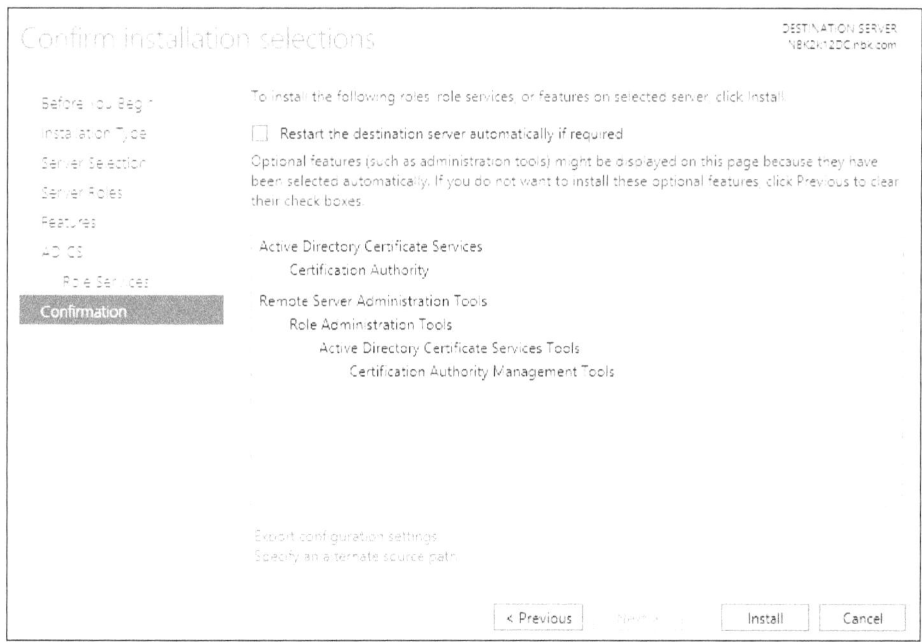

8. Wait for the installation progress bar to complete and the click on **Close** to complete the installation:

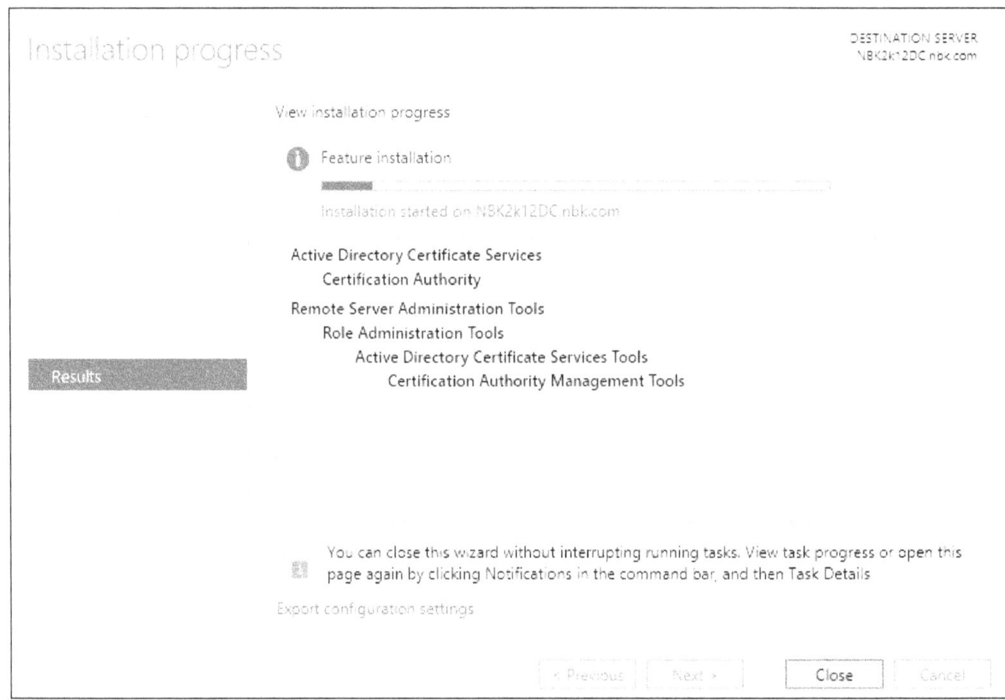


# Configuring the certificate authority

In this selection, we will do the post-installation configuration of active directory certificate services. Follow these steps:

1. Click on the exclamation mark flag, which is inside the server manager. On clicking, it will show you the following options. Click on **Configure Active Directory Certificate Services on th...**:

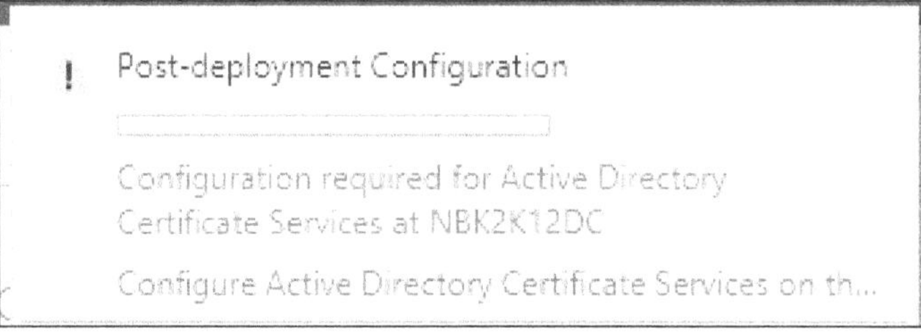

2. On the next screen, we have to specify the credentials to configure the role. It can be the enterprise admin account. Click on **Next**:

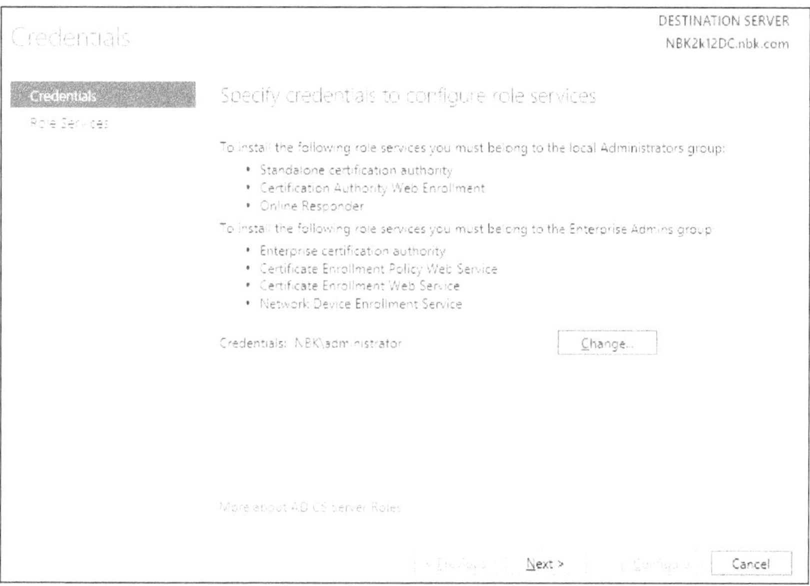


3. Select the role you want to configure. In the installation selection, we have only installed the certificate authority. It will be selected by default. Click on **Next**:

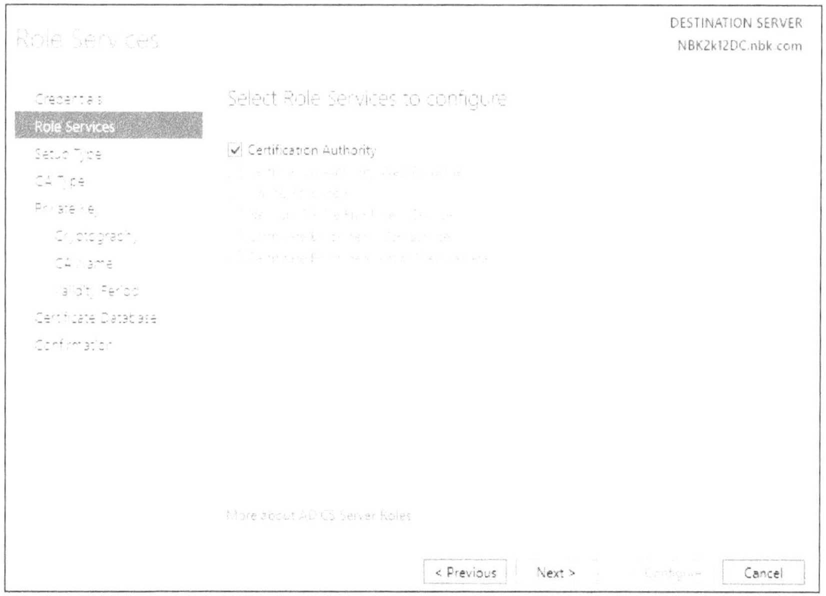

4. On the next screen, choose the setup type. Choose **Enterprise CA** and click on **Next**:

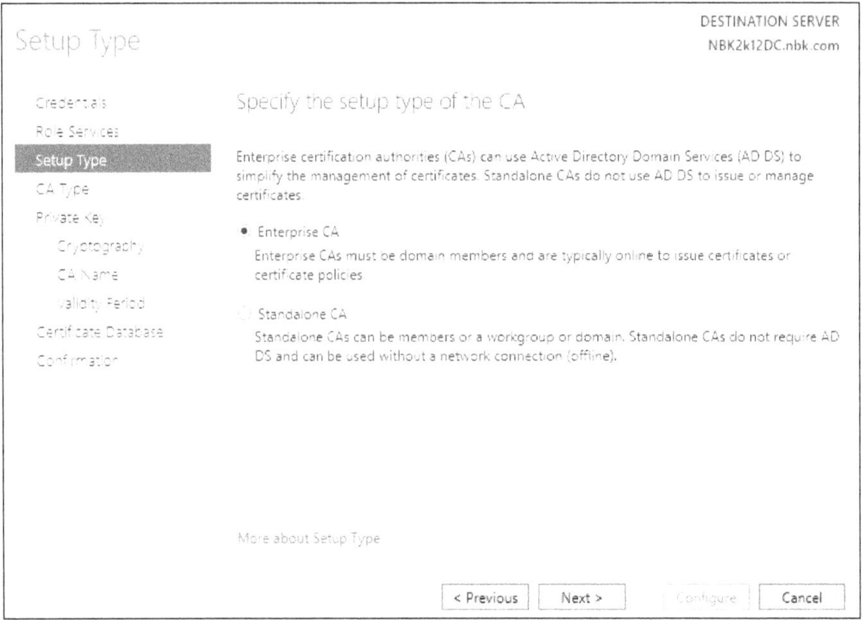


5. This CA will be our root CA. Choose **Root CA** and click on **Next**:

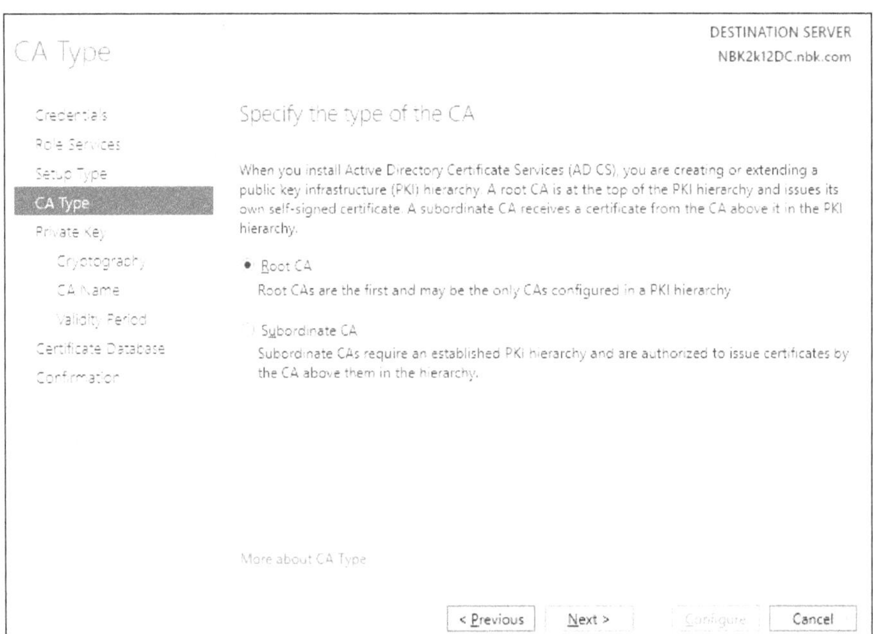

6. In the next window, we will get the option to either create a new private key or to use an existing one. Choose **Create a new private key** and click on **Next**:

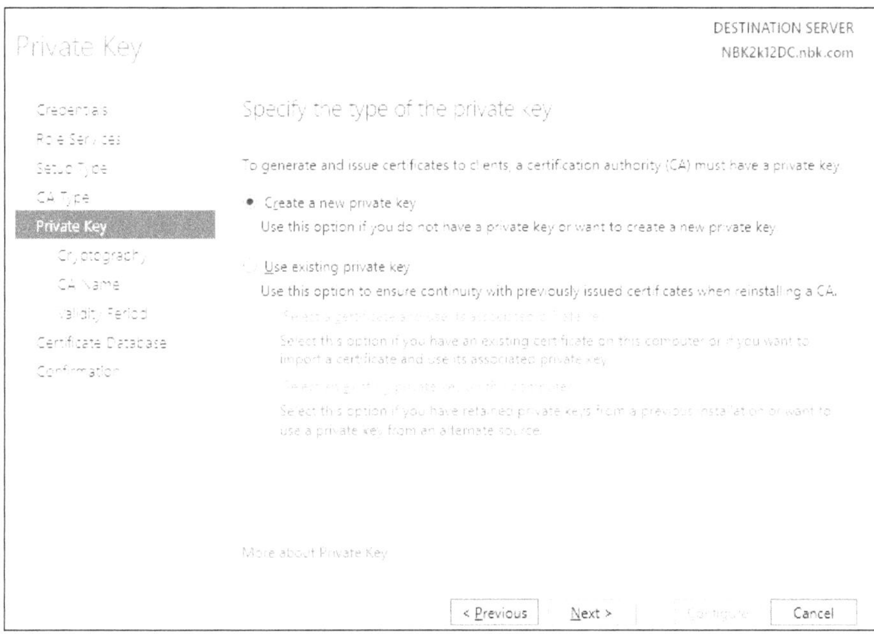

7. The next screen will give you the option to select the cryptography option. Choose the required one and click on **Next**:

8. On the next screen, you have to give the CA a name. Click on **Next**:

9. Specify the validity period of the certs, which will be generated from CA. Click on **Next**:

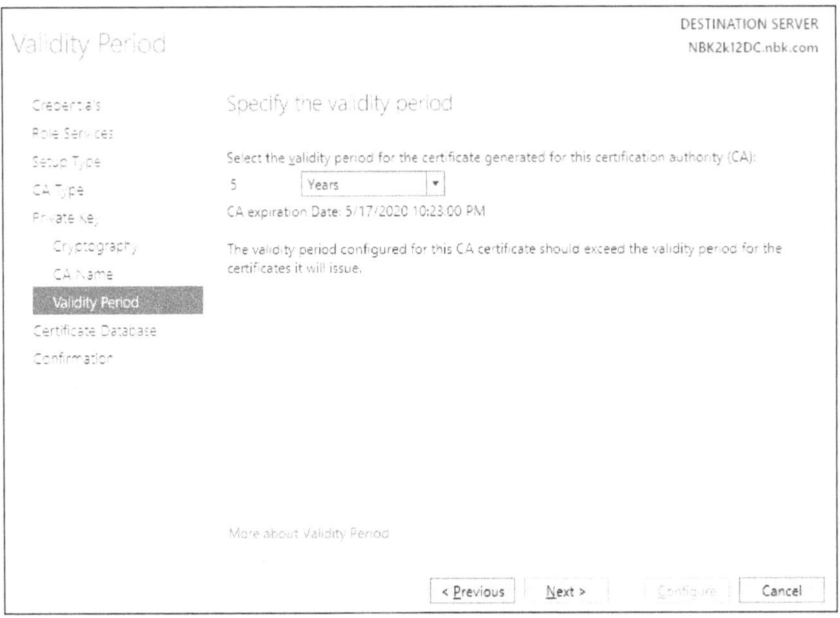

10. Specify the database location where you want to keep the database and database log file. Click on **Next**:

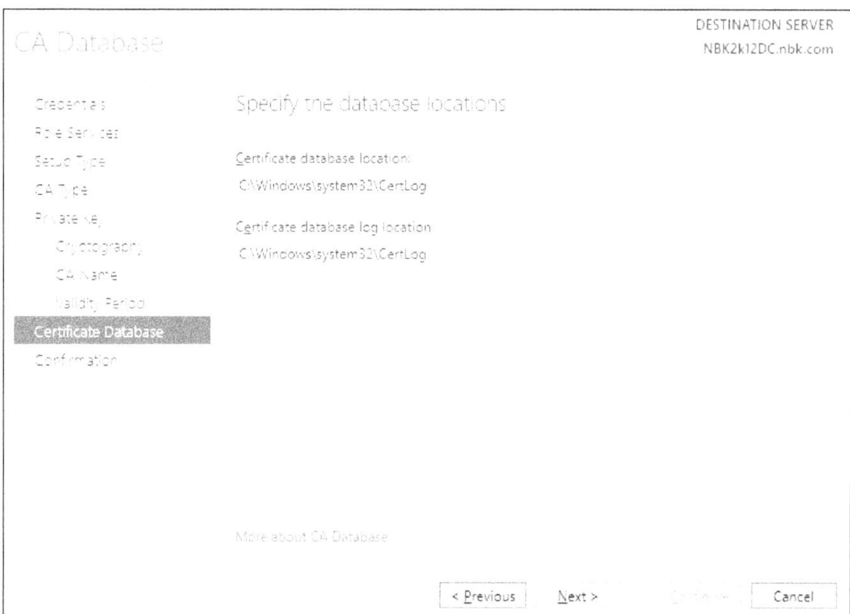


11. Confirm the selection that you have made in the configuration wizard so far by clicking on **Configure**:

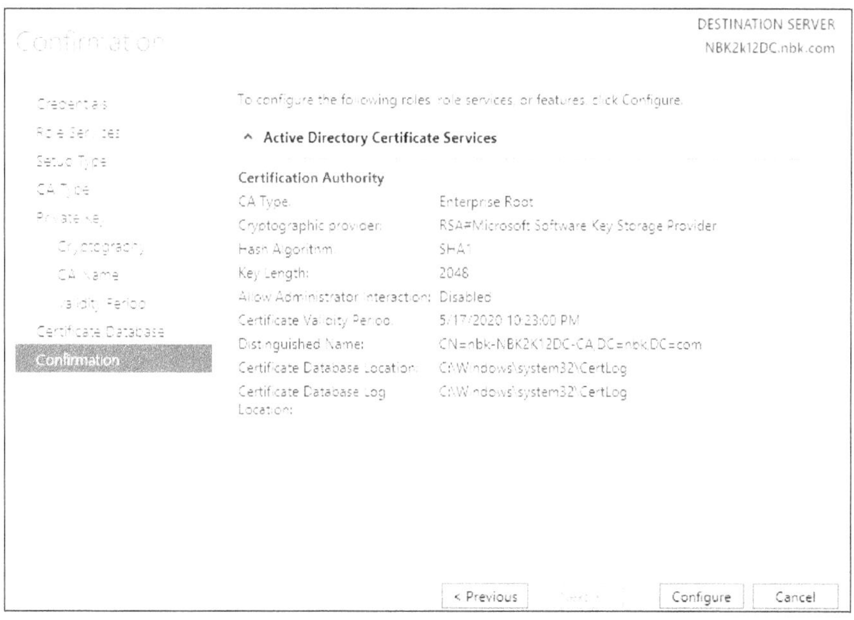

12. It will go through the configuration process as follows:

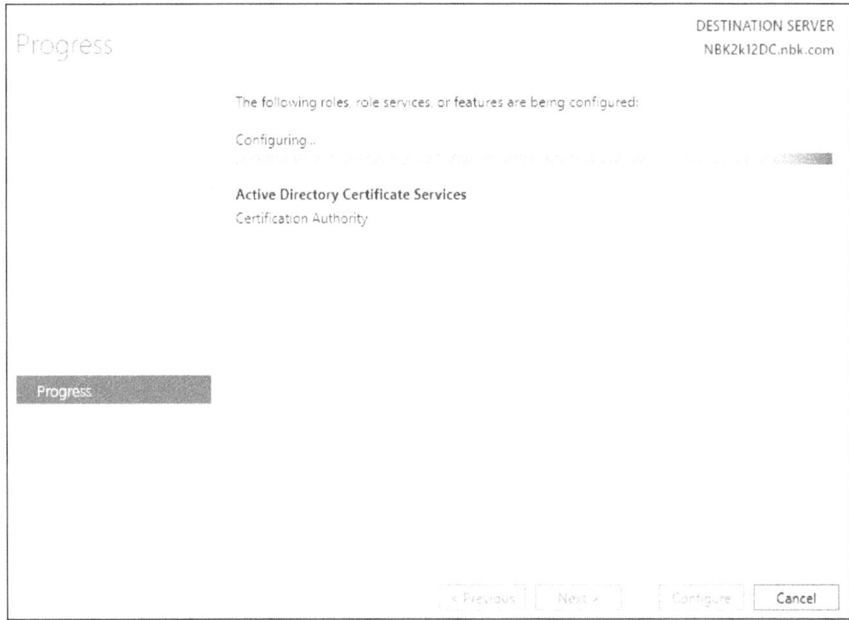


13. Once configured, it will show you the following result:

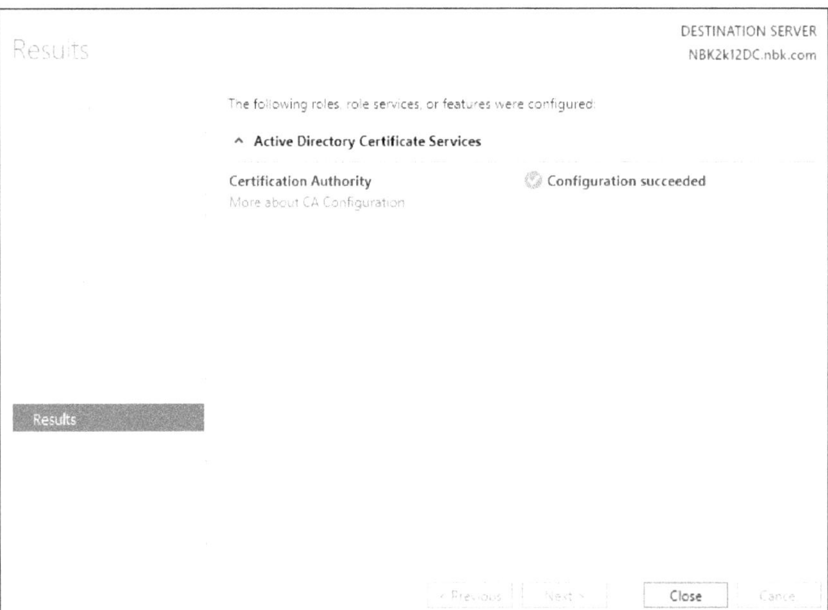

14. Click on **Close** to complete this certificate authority configuration wizard.

Now, we can use this server role whenever we need the certificate for the domain components. It will be useful when we will install the StoreFront.

# Setting up SQL server 2012

In this section, I will walk you through the steps of setting up the SQL server for our Citrix XenApp 7.6 site. The role of SQL server is to host the database, which will contain all the static configuration of Citrix XenApp 7.6. When we say static configuration, it means it will store the information such as configuration, policy created inside the Citrix studio, user preferences, and utilization reports.

Let's start the installation. I already have the server ready for the installation, which is Microsoft Windows 2012 R2 with 2 vCPU and 2 GB RAM installed on it. Follow these steps:

1. Mount the SQL server 2012 ISO to the server for installation. You can download your copy from `http://www.microsoft.com/en-us/download/details.aspx?id=29066`.
2. Browse the mounted ISO and look for the `setup` file and run it as an administrator:

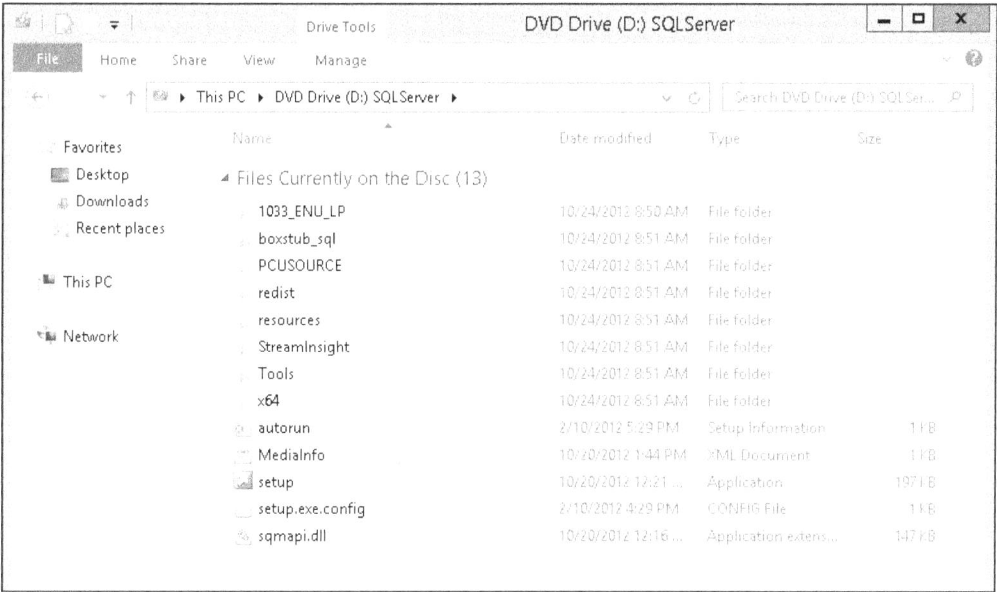

3. It will bring up **SQL Server Installation Center**. From the **Planning** section, chose **System Configuration Checker** to make sure your server is passing all the checks to install SQL on it:

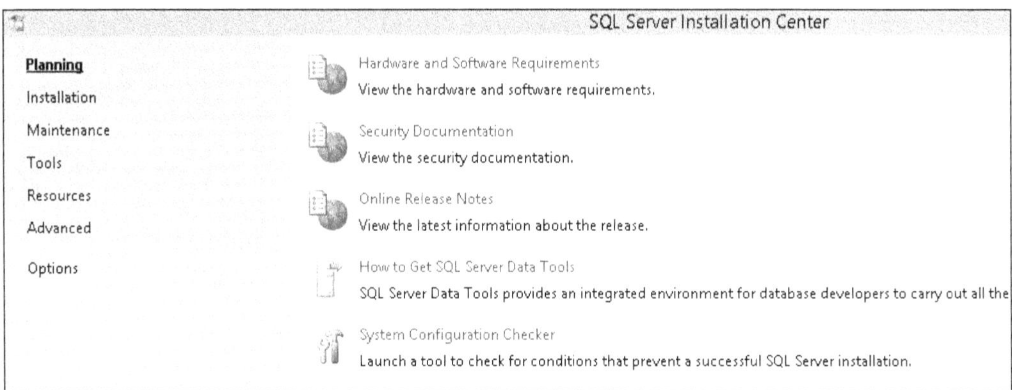


4. It will bring up another window and it will go through the checklist and show the report whether they passed or failed:

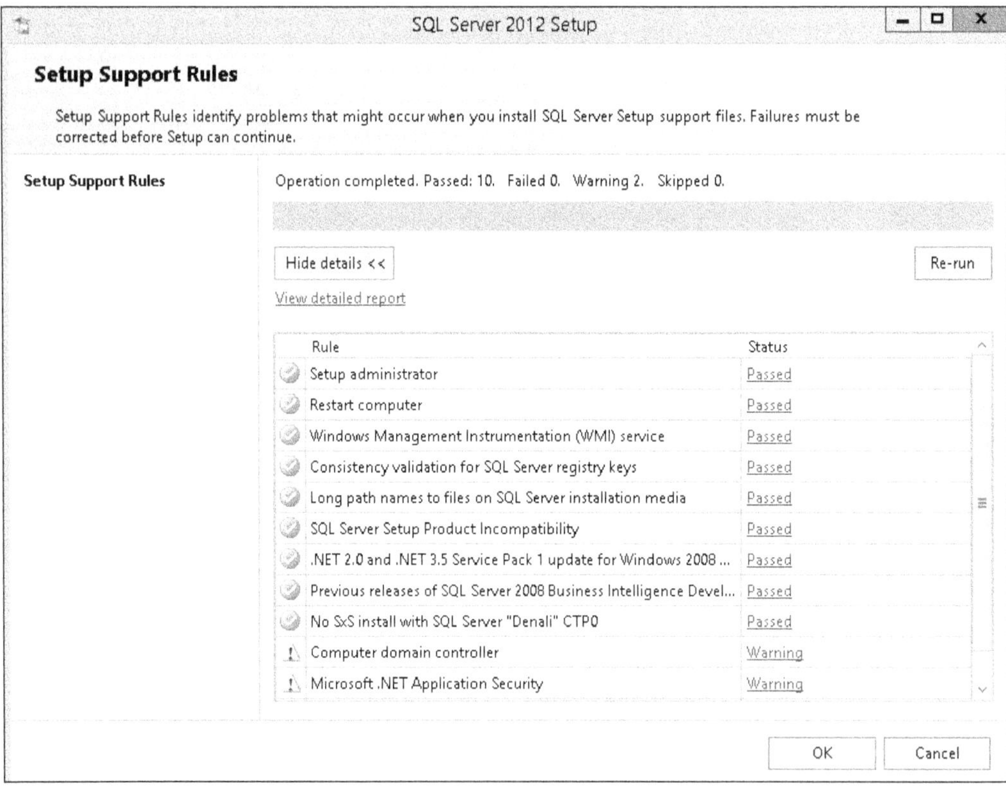

As this is the proof of concept environment, I am installing most of the components on single server, which is also the domain controller. In the production, it is recommended to install every component on different servers to avoid a single point of failover.

5. Once the server has passed all the tests, click on **OK** and go back to **SQL Server Installation Center** and in the **Installation** section, click on **New SQL Server stand-alone installation or add features to an existing installation**:

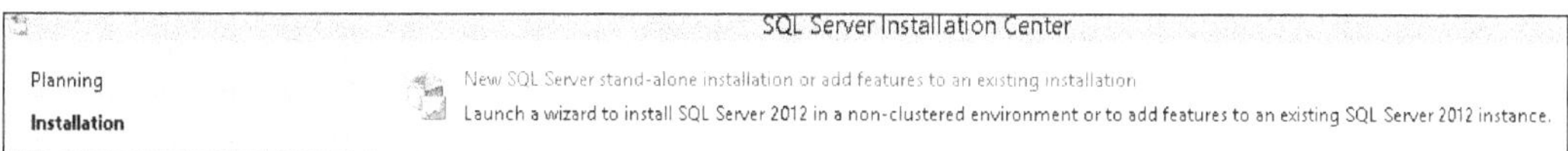


6. After clicking on the stand-alone mode of install, it will ask you for the product key or you can also use it for free for a limited amount of time in the evaluation mode. Click on **Next** after making the selection:

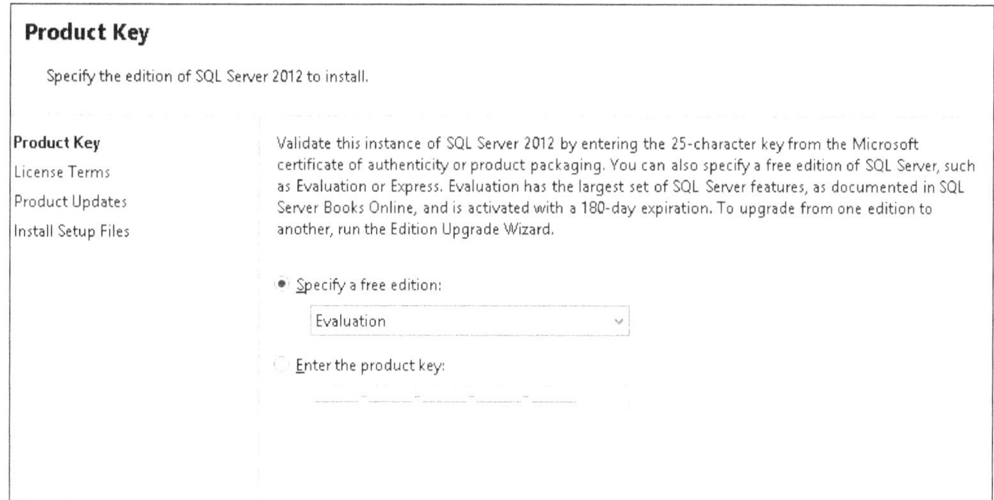

Product Key
Specify the edition of SQL Server 2012 to install.
Product Key
License Terms
Product Updates
Install Setup Files
Validate this instance of SQL Server 2012 by entering the 25-character key from the Microsoft certificate of authenticity or product packaging. You can also specify a free edition of SQL Server, such as Evaluation or Express. Evaluation has the largest set of SQL Server features, as documented in SQL Server Books Online, and is activated with a 180-day expiration. To upgrade from one edition to another, run the Edition Upgrade Wizard.
Specify a free edition:
Evaluation
Enter the product key:

7. On the next screen, you have to accept the agreement from Microsoft for **MICROSOFT SQL SERVER 2012 EVALUATION**. Go through it, accept it, and click on **Next**:

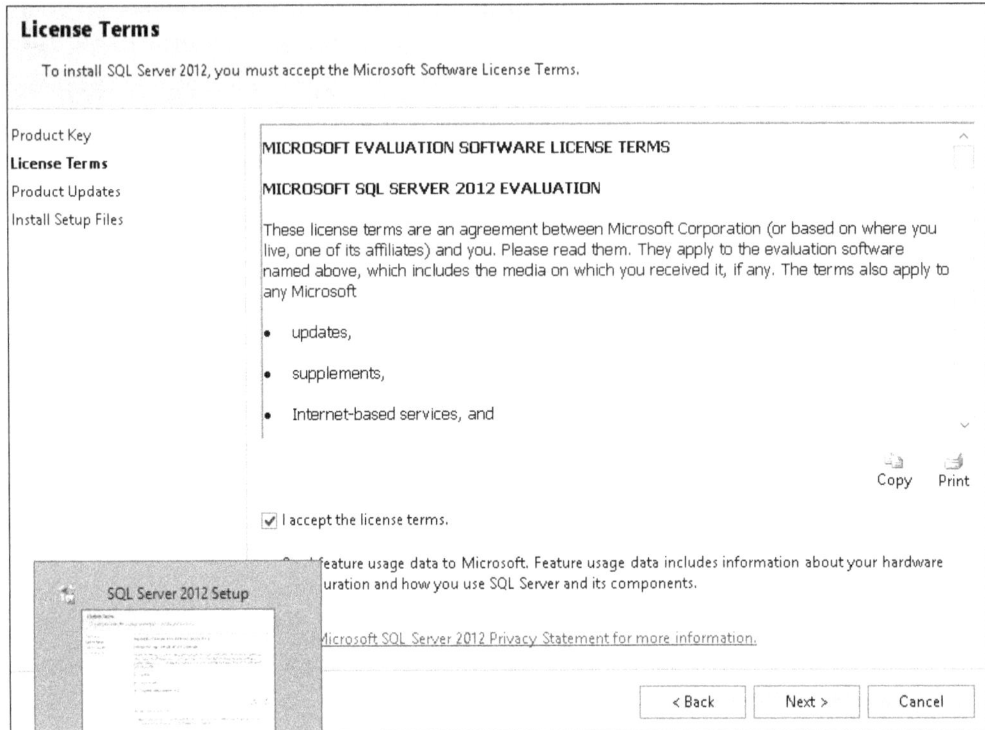


8. Post clicking on **Next**, it will look for the product updates. As my server is not connected, it will show some error that it was not able to communicate to get the update. Ignore the window and click on **Next**, and it will start the installation of setup files:

**Install Setup Files**

SQL Server Setup will now be installed. If an update for SQL Server Setup is found and specified to be included, the update will also be installed.

Product Key
License Terms
Product Updates
**Install Setup Files**

SQL Server Setup files are being installed on the system.

| Task | Status |
| --- | --- |
| Install Setup files | In Progress |

< Back     Install     Cancel

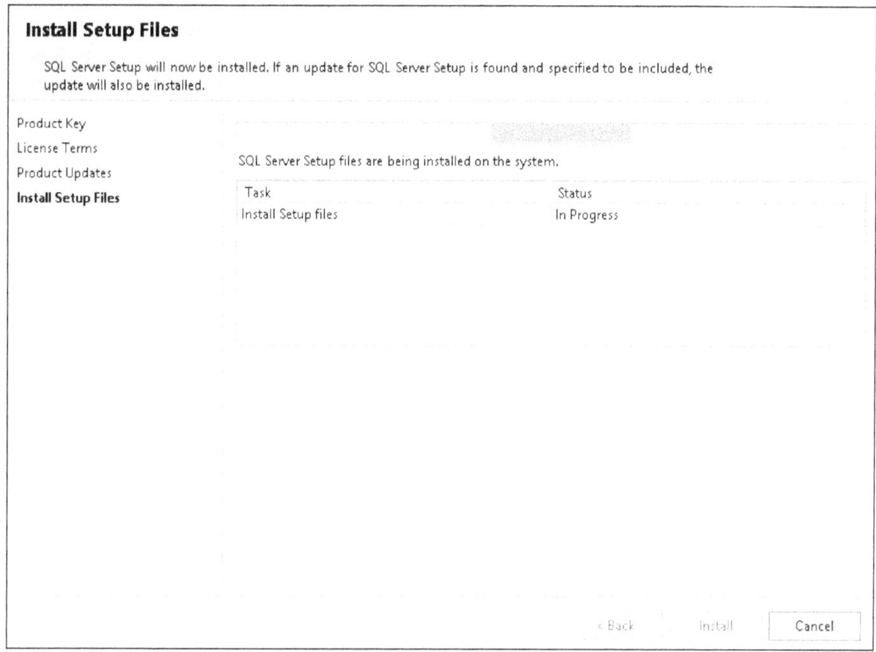

9.  Post installation, it will bring up another window to choose the setup role. Choose **SQL Server Feature Installation** and click on **Next**:

**Setup Role**

Click the SQL Server Feature Installation option to individually select which feature components to install, or click a feature role to install a specific configuration.

Setup Support Rules
**Setup Role**
Feature Selection
Installation Rules
Disk Space Requirements
Error Reporting
Installation Configuration Rules
Ready to Install
Installation Progress
Complete

● SQL Server Feature Installation

Install SQL Server Database Engine Services, Analysis Services, Reporting Services, Integration Services, and other features.

○ SQL Server PowerPivot for SharePoint

Install PowerPivot for SharePoint on a new or existing SharePoint server to support PowerPivot data access in the farm. Optionally, add the SQL Server relational database engine to use as the new farm's database server.

○ All Features With Defaults

Install all features using default values for the service accounts.

< Back     Next >     Cancel     Help

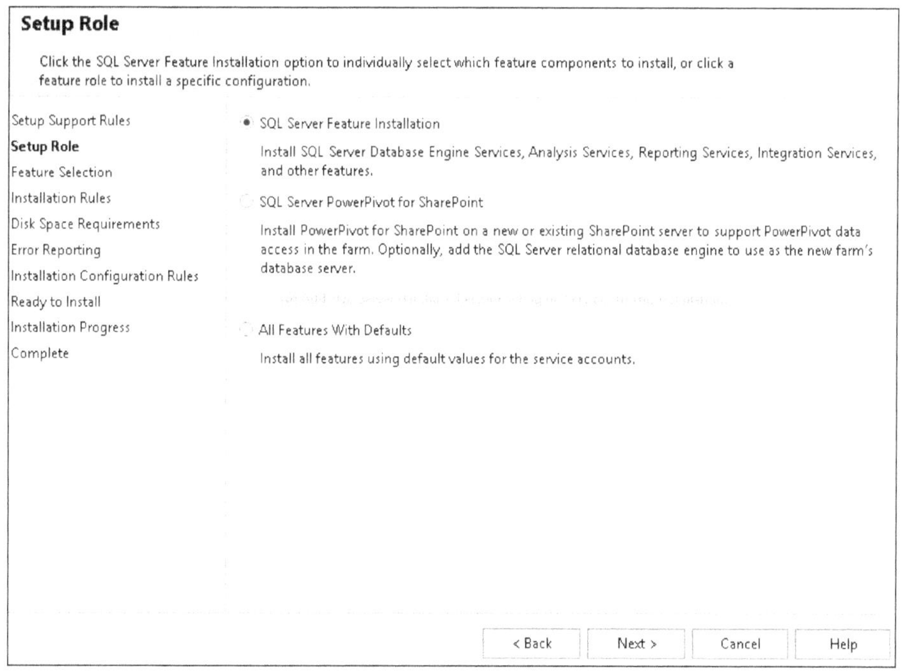

10. The next window will give you the list feature to select, and you have to make the following selections:
    - **Database Engine Services** and its sub-option **SQL Server Replication**
    - From **Shared Features**, choose **Management Tools**
11. Click on **Next**:

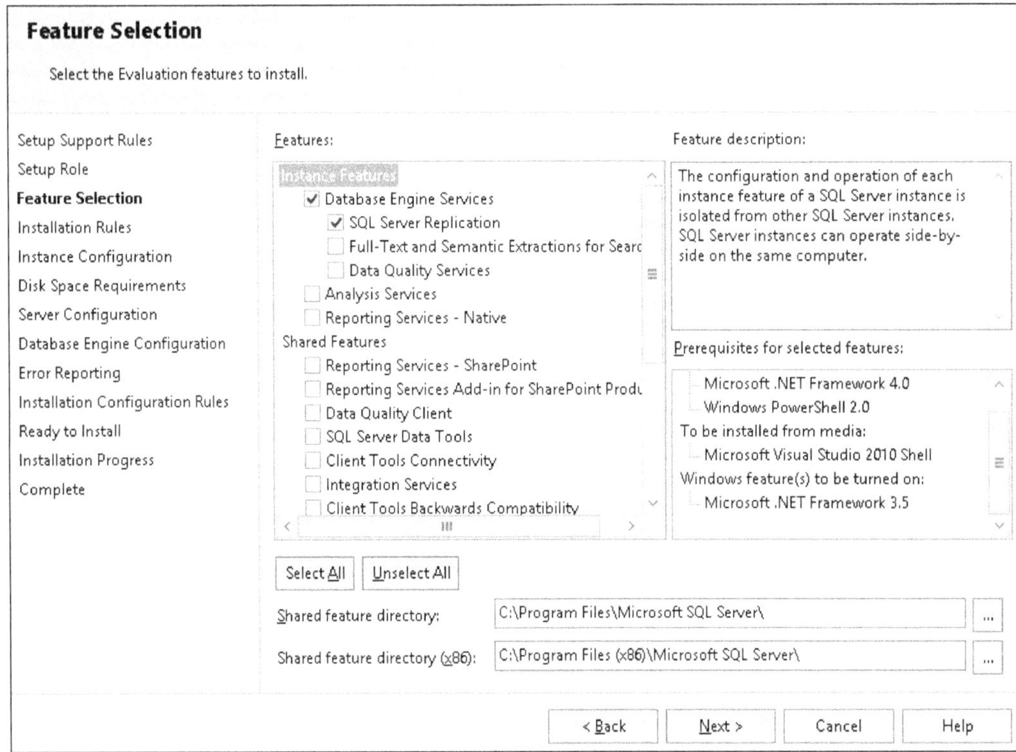


12. Follow the installation wizard and choose **Instance Configuration** as a default or you can change it as per the design.

13. In **Server Configuration**, change the account name for **SQL Server Agent** and **SQL Server Database Engine** to database service account and leave **SQL Server Browser** to **NET AUTHORITY\LOCAL SERVICE** and change **Startup Type** to **Automatic** for all the three SQL server services and then click on **Next**:

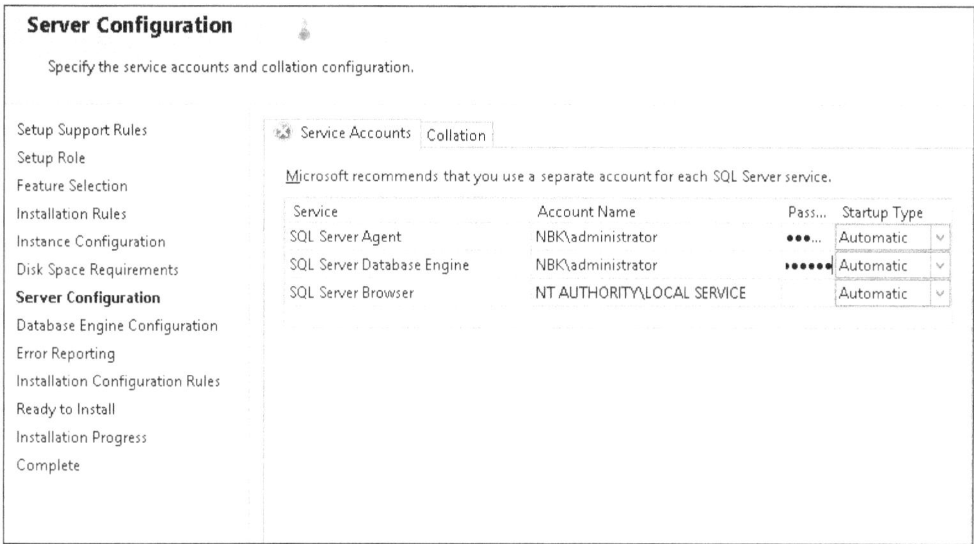


14. In **Database Engine Configuration**, choose the windows authentication mode, add the SQL services account, and verify the data directories for the different database. Once done, click on **Next** to continue.
15. In **Installation Configuration Rules**, it will run the checks for the rules related to `FAT32` file system, existing clustered or cluster-prepared installation, and so on. Check the result and click on **Next**.

16. After giving all the inputs for the configuration, the installation will now show you the **Ready to Install** window with the summary of configuration input provided. Go through it and click on **Install**:

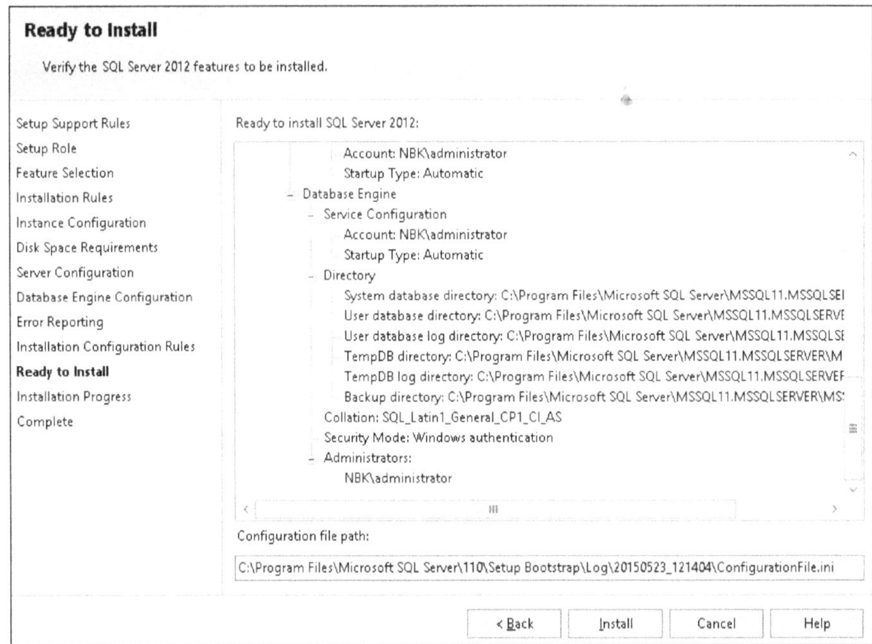


17. Monitor the installation progress and once completed, click on **Finish**.

# Setting up SQL mirroring

SQL mirroring is generally used for the disaster recovery model to provide high availability to the database. To implement SQL mirroring, you need at least two SQL server instances on the same server or the different server. One of the SQL server instances acts as the primary database instance, known as principal, while the other one is a mirror instance, know as mirror instance.

While configuring SQL mirroring for Citrix database, make sure the database is in full recovery mode and follow these steps:

1. Make sure the Citrix database that requires mirroring is in full recovery model.
2. Then, take a backup of the Citrix database with the transaction log and restore it on another SQL server instance, which will act as a mirror.

While restoring the database, the process should be executed using No recovery option.

3. To enable database mirroring, go to the primary SQL server instance using SQL server management studio; go to the properties of the Citrix database and then go to the **Mirror** tab.
4. When you click on **Configure Security**, it will ask you for the witness server. If you have it available, you can click on **Yes**, else click on **No**. In our case, we can click on **Yes** and then on **Next**.

   Witness server is basically required when you want automatic failover.

5. The next screen will ask you for the port, which will be 5022, and the endpoint name. You can name it `Mirror`. Click on **Next**.
6. In the next window, choose your mirror database. If you are using the same server with different database instances as in our scenario, change the port number to 5023 and enter the endpoint name as `Mirror` and then click on **Next**.
7. On the next screen, you have to repeat the steps this time for the witness server. Don't forget change the port number to 5024.
8. In the next window, enter the service account which you want to use and then click on **Next**.
9. The next screen will be a summary screen where you can review your configuration. Review it and click on **Finish**.

It will take you back to the mirror properties of the database, which will give you the details about the principal, mirror, and witness, and in the status box, you can see the synchronization status.

# Summary

In this chapter, we learned about setting up some core infrastructure components required for XenApp 7.6 site, including the domain controller for authentication purpose, DHCP for assigning the automatic IP configuration, PXE boot for Citrix Provisioning Services, certificate authority to generate certificates for the secure communication and identification, and SQL server, which will hold the static configuration of XenApp 7.6 site.

In the next chapter, we will set up the Citrix component, which is required to set up the XenApp 7.6 site.

# 4
# Setting Up the Citrix® Components

In this chapter, we are going to implement the Citrix XenApp infrastructure components, which are going to work together to deliver the applications. The components we will be implementing are as follows:

- Setting up Citrix License Server
- Setting up Delivery Controller
- Setting up Director
- Setting up StoreFront
- Setting up Studio

Once you will complete this chapter, you will be able to understand how to install the Citrix XenApp infrastructure components for effective delivery of applications.

## Setting up the Citrix® infrastructure components

You must be aware of the fact that Citrix reintroduced Citrix XenApp in the version Citrix XenApp 7.5 with the new FMA-based architecture, replacing IMA. In this chapter, we will be setting up different Citrix components so that they can deliver the applications.

As this is proof of concept, I will be setting up almost all the Citrix components on the single Microsoft Windows 2012 R2 machine, where it is recommended that in the production environment, you should keep the Citrix components such as License Server, Delivery Controller, and StoreFront. These need to be installed on separate servers to avoid a single point of failure and provide better performance.

The components that we will be setting up in this chapter are:

- Delivery Controller: This Citrix component will act as broker, and the main function is to assign users to a server, based on their selection of application published.
- License Server: This will assign the license to the Citrix components as every Citrix product requires a license in order to work.
- Studio: This will act as the control panel for Citrix XenApp 7.6 delivery. Inside Citrix, studio administrator makes all the configuration and changes.
- Director: This component is basically for monitoring and troubleshooting, and is a web-based application.
- StoreFront: This is the frontend of the Citrix infrastructure by which users connect to applications, either via the Citrix Receiver or Web.

# Installing the Citrix® components

In order to start the installation, we need the Citrix XenApp 7.6 DVD or ISO image. You can always download, from the Citrix website, all you need to have in the MyCitrix account.

Follow these steps:

1. Mount the disc/ISO you have downloaded.
2. When you will double-click on the mounted disc, it will bring up a nice screen where you have to make the selection between **XenApp Deliver applications** or **XenDesktop Deliver applications and desktops**:

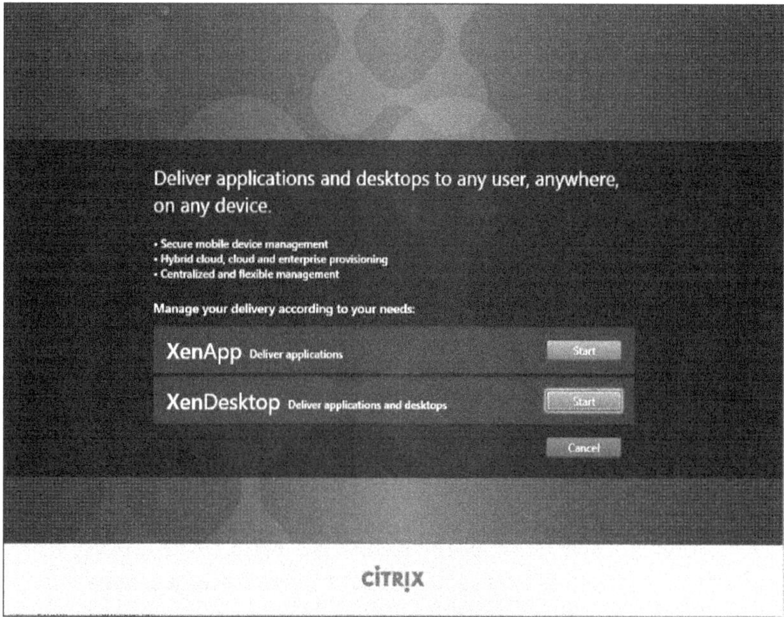


3. Once you have made the selection, it will show you the next option related to the product. Here, we need to select **XenApp**.
4. Choose **Delivery Controller** from the options:

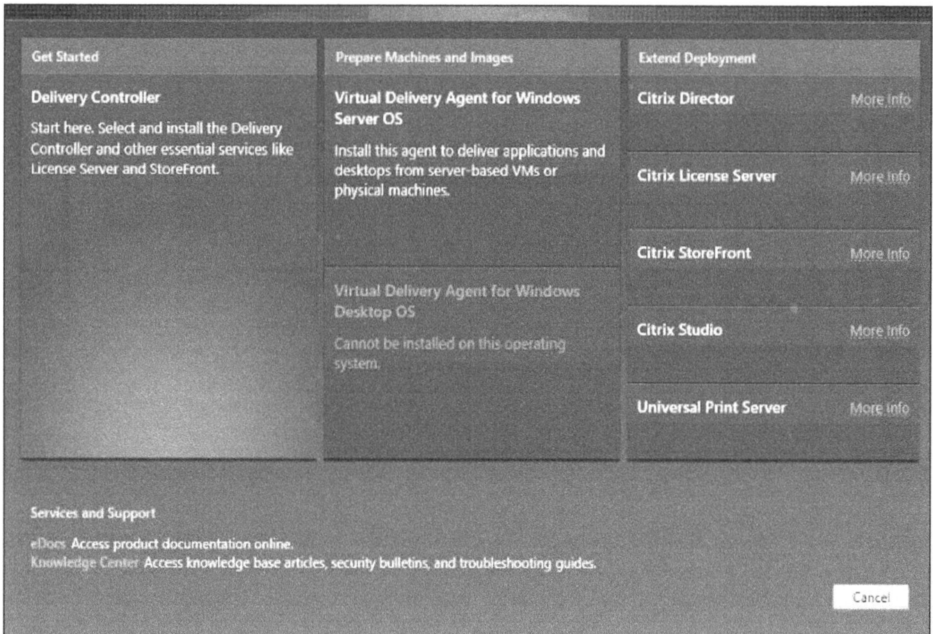

5. The next screen will show you the **License Agreement**. You can go through it, accept the terms, and click on **Next**:

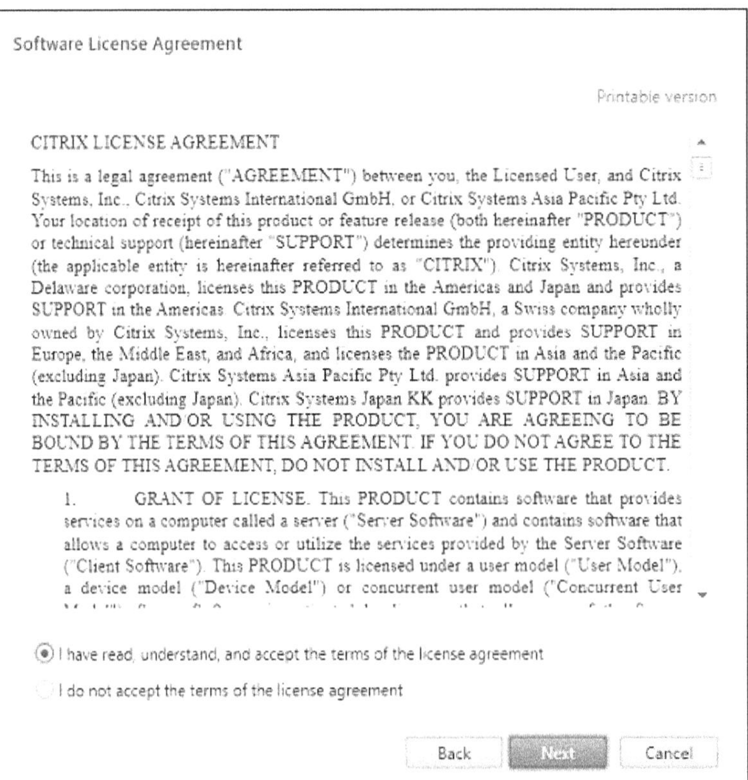

Software License Agreement
Printable version
CITRIX LICENSE AGREEMENT
This is a legal agreement ("AGREEMENT") between you, the Licensed User, and Citrix Systems, Inc., Citrix Systems International GmbH, or Citrix Systems Asia Pacific Pty Ltd. Your location of receipt of this product or feature release (both hereinafter "PRODUCT") or technical support (hereinafter "SUPPORT") determines the providing entity hereunder (the applicable entity is hereinafter referred to as "CITRIX"). Citrix Systems, Inc., a Delaware corporation, licenses this PRODUCT in the Americas and Japan and provides SUPPORT in the Americas. Citrix Systems International GmbH, a Swiss company wholly owned by Citrix Systems, Inc., licenses this PRODUCT and provides SUPPORT in Europe, the Middle East, and Africa, and licenses the PRODUCT in Asia and the Pacific (excluding Japan). Citrix Systems Asia Pacific Pty Ltd. provides SUPPORT in Asia and the Pacific (excluding Japan). Citrix Systems Japan KK provides SUPPORT in Japan. BY INSTALLING AND/OR USING THE PRODUCT, YOU ARE AGREEING TO BE BOUND BY THE TERMS OF THIS AGREEMENT. IF YOU DO NOT AGREE TO THE TERMS OF THIS AGREEMENT, DO NOT INSTALL AND/OR USE THE PRODUCT.
1. GRANT OF LICENSE. This PRODUCT contains software that provides services on a computer called a server ("Server Software") and contains software that allows a computer to access or utilize the services provided by the Server Software ("Client Software"). This PRODUCT is licensed under a user model ("User Model"), a device model ("Device Model") or concurrent user model ("Concurrent User
I have read, understand, and accept the terms of the license agreement
I do not accept the terms of the license agreement
Back
Next
Cancel

> As described earlier, this is proof of concept. We will install all the components on a single server, but it is recommended to put each component on different servers for better performance.

6. Select all the components and click on **Next**:

Core Components

For scale and performance reasons, it is recommended that Director and the License Server be installed on separate servers.

Location: C:\Program Files\Citrix   [ Change... ]

✓   Component (Select all)

✓   Delivery Controller
    Distributes applications and desktops, manages user access, and optimizes connections

✓   Studio
    Create, configure, and manage infrastructure components, applications, and desktops.

✓   Director
    Monitor performance and troubleshoot problems

✓   License Server
    Manages product licenses

✓   StoreFront
    Provides authentication and resource delivery services for Citrix Receiver, enabling you to create centralized enterprise stores to deliver applications, desktops, and other resources to users on any device, anywhere.

[ Back ]   [ Next ]   [ Cancel ]

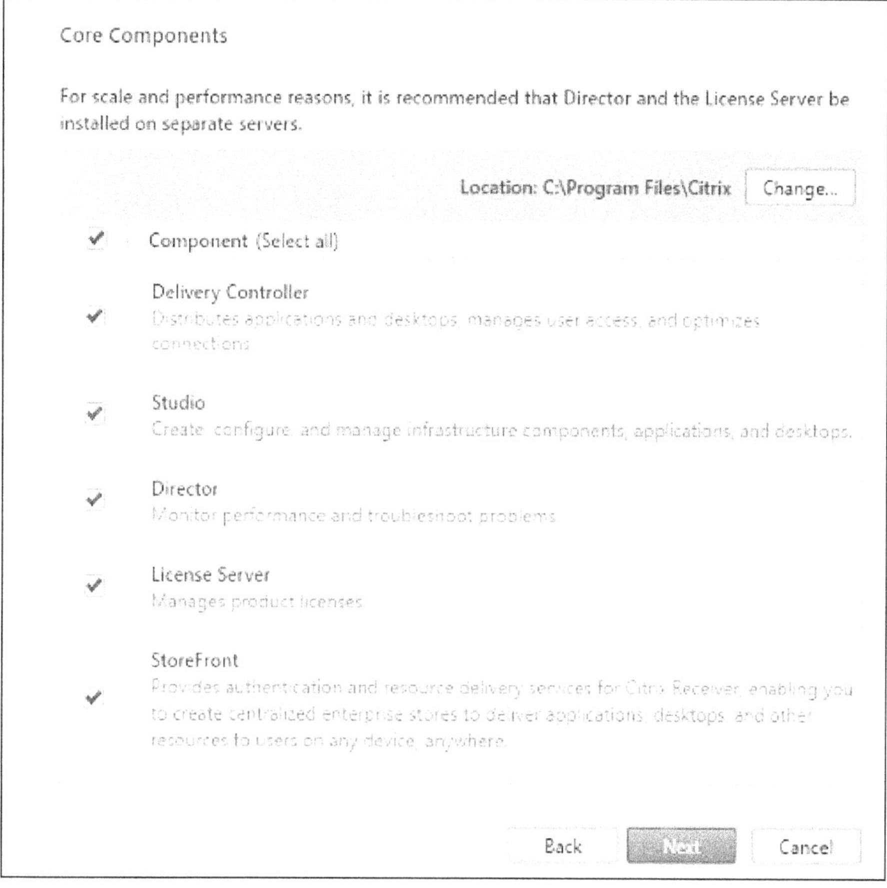

7. The next screen will show you the features that can be installed. As we have already installed the SQL server, we don't have to select the SQL Express, but we will choose **Install Windows Remote Assistance**. Click on **Next**:

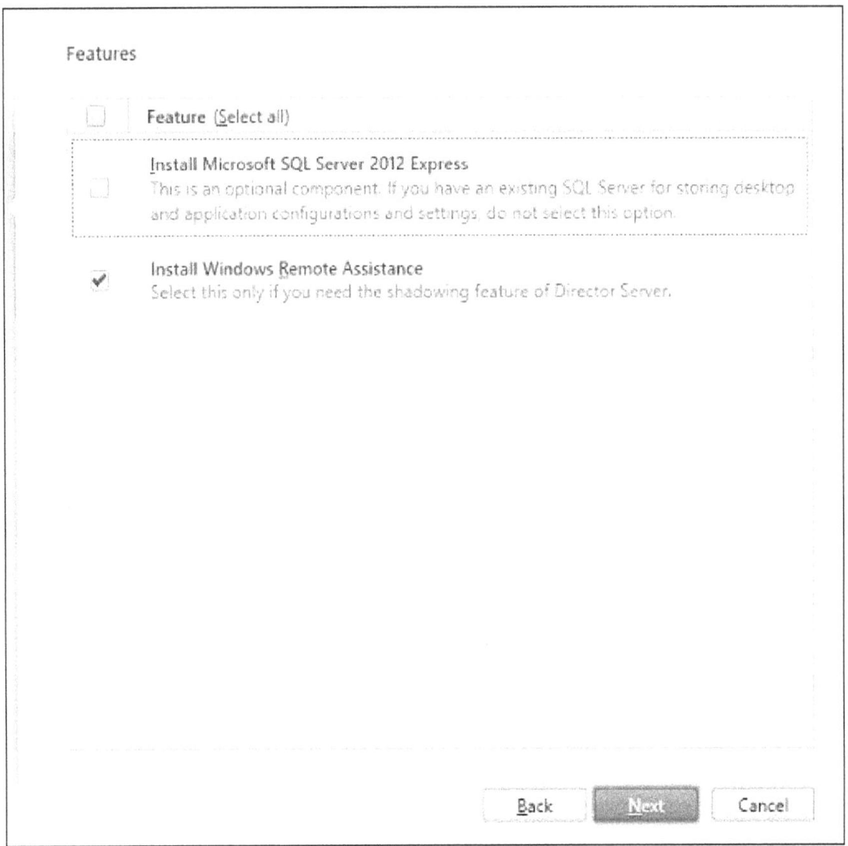
Features
Feature (Select all)
Install Microsoft SQL Server 2012 Express
This is an optional component. If you have an existing SQL Server for storing desktop and application configurations and settings, do not select this option.
Install Windows Remote Assistance
Select this only if you need the shadowing feature of Director Server.
Back
Next
Cancel

8. The next screen will show you the firewall ports that need to be allowed to communicate, and it can be adjusted by Citrix as well. Click on **Next**:

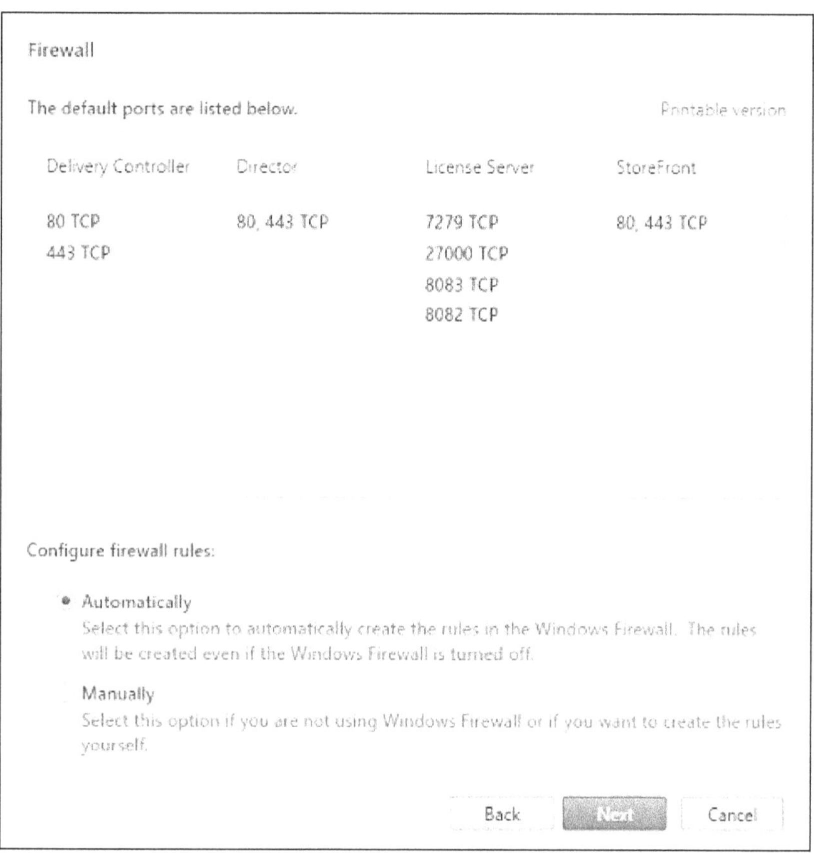
Firewall
The default ports are listed below.
Printable version
Delivery Controller
Director
License Server
StoreFront
80 TCP
443 TCP
80, 443 TCP
7279 TCP
27000 TCP
8083 TCP
8082 TCP
80, 443 TCP
Configure firewall rules:
Automatically
Select this option to automatically create the rules in the Windows Firewall. The rules will be created even if the Windows Firewall is turned off.
Manually
Select this option if you are not using Windows Firewall or if you want to create the rules yourself.
Back
Next
Cancel

9. The next screen will show you the summary of your selection. Here, you can review your selection and click on **Install** to install the components:

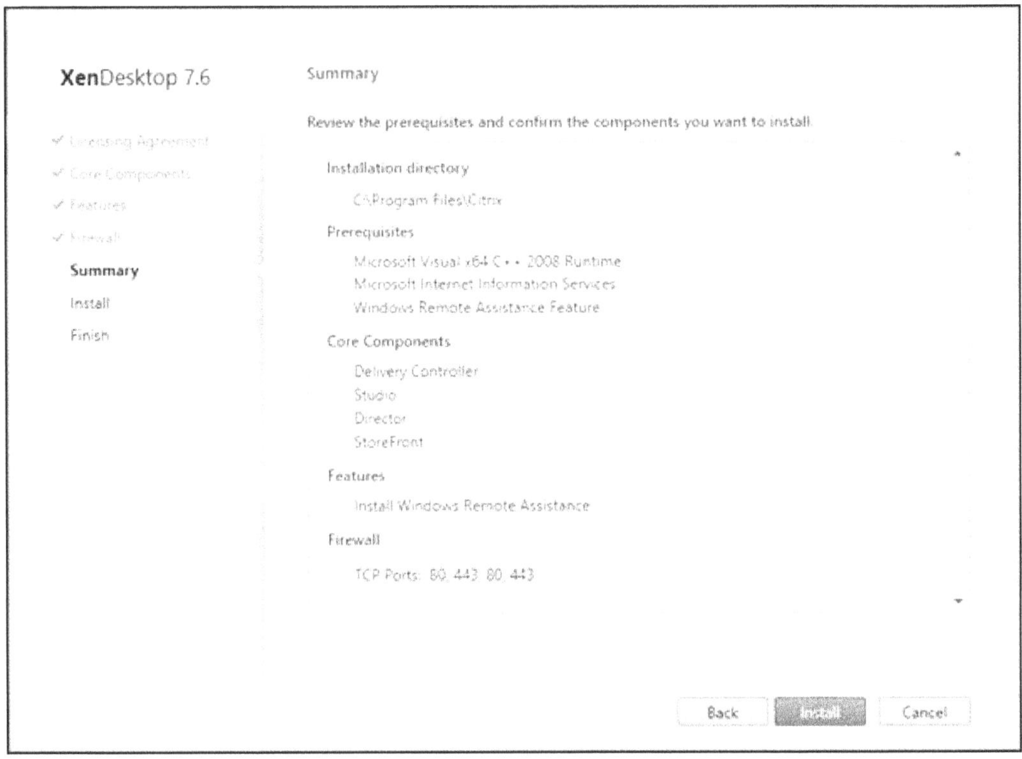


10. After you click on **Install**, it will go through the installation procedure, and once the installation is complete, click on **Next**.

By following these steps, we completed the installation of the Citrix components such as Delivery Controller, Studio, Director, and StoreFront. We also adjusted the firewall ports as per the Citrix XenApp requirement.

# Configuring the Citrix® components

In the last section, we went through the steps to install the Citrix components, and in this section, we will spend some time configuring them so that they are ready to use.

# Configuring Delivery Controller

As I said, almost all of the setting needs to be configured inside Citrix Studio, so you have to launch Citrix Studio. Following are the steps to configure Delivery Controller:

1. Launch Citrix Studio by going to **Start** | **Administrative tools** | **Citrix Studio**, and it will offer three options, as shown in the following screenshot:

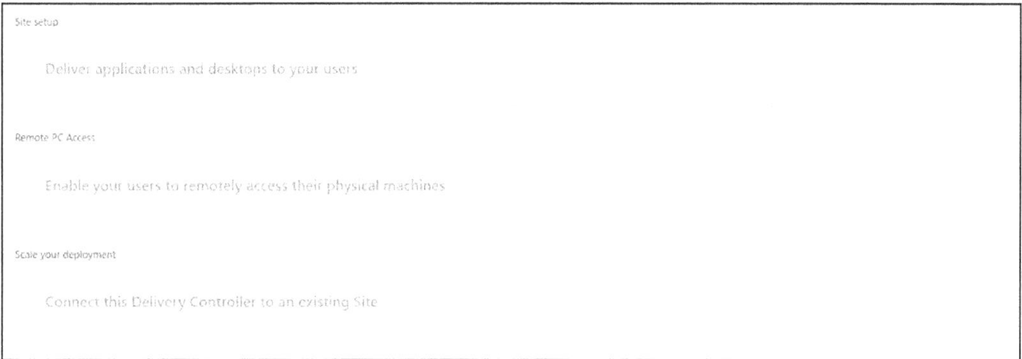


2. As this is the first Delivery Controller, we will choose the first option, which is **Deliver application and desktops to your users**. It will bring up the following screen where we will choose **A fully configured, production-ready Site (recommended for new users)** and then click on **Next**:

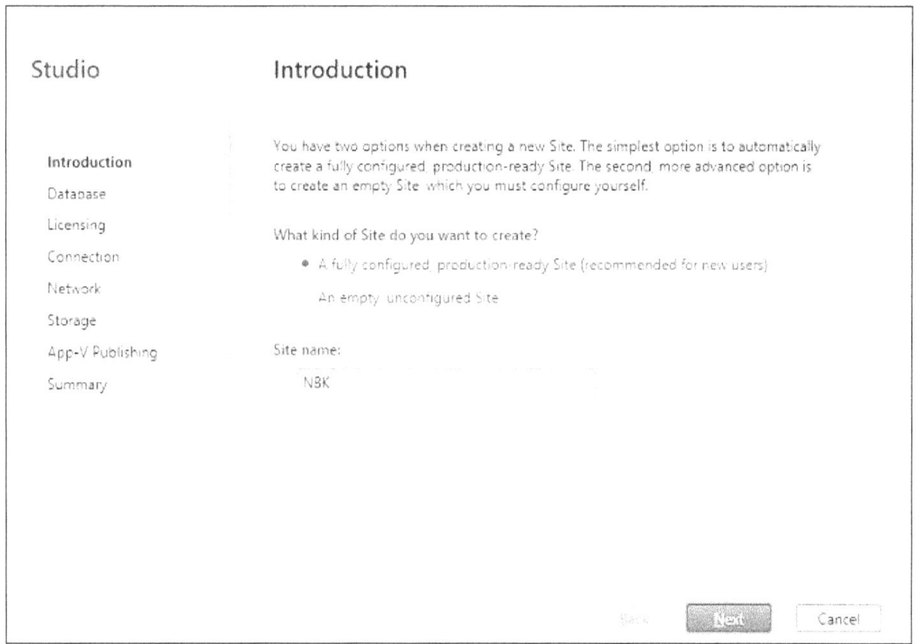

3. On clicking **Next**, it will ask you to enter the site database information where Citrix XenApp will store all the site configuration, logging, and monitoring data. Enter the information, test the connection, and click on **Next**:

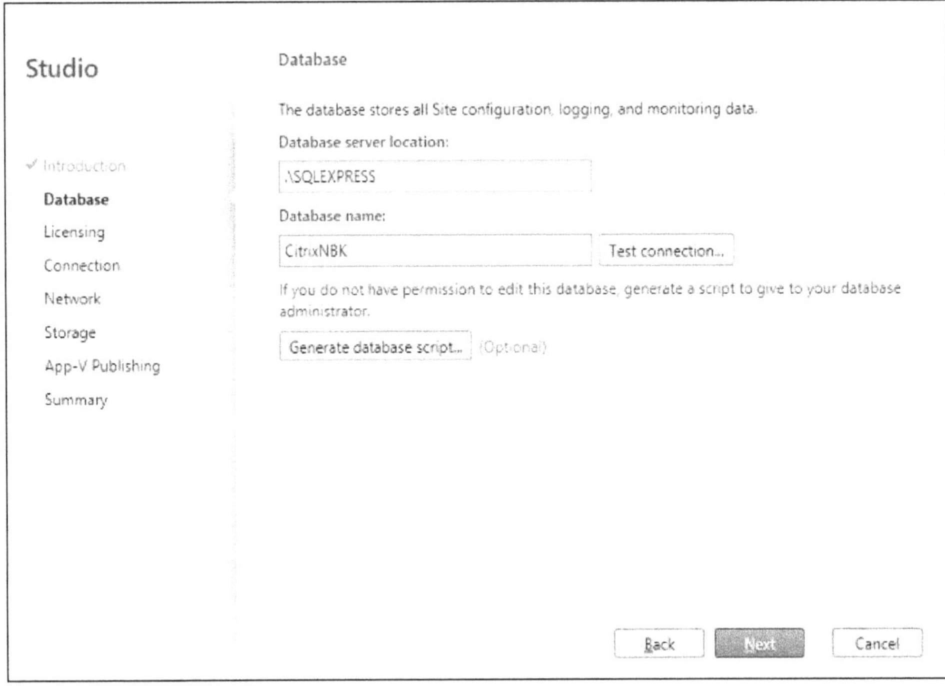


4. The next screen will ask you to enter the License Server information. Enter the information, click on test connection, and choose the required license if allocated already. Click on **Next** to continue with the configuration:

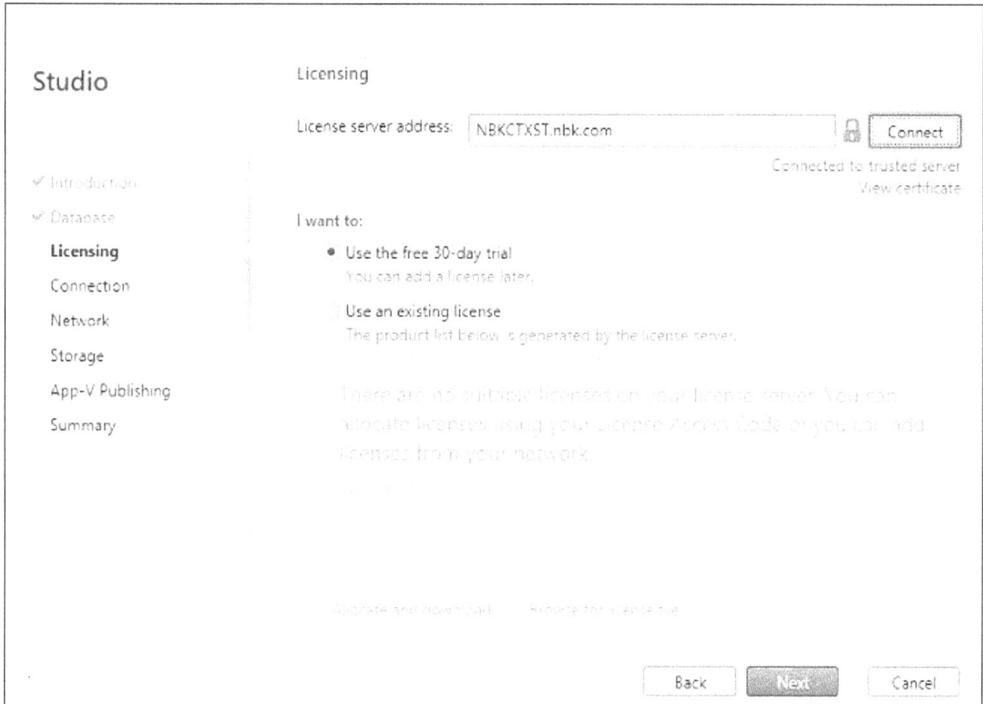

Please note that in this case, I am yet to allocate the license file.

5. On the next screen, it will ask you the connection information, which is basically used for machine management and needs to be configured if you are planning to use MCS or Citrix Provisioning Services. Enter your hypervisor information that you are planning to use and click on **Next**.

In this case, we are going to use Citrix Provisioning Services. Hypervisor with XenServer and VMware ESX and Microsoft can also be used:

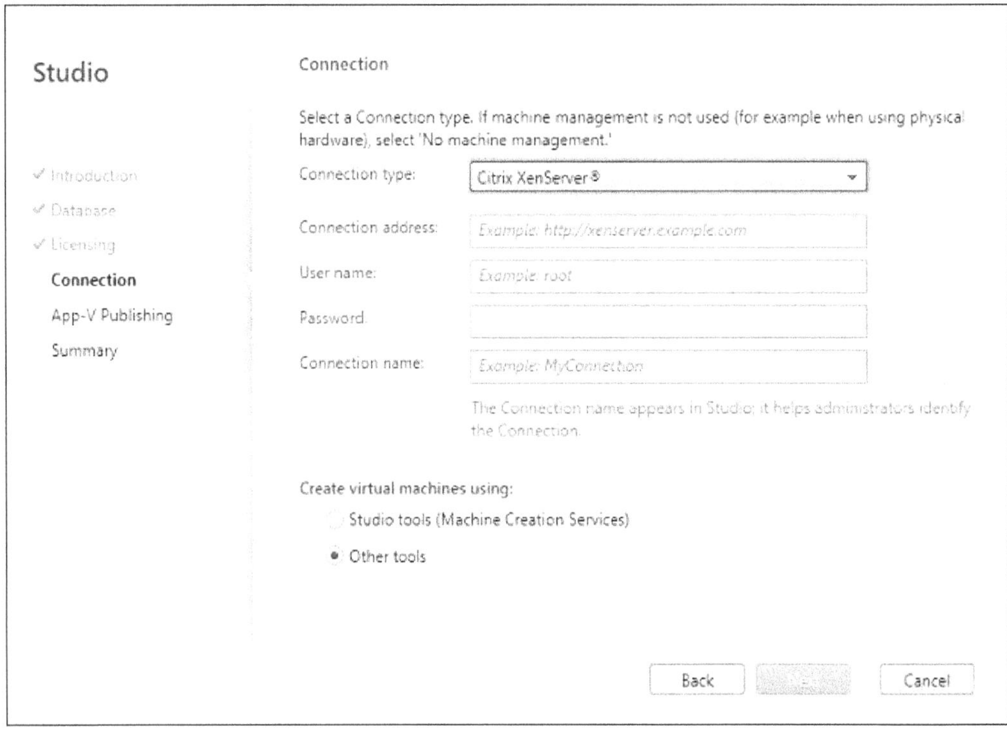

6. The next screen will ask whether you want to use **App-V** for publishing the streamed application. If you already have the App-V in the infrastructure, you can integrate with your XenApp environment, if you don't, then choose **No** and then click on **Next**:

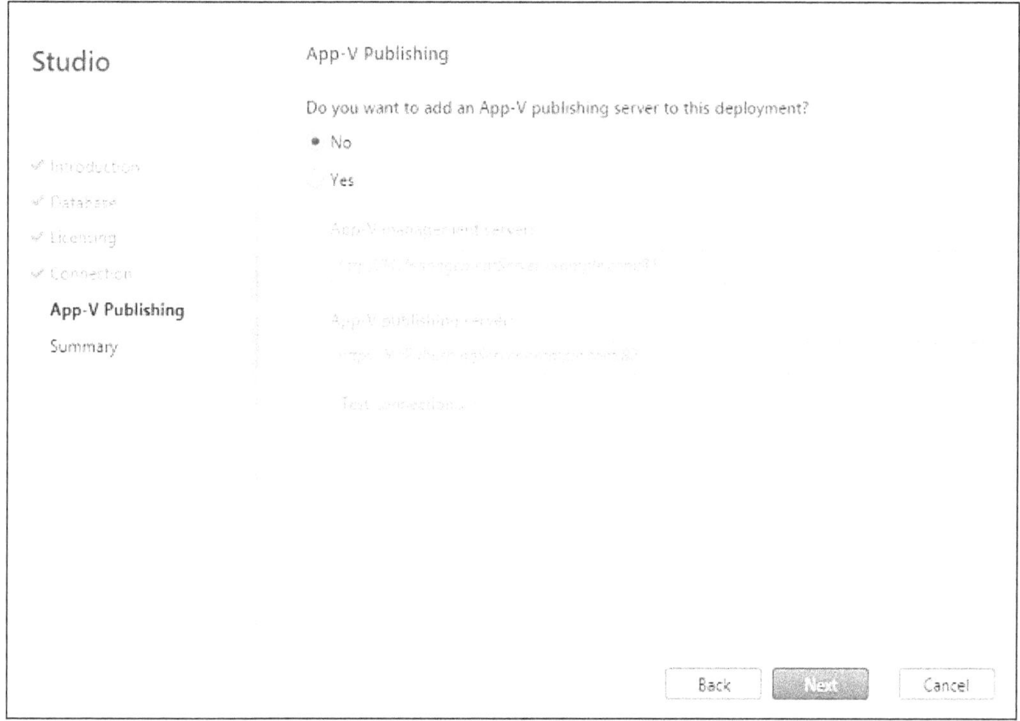

7. In the end, you will get the summary where you can review all the configuration options you have selected so far and then click on **Finish** to configure the settings. It will take a while to configure your Citrix Delivery Controller and once done, it will show you the following screen:

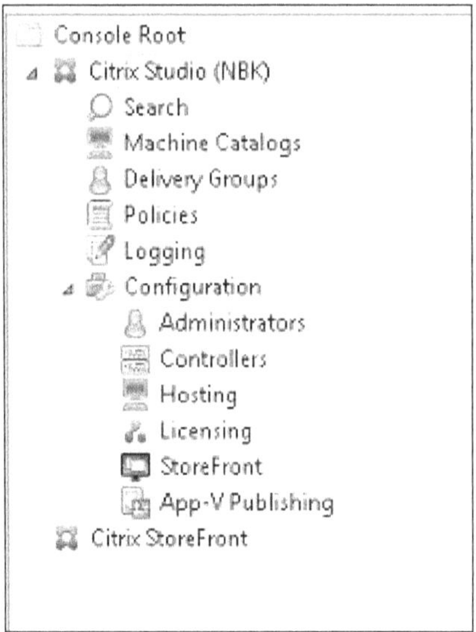


## Configuring the secondary Delivery Controller

For high availability, we are going to configure the secondary Delivery Controller by following these steps:

1. Once you have installed the Delivery Controller on the second server, after launching it, you will again get the same three options that we got earlier while setting up the first controller, and this time you have to choose **Connect this Delivery Controller to an existing Site**:

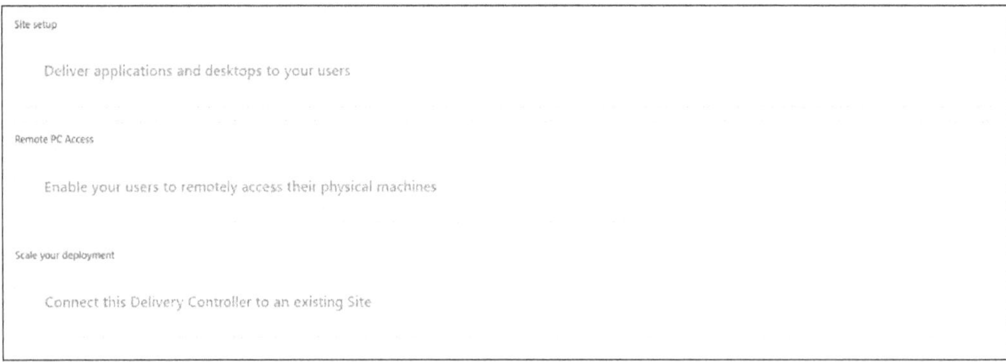

2. Post that, you will get the prompt to specify the name of the Delivery Controller already on the site:

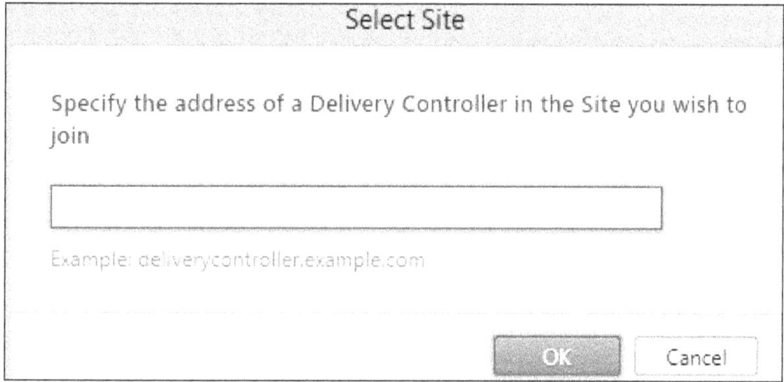


3. After entering the Delivery Controller, it will give you the option to automatically update the site database about the second Delivery Controller. Click on **Yes**:

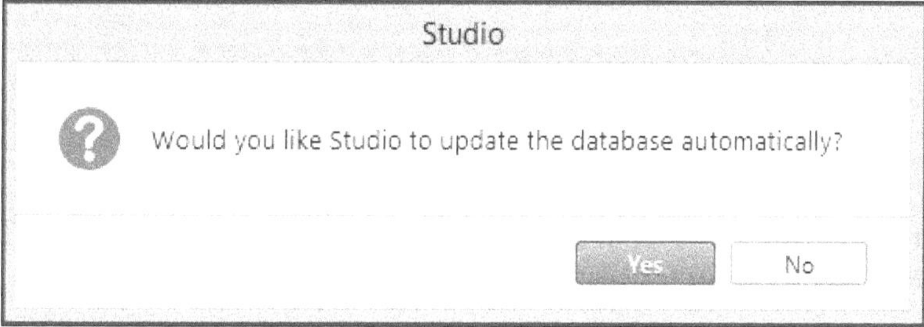

Studio
Would you like Studio to update the database automatically?
Yes
No

It will take some time, and once the database is updated second Delivery Controller will be ready for the use.

# Configuring StoreFront™ server

Before we start configuring the StoreFront, this is just to let you know that StoreFront only use secure HTTP connections, so we need a certificate for the StoreFront server. We will use the certificate authority that was set up in the last chapter to issue the certificate.

You can do that using the article published by me on the blog, `https://sjnbk.wordpress.com/2015/02/03/how-to-add-local-certificate-for-storefront-store-to-use-https/`.

Follow the steps:

1. Once you have the certificate issued, you can go ahead and launch the StoreFront by navigating to **Start** | **Administrative tools** | **Citrix StoreFront**, and it will show you the following screen:

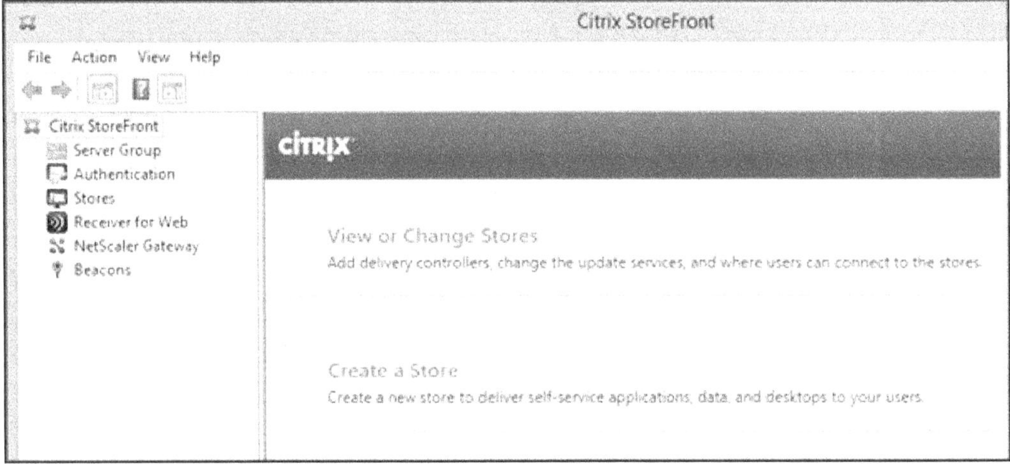


2. Click on **Create a Store**, and it will ask for the store name. Enter the store name that you want to assign and click on **Next**:

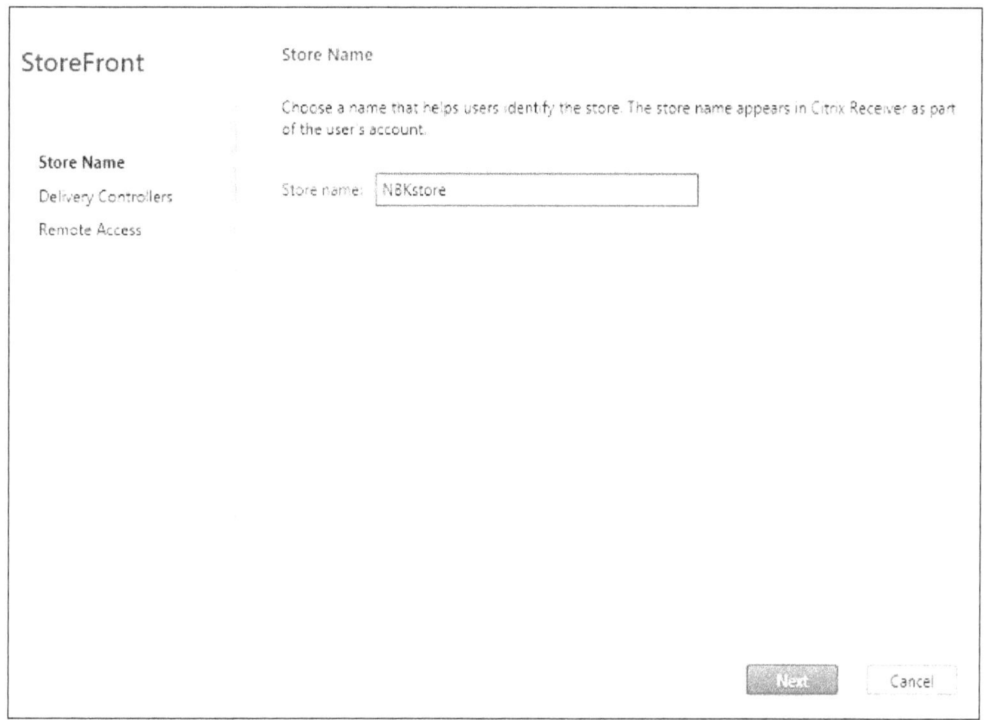


3. The next window will appear and it will ask for the Delivery Controller information for the site, which will act as a broker between the users and site. Click on **Add...** and specify the **Delivery Controllers**. Once done, click on **Next**:

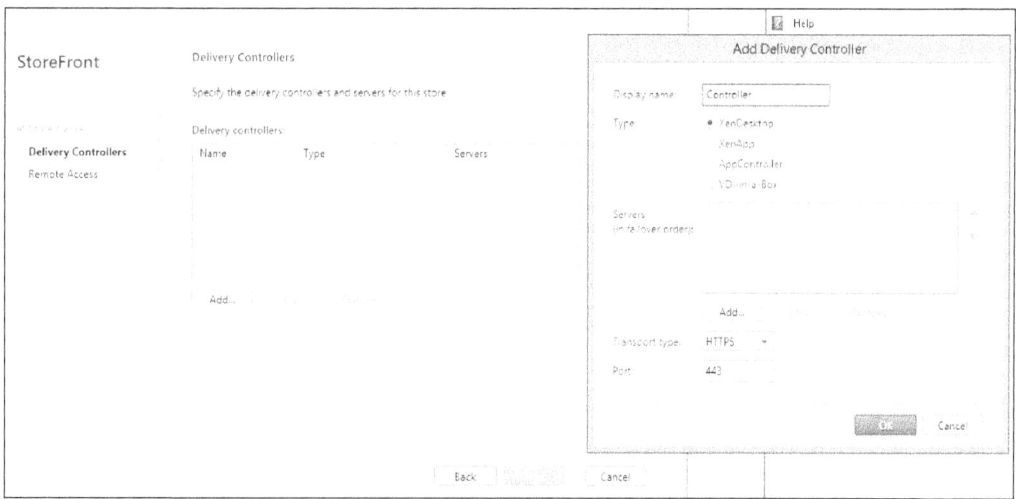

4. The next screen will ask you for the remote access for the users coming from external networks. As of now, we don't have the **NetScaler** set up, so we will choose **None** and then click on **Create** to create the store:

We will cover this topic in *Chapter 8, Setting Up NetScaler*.

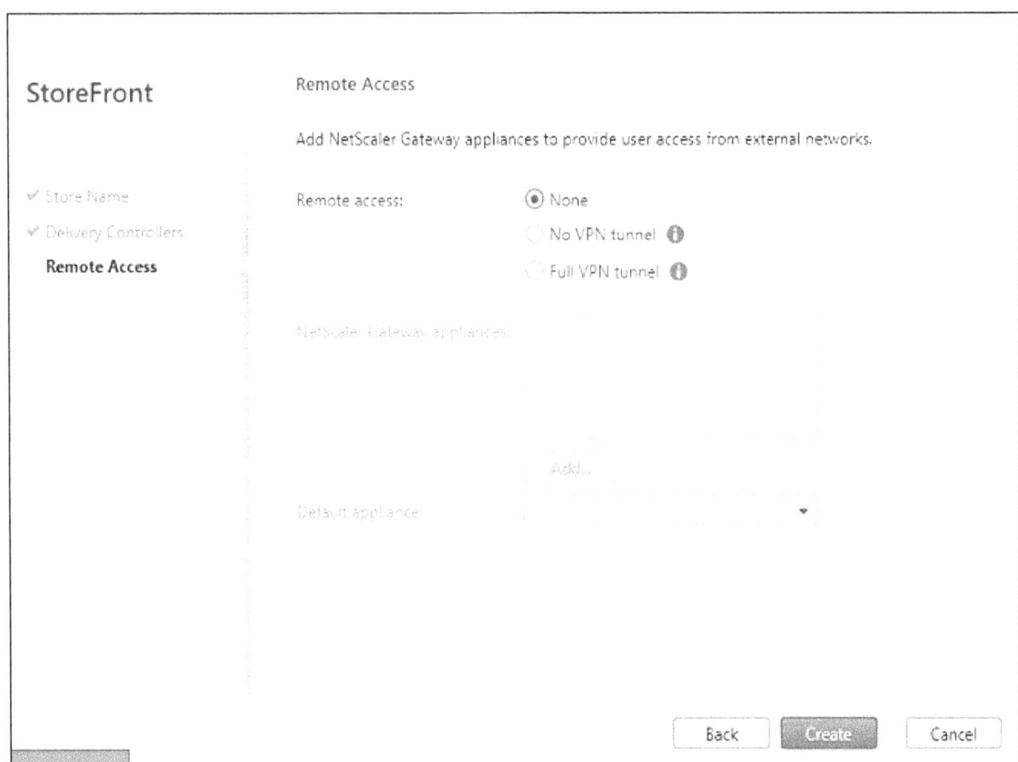

5. It will go through the configuration process and once done, it will show you the URL that is created:

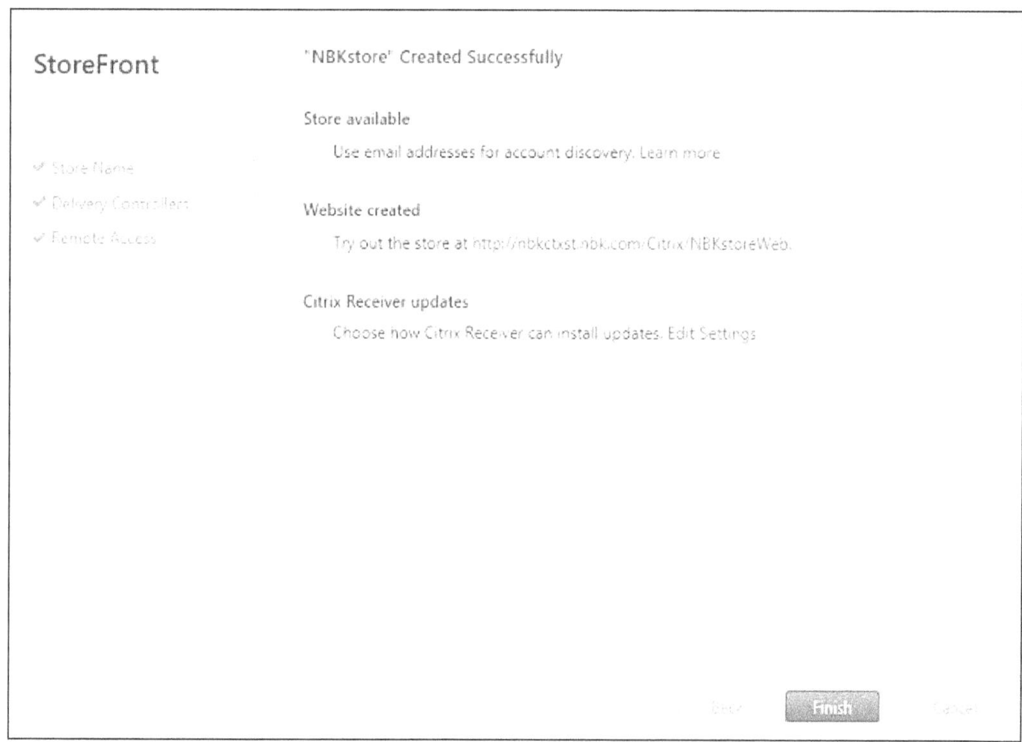
StoreFront
'NBKstore' Created Successfully
Store available
Use email addresses for account discovery. Learn more
Website created
Try out the store at http://nbkctxst.nbk.com/Citrix/NBKstoreWeb.
Citrix Receiver updates
Choose how Citrix Receiver can install updates. Edit Settings
Finish

6. You can also test the URL by accessing it via a browser:

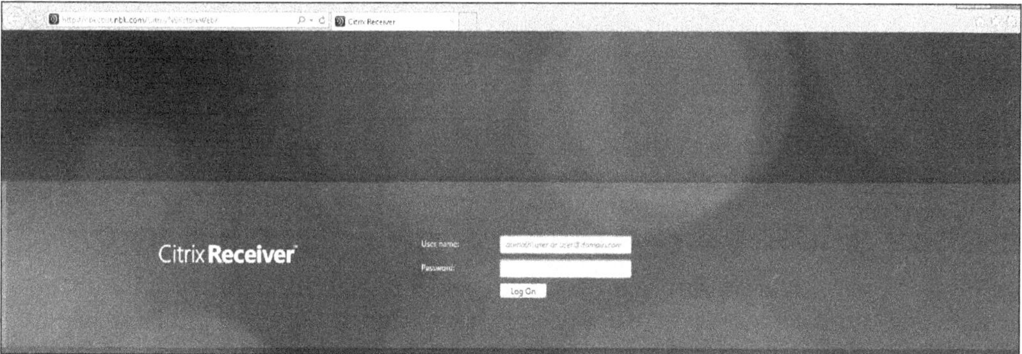
Citrix Receiver
User name:
Password:
Log On

# Configuring Citrix Receiver™

In this section, we will configure Citrix Receiver for web access and e-mail address discovery, and enable the HTML5 client when the Citrix Receiver installation fails.

## Configuring Citrix Receiver™ for web

To configure the Citrix Receiver for web access, you need to click on **Receiver** for web and from the right pane, click on **Create Website** and then click on **Create**.

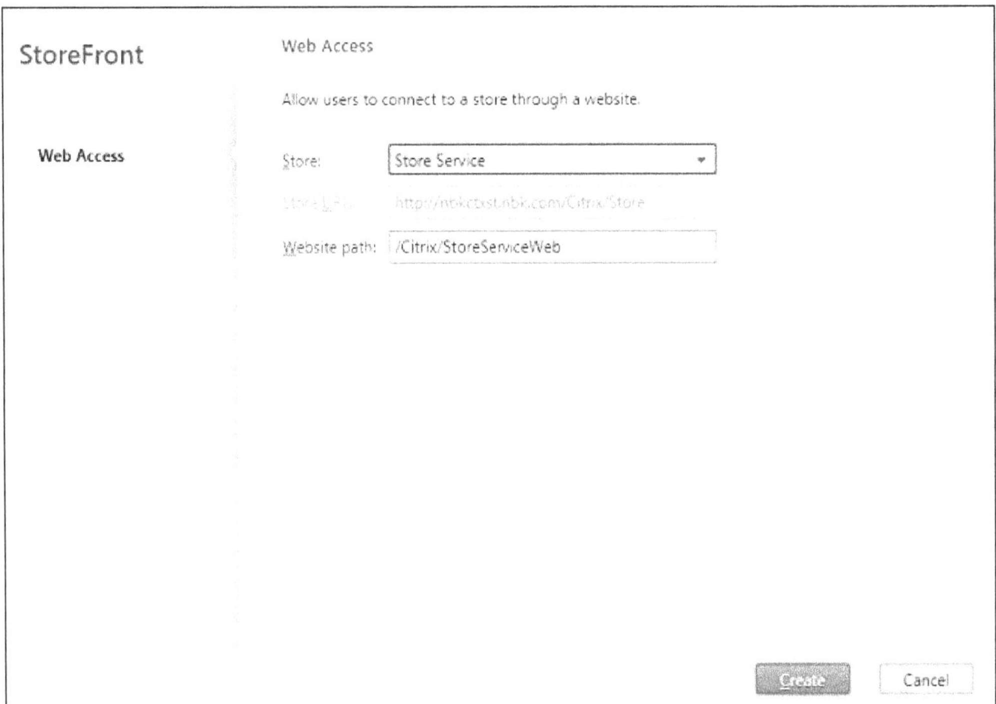


It will create the website for web access.

# E-mail address discovery via Citrix Receiver™

In this section, we will configure the Citrix Receiver so that it can allow users to log in with their e-mail address. In order to implement this, we need to put in some of the DNS entry to make sure that it works, and for that, you have to create DNS SRV record by following these steps:

1. Launch the DNS management console.
2. Expand the forward look up zones.

3. Right-click on your domain and choose **other new records**.
4. Scroll down, choose **SRV (service location)**, and click on **Create Record...**.
5. Enter the information as shown in the following screenshot:

Please note that the host offering this service will be the StoreFront server.

After making the above changes, users will be able to log in to Citrix Receiver via their e-mail address.

# Using HTML5 as a replacement client of Citrix Receiver™

Citrix always recommends using Citrix Receiver to access your application via your laptop or desktop, but there are situations when users don't have the permission to install the Citrix Receiver client; for such cases, we can enable the HTML5 support for our Citrix StoreFront.

In order to enable HTML5 support for StoreFront, you need to click on **Receiver for web** from the right-hand side pane of the StoreFront panel and then from the left-hand side panel, choose **Deploy Citrix Receiver**. It will bring up the following window:

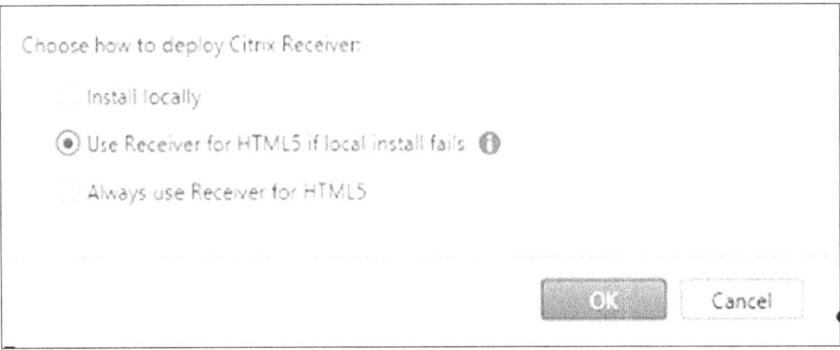


Choose **Use Receiver for HTML5 if local install fails** and then click on **OK**. This will enable HTML5 support for your StoreFront servers.

You have to enable the additional setting in the Citrix policies (HTML5 web sockets settings) for full functionality of HTML5 Receiver.

# Summary

In this chapter, you learned about setting up the Citrix infrastructure components and also how to install and configure Delivery Controller, License Server, Studio, Director, StoreFront.

In the next chapter, we will be using these Citrix components to create Machine Catalogs and delivery groups to deliver the applications to the users.

# 5
# Setting Up the XenApp® Resources

In this chapter, we are going to start preparing the Citrix components to host the application. Preparation will be done from the components that we installed in the previous chapter.

Things that we will be doing in this chapter are as follows:

- Preparing the master virtual machine
- Setting up server OS for Master Image
- Creating Machine Catalogs
- Creating delivery groups

Once you complete the chapter, you will be able to create master images for server OS and deliver the application via Machine Catalogs and delivery groups.

## Preparing the master virtual machine

As we are deploying Citrix XenApp to deliver the hosted application, in this section, we will be doing the basic task of preparing our virtual machine so that it can be used as a master template to deploy the virtual machine, which will be used in Machine Catalog to deliver the application.

For this section, I have already created a virtual machine with Windows server OS 2012 R2. To start preparing the master VM, we have to do the following things to avoid any issues:

- Join the virtual machine to an active directory domain.
- License and activate the operating system: This is important because once we create the machine from Master Image, it should contain the licensing information so that we don't have to do this task again and again.
- DHCP for network addressing: This is also important to avoid the IP conflicts if we don't use the DHCP.
- Install Virtual Delivery Agent: VDA is one of those plugins which facilitates the communication between the virtual machine and the Delivery Controller. Also, when users establish the hosted application connection, it will help in communication between the user and virtual machine.

As this is the basic operating system configuration task, I have already done the following things:

- Windows server 2012 R2: This template is joined to the active directory domain
- Master VM is in trial period: This is the POC but it is recommended to activate the server in a production environment
- Master VM is talking to DHCP server to get the IP address

The next step to install the Virtual Delivery Agent will be taken in the next section in which we will prepare this Master VM for Master Image of Server OS.

# Setting up server OS for Master Image

In the last section, we prepared the virtual machine for the master virtual machine, and now, it is time to set up the operating system for the Master Image so that we can use this image to build worker servers to deliver the applications. Follow these steps:

1. Mount the ISO image of Citrix XenApp 7.6 to the master virtual machine and click on it launch the installation wizard:

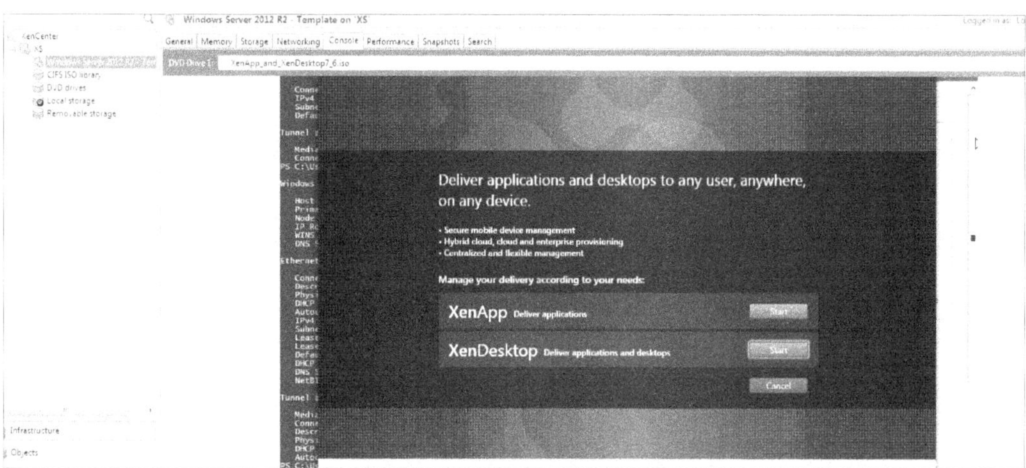


2. Click on **XenApp Deliver applications**, and it will take you to the next screen. Here, in the **Prepare Machines and Images** section, click on **Virtual Delivery Agent for Windows Server OS**.

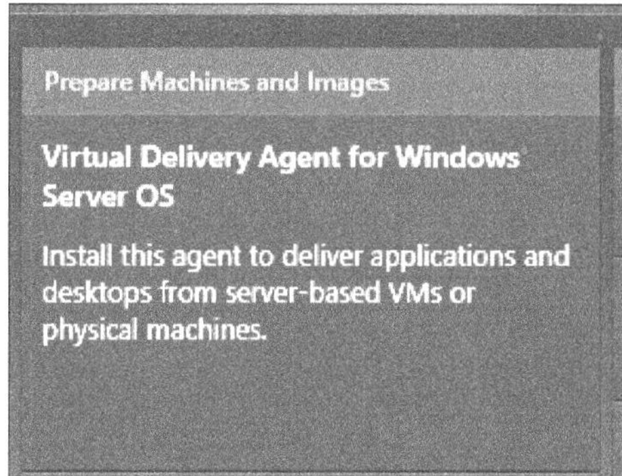

3. It will bring up the installation wizard and will give you the screen where you can choose from **Create a Master Image** or **Enable connections to a sever machine**. As we are preparing this server to be a master image, we will click on **Create a Master Image**:

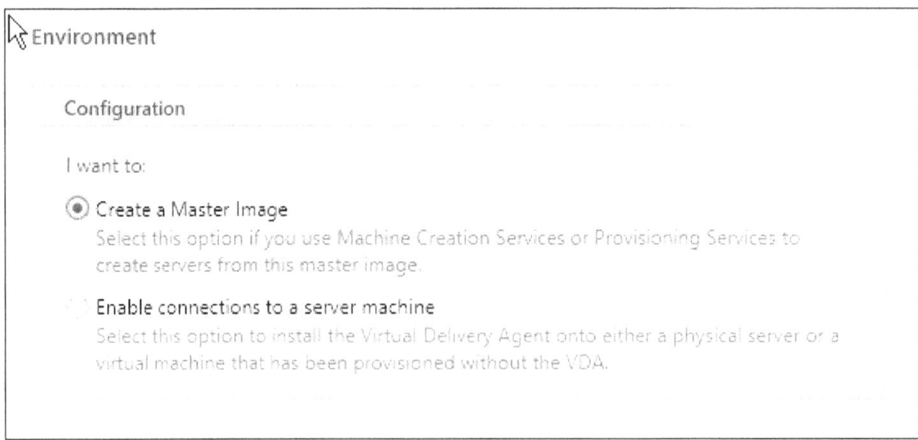
Environment
Configuration
I want to:
Create a Master Image
Select this option if you use Machine Creation Services or Provisioning Services to create servers from this master image.
Enable connections to a server machine
Select this option to install the Virtual Delivery Agent onto either a physical server or a virtual machine that has been provisioned without the VDA.

4. This will take us to the next screen, where we will get the option to choose the core components required to install. The options will be **Virtual Delivery Agent** and **Citrix Receiver**. Select both of them and click on **Next**:

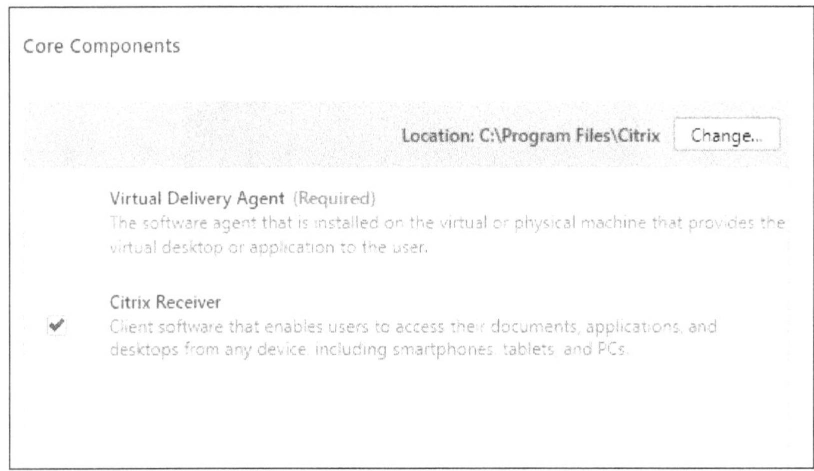
Core Components
Location: C:\Program Files\Citrix
Change...
Virtual Delivery Agent (Required)
The software agent that is installed on the virtual or physical machine that provides the virtual desktop or application to the user.
Citrix Receiver
Client software that enables users to access their documents, applications, and desktops from any device, including smartphones, tablets, and PCs.

5. On the next screen of the installation wizard, we have to specify the Delivery Controller. It is recommended to use the group policy to specify the Delivery Controller, but as this is the POC environment, we will use the **Do it manually** option, or we could use the **Let Machine creation services do it automatically** option if we are using the MCS to create our virtual machine. So, specify the controller, add it, and click on **Next**:

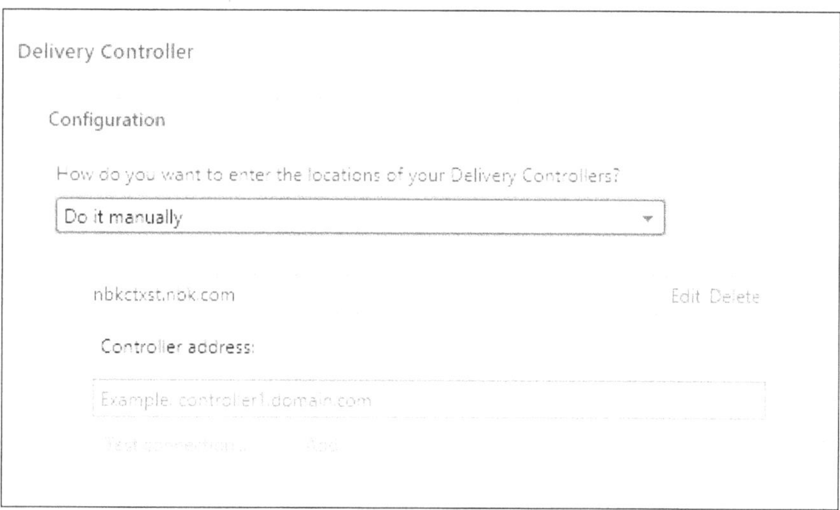


6. The next screen will list the features to select from. Here, we will select all of them to increase your knowledge:
   - **Optimize performance**: This option runs the target OS optimizer tool to improve the performance of the operating system when a machine is used as a virtual desktop. For more information on what optimization will be done, you can refer to the Citrix Article—CTX125874.
   - **Use Windows Remote Assistance**: This feature will enable the Windows remote assistance for use with the users' shadowing feature of Citrix Director.
   - **Use Real-Time Audio Transport for audio**: This option should be selected if VOIP is widely used in your network. It reduces latency and improves audio resilience over lossy network. Selecting this feature will allow audio data to be transmitted using RTP over UDP transport.

Please make the selection based on your requirement. In this installation, I will choose **Optimize performance** and **Use Windows Remote Assistance** and then click on **Next**:

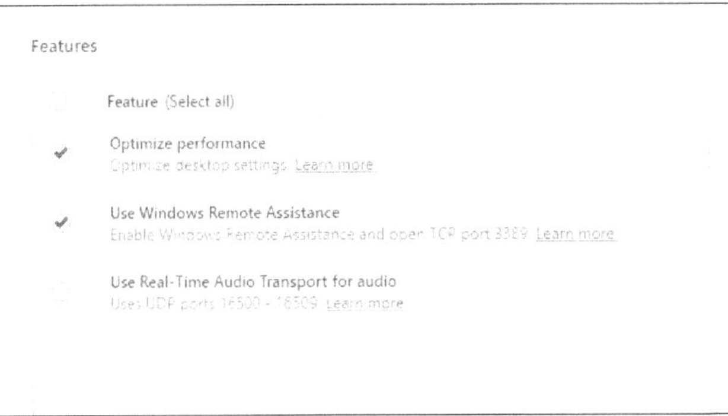
Features
Feature (Select all)
Optimize performance
Optimize desktop settings. Learn more
Use Windows Remote Assistance
Enable Windows Remote Assistance and open TCP port 3389. Learn more
Use Real-Time Audio Transport for audio
Uses UDP ports 16500 - 16509. Learn more

7. Once you move to the next screen, it will give you the list of Firewall ports, which is required for controller communication and remote assistance purpose. It will also give you the option to configure the Firewall rules automatically or manually.
8. I will choose **Automatically**; and in your case, please choose **Manually** if you are using some other Firewall devices. Click on **Next**:

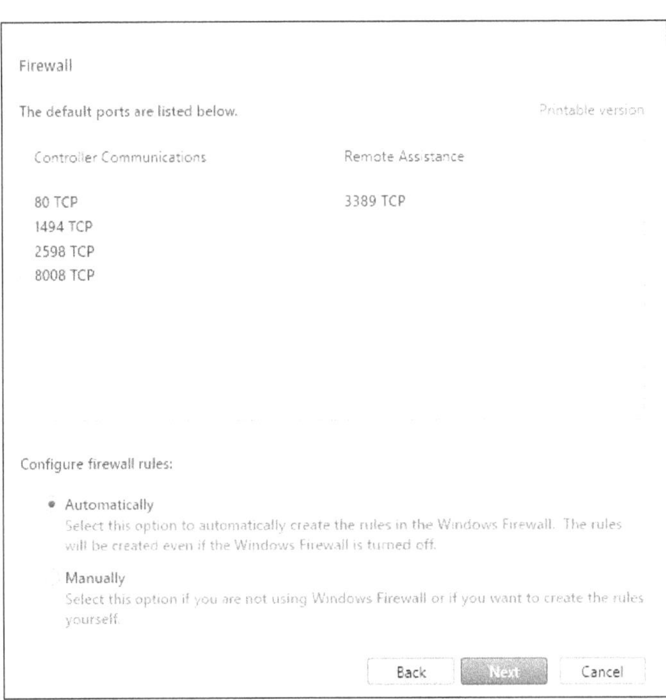
Firewall
The default ports are listed below.
Printable version
Controller Communications
Remote Assistance
80 TCP
1494 TCP
2598 TCP
8008 TCP
3389 TCP
Configure firewall rules:
Automatically
Select this option to automatically create the rules in the Windows Firewall. The rules will be created even if the Windows Firewall is turned off.
Manually
Select this option if you are not using Windows Firewall or if you want to create the rules yourself.
Back
Next
Cancel

9. The next screen will be a summary screen of all the options that we have selected so far. You can review them and make any changes if you want by going back. Here, we will click on **Install** to make the configuration:

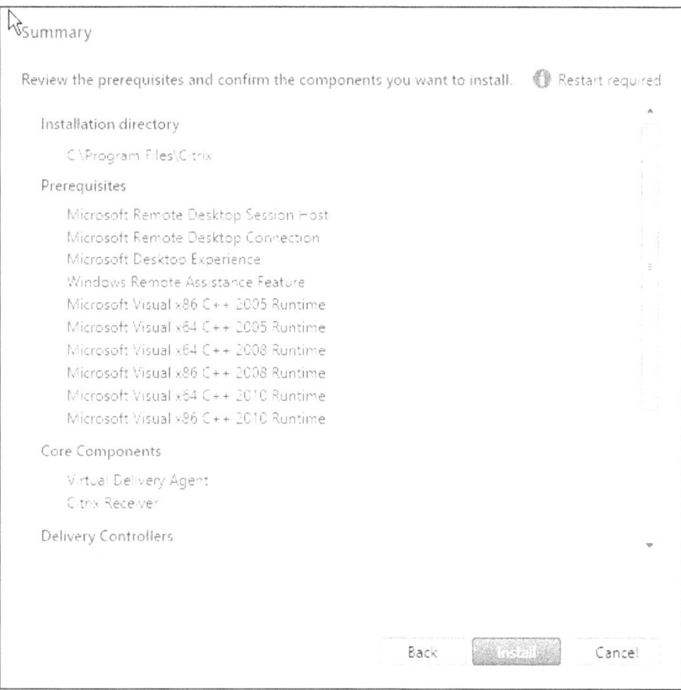


It will take a while to perform the installation and will be restarted multiple times. Once done, you have to restart the machine again and just power off. After that, your Master Image will be ready for virtual machine deployment.

# Creating a Machine Catalog

In the previous section, we prepared the source master image, which makes us ready to create a Machine Catalog for the servers from which we will deliver the application via the delivery group.

In this section, we will spend some time creating a Machine Catalog for Windows server 2012 R2 for server-based computing via which users will access the application. Follow these steps:

1. Launch Citrix Studio as it is the central console from where most of the administrative tasks can be done. Choose the **common tasks node** and in that section, you will see the **Create a new Machine Catalog** option. Click on it:

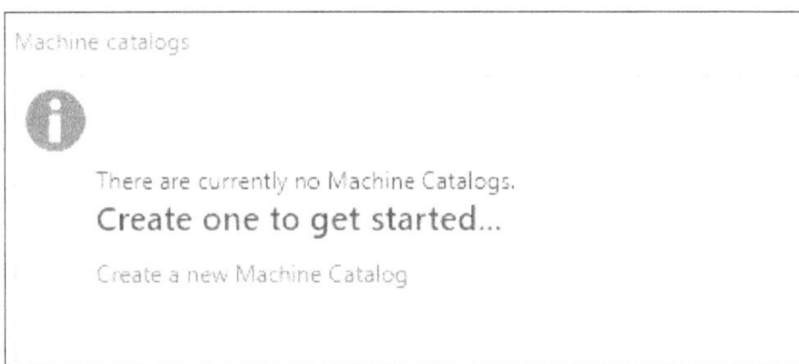


2. It will bring up the Machine Catalog creation wizard with the very first screen, which gives the introduction about what Machine Catalog is. Please spend some time understanding what Machine Catalog is by going through the description and then click on **Next**:

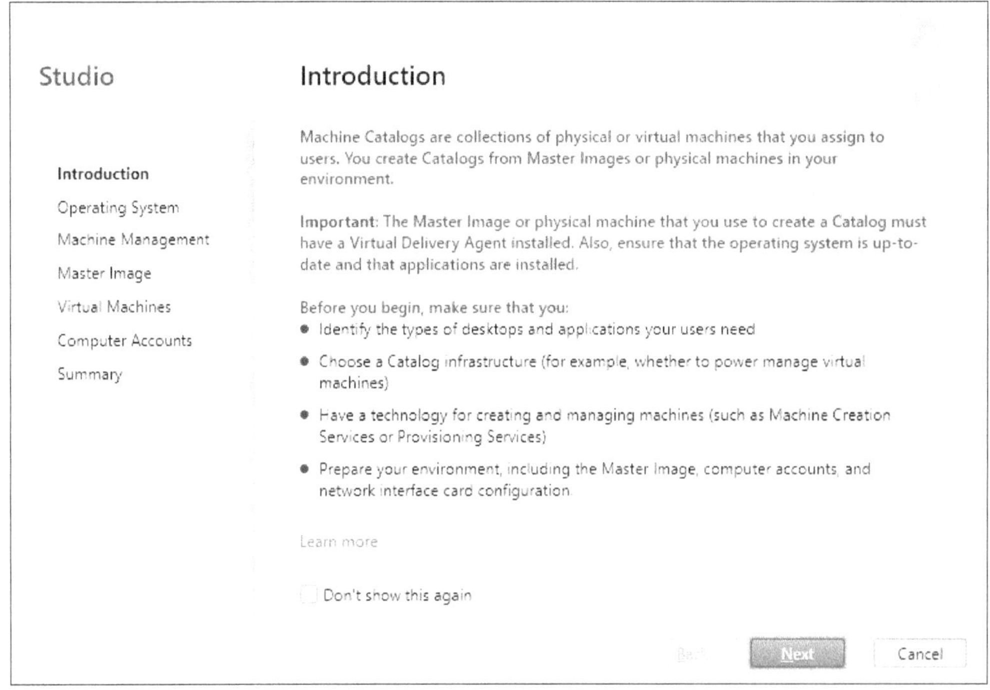

Studio
Introduction
Introduction
Operating System
Machine Management
Master Image
Virtual Machines
Computer Accounts
Summary
Machine Catalogs are collections of physical or virtual machines that you assign to users. You create Catalogs from Master Images or physical machines in your environment.
Important: The Master Image or physical machine that you use to create a Catalog must have a Virtual Delivery Agent installed. Also, ensure that the operating system is up-to-date and that applications are installed.
Before you begin, make sure that you:
Identify the types of desktops and applications your users need
Choose a Catalog infrastructure (for example, whether to power manage virtual machines)
Have a technology for creating and managing machines (such as Machine Creation Services or Provisioning Services)
Prepare your environment, including the Master Image, computer accounts, and network interface card configuration.
Learn more
Don't show this again
Next
Cancel

3. The next screen will give you three options:
    - **Windows Server OS**: Server OS Machine Catalog provides hosted shared desktops and applications for a large-scale deployment of standardized machines
    - **Windows Desktop OS**: Desktop OS Machine Catalog provides VDI desktop ideal for a variety of different users
    - **Remote PC Access**: Remote PC access Machine Catalog provides users with remote access to their physical office desktops, allowing them to work from anywhere

   Here, we will choose **Windows Server OS** as we want to deliver the hosted applications to the users and then click on **Next**:

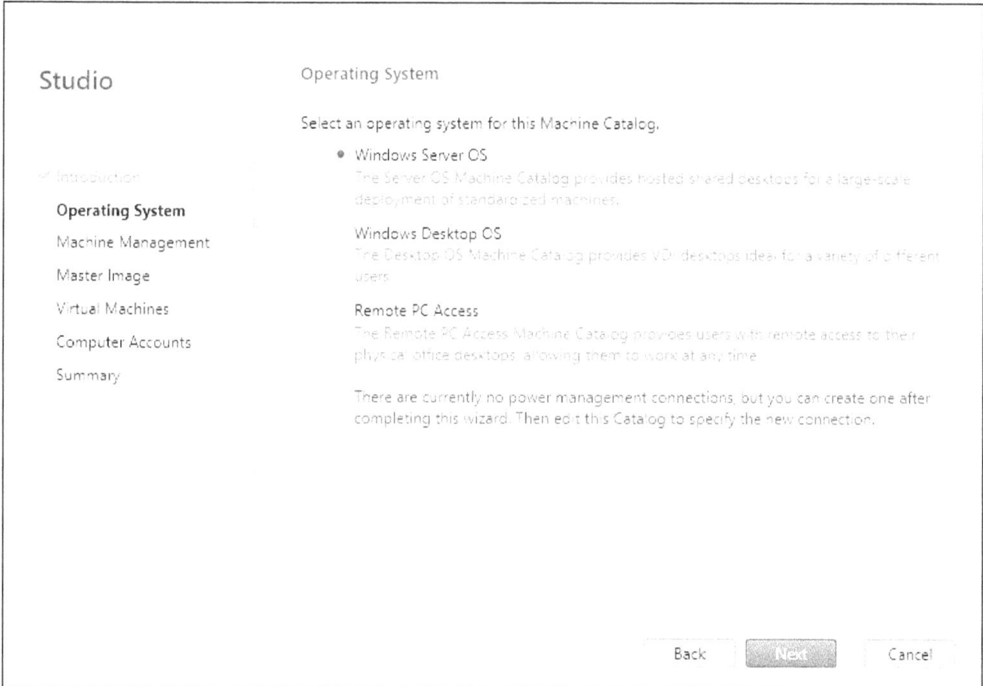


   As of now, we will use machine creation service to deploy our machines as we don't have PVS set up yet. We will be spending some time later in this book setting up PVS to deliver the virtual machine.

4. So, in the machine management selection, we will choose **Citrix Machine Creation Services (MCS)** to deploy the machines and then click on **Next**:

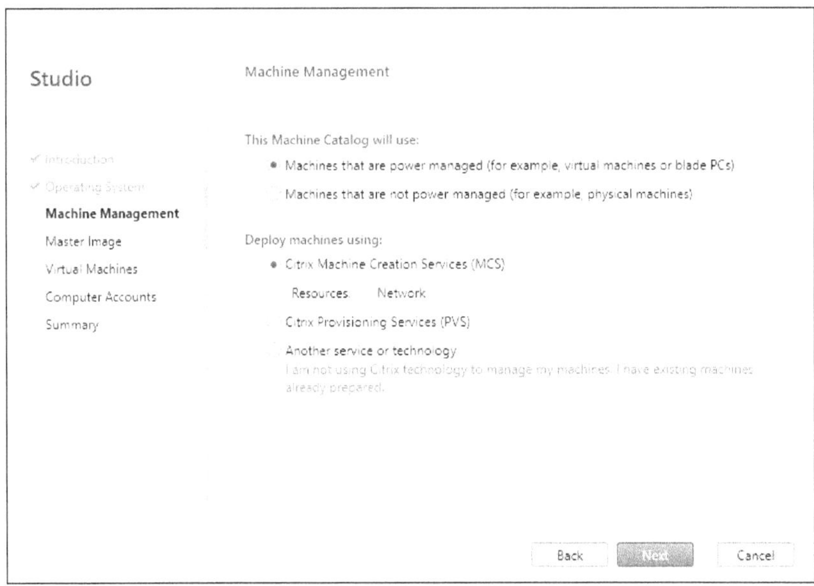


5. On the next screen, we will be asked to choose the **Master Image**, and we will choose the **Master Image** that we prepared in the last section and click on **Next**:

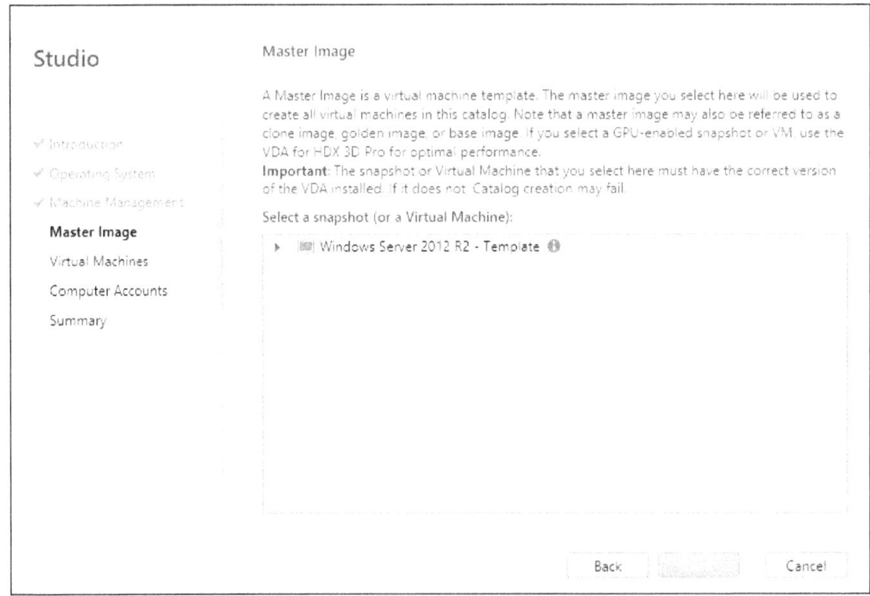

6. On the next screen, you will be asked to choose the memory and processor required for the new VM and in this case, we will keep it to one vCPU, 2 GB memory, and 40 GB hard disk. Click on **Next**:

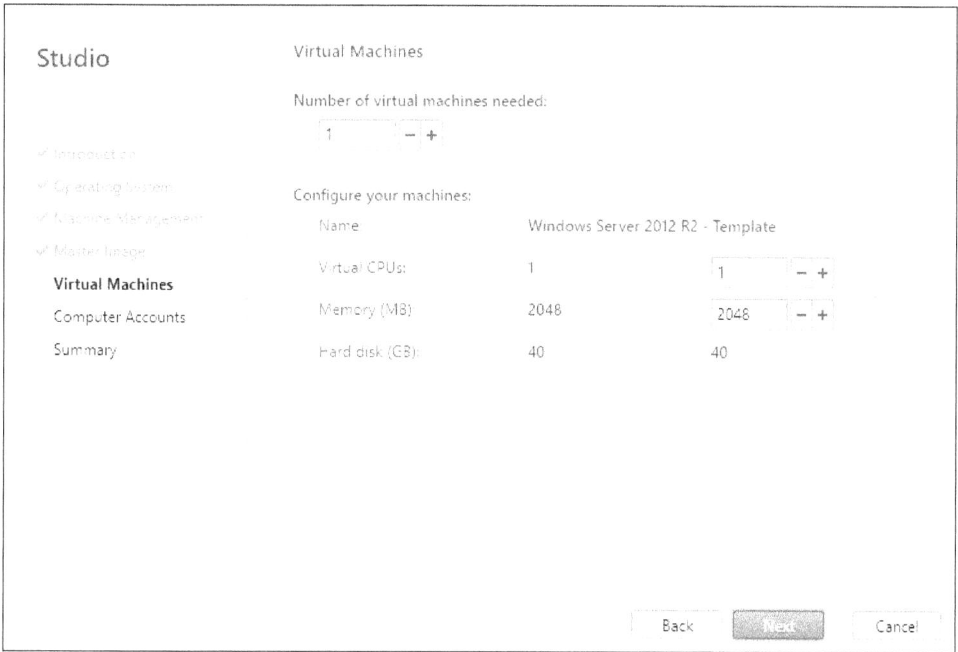


7. In the next section, the Machine Catalog creation wizard will ask for the computer account because since this is in domain, every computer will have the computer account in the active directory. On this screen, you can create a custom organization unit to keep the computer account or use the existing one. Also, you have to enter the Machine Naming Scheme.

8. As this is Windows Server 2012 R2, I will enter the scheme as `WS2012-##`, where `##` will dynamically enter the numbers. You can see the following screenshot for the example. Click on **Next**:

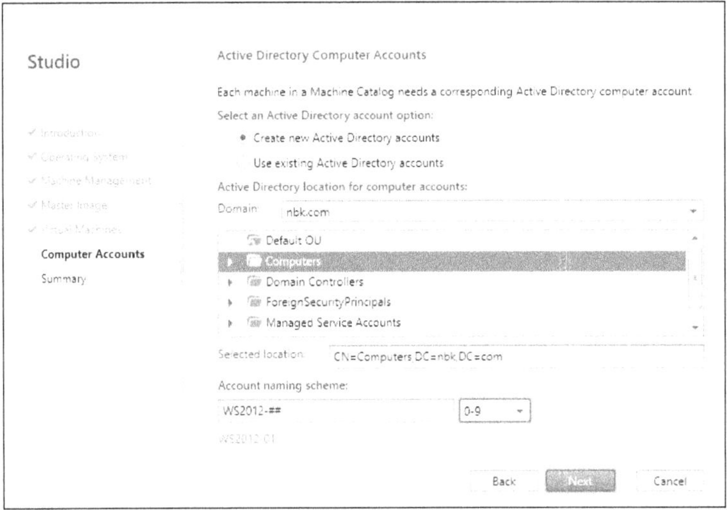


9. In the summary screen, it will give you the list of options you have selected. You also have to enter the name of the Machine Catalog. Once you click on **Finish**, it will take some time to make the connection to the hypervisor and create a snapshot of the template you have selected as the master image and that snapshot will be used as a source for a new virtual machine. With this, our original template will stay intact, and we can make the updates if required.

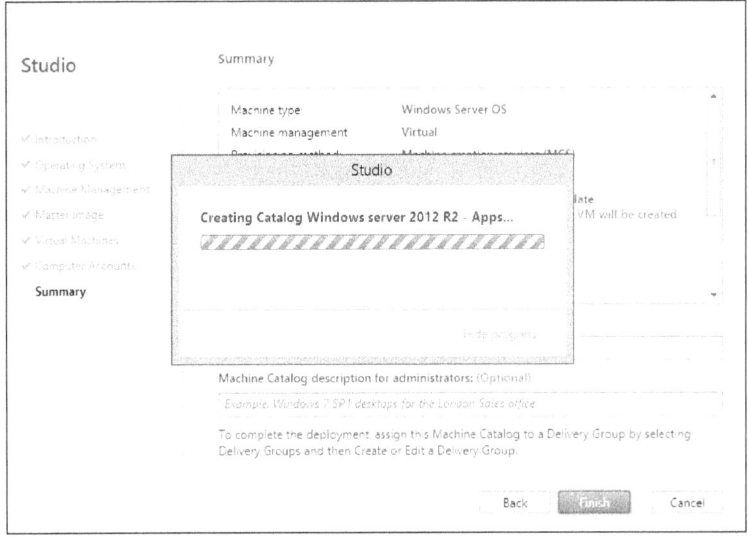

10. Once the catalog is created, if you go back to XenCenter, you can see the new snapshot created for the master template:

11. Once the catalog is created, you can check it in **Machine Catalog**:

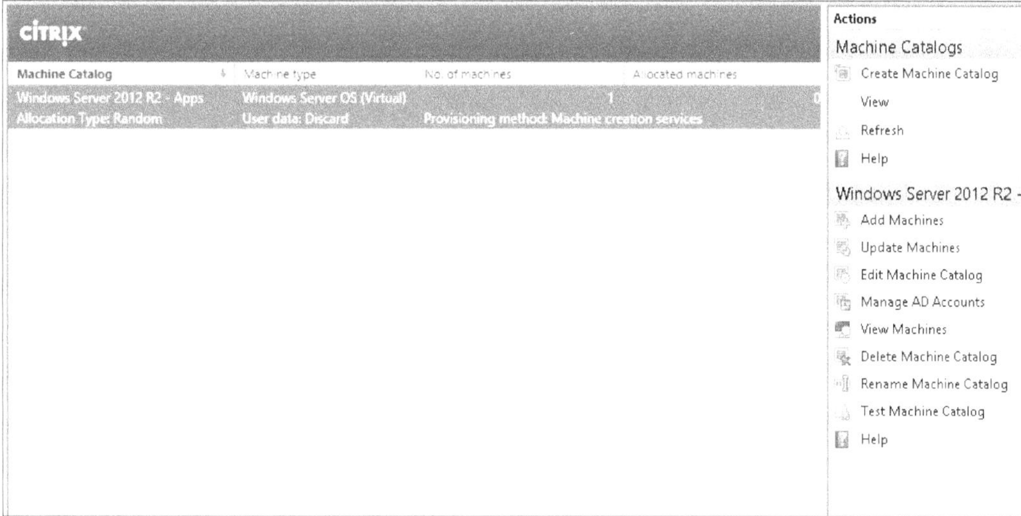

# Creating a delivery group

This is a relatively easier task and is less time-consuming. Delivery group is basically a collection of applications that are created from the Machine Catalog. Follow these steps:

1. In order to start the steps, first you have to move to the common task screen again. In that section, there is an option at the bottom that says **Create a new Delivery Group**. Click on it:

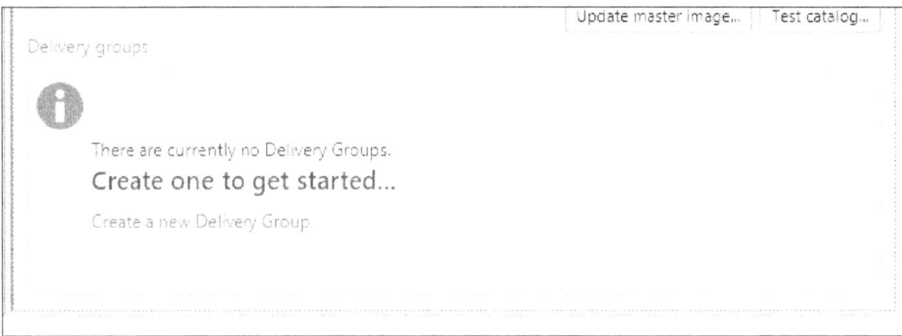


2. It will bring up the **Introduction** screen, where it will have the information about the delivery group and why we create a delivery group. Please spend some time to understand it and then click on **Next**:

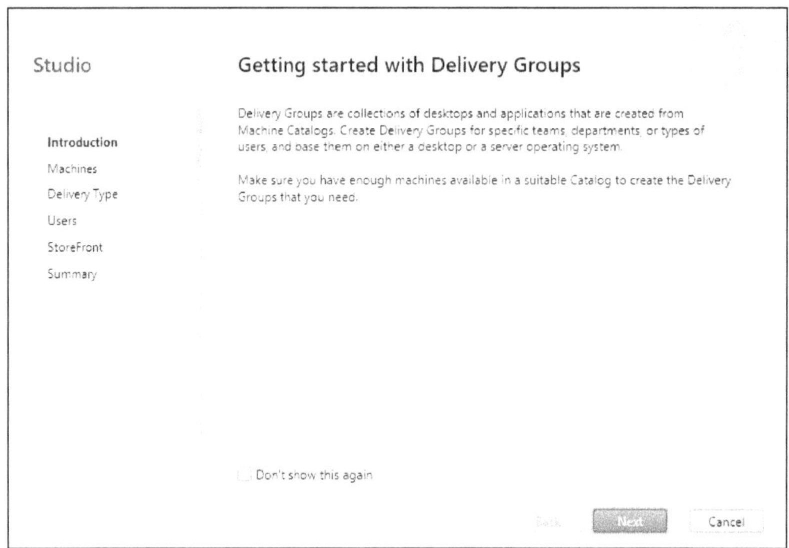

3. On the next screen, you will get the option to choose the Machine Catalog to publish the application from. We only have one catalog available which was created in the last section. Also, you have to choose the number of machines that you want to use in this delivery group. Click on **Next**:

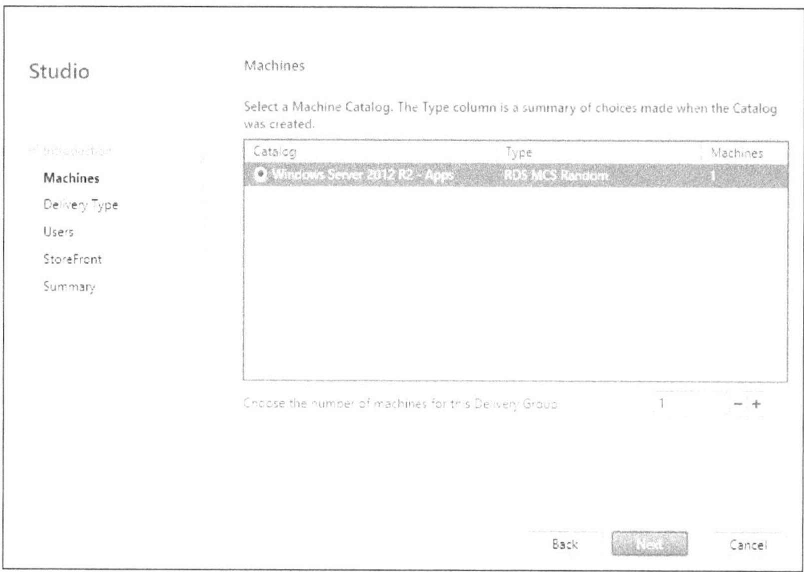


4. On the next screen, you will get three options of delivery type:

   **Desktops**

   **Desktop and applications**

   **Applications**

We will choose **Applications** and then click on **Next**:

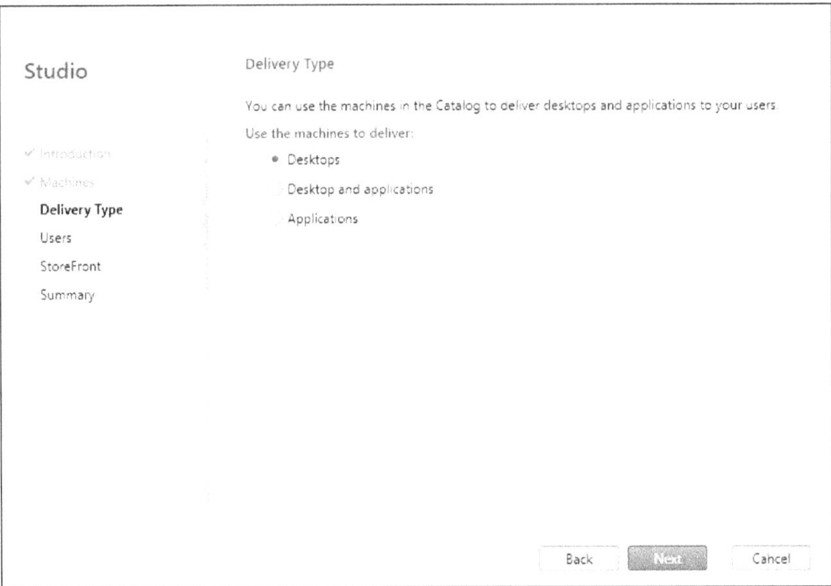


5. On the next screen, you have to select the users or the user group that will get access to the application. In this case, I will grant the permission to the domain users so that everybody has the access to the application of this delivery group:

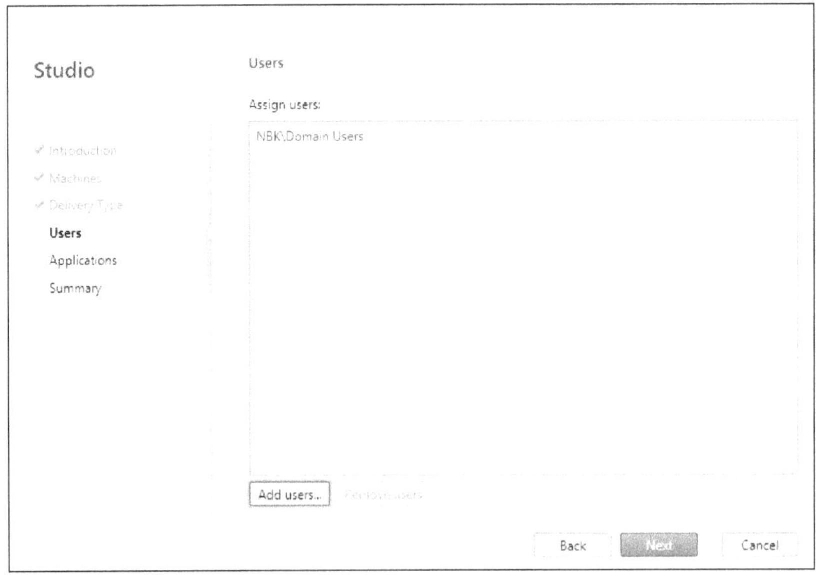

6. The next section will be the main part where it will show you the list of applications that can be published via the delivery group. If the application you want to publish is not listed automatically, you can use the option at the bottom which says **Add applications manually...**. Most of the internally developed applications don't populate in the list.
7. I will choose **Calculator** to publish in this delivery group and then click on **Next**:

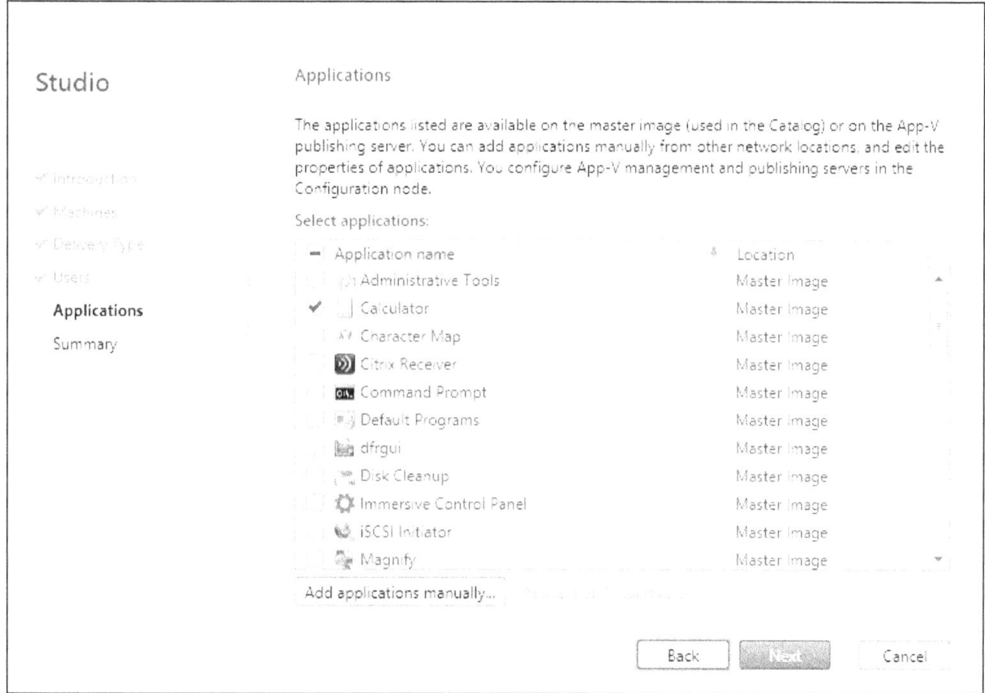

8. At last, on the summary screen, you can name the delivery group. I will name it `Calculator` and then click on **Finish**:

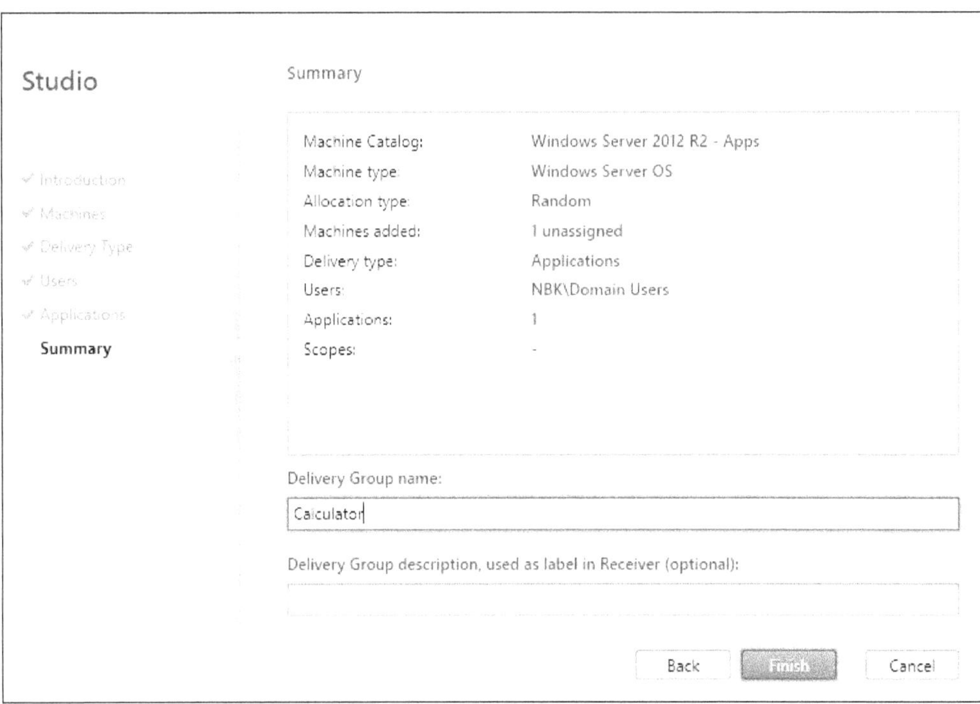


9. The **Delivery Groups** node will look similar to the following:

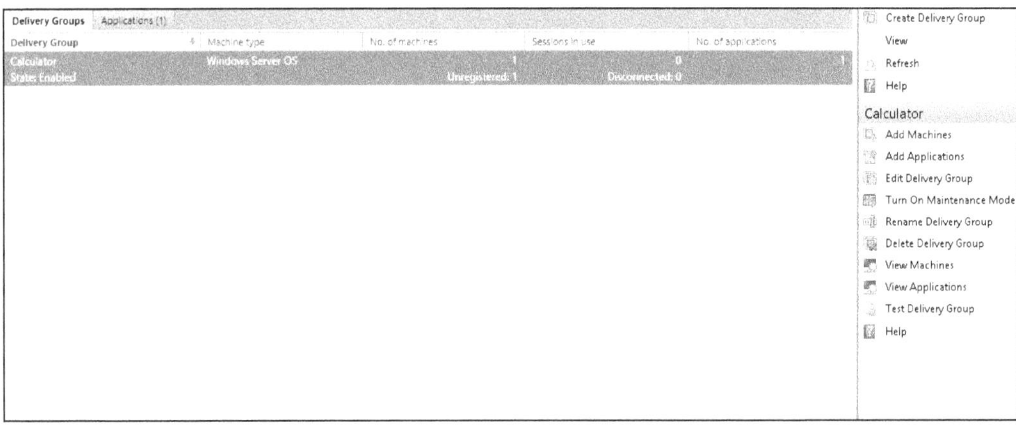

10. You can also verify whether the application is visible or not by logging on to the StoreFront website. By doing this, you will be able to see the new icon:

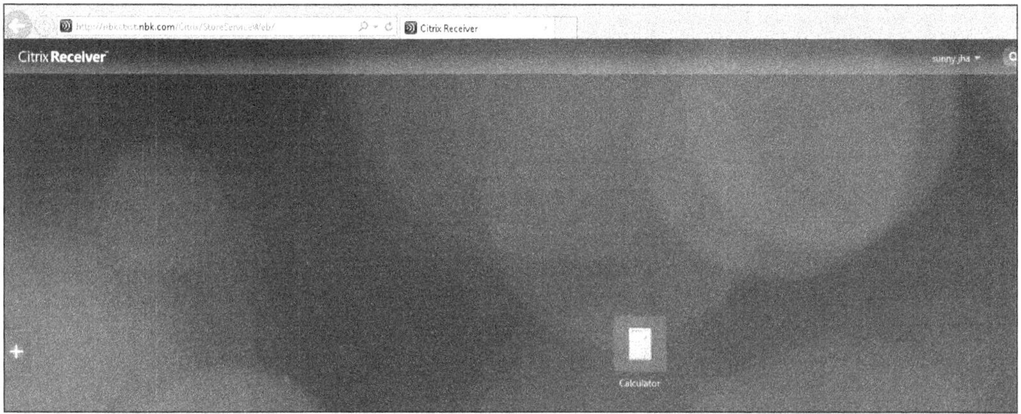


# Summary

In this chapter, we learned about setting up XenApp resources to prepare Machine Catalog and delivery group. We learned how to prepare and customize a master virtual machine, set up the Master Image for server OS, create a Machine Catalog via MCS, and create a delivery group to publish the applications.

In the next chapter, we will spend some time understanding the most important part of XenApp, which is group policy, and we will work on configuring the XenApp group policy for the smooth and better functioning of the hosted application when it is accessed by the user.

# 6

# Configuring Policies

In this chapter, we are going to spend some time working with one of the crucial parts of XenApp deployment. In this section, we will learn about the policies that are sets of settings that we force on the users' session for better user experience and effective bandwidth utilization, and at the same time, make sure that the enterprise security is in place.

Things we will be doing in this chapter are as follows:

- Setting up policies
- Installing the group policy management feature
- Printing policies
- Configuring remote assistance
- Citrix profile management

Once the chapter is completed, you will be able to implement group polices for a better user experience and effective bandwidth management while keeping the enterprise security in place.

## Setting up policies

Policies are set of the configuration settings that are applied to set the behavior of how the session will work, how bandwidth will be used for better user experience, and how the enterprise data is kept secure at the same time. These policies are based on the user group, devices that they are using, and the type of connection.

We can force these policies to physical server, virtual servers, or to the users. Polices are applied in the following manner:

```
Processing →
Local policies > Citrix Polices > Site GPO > Domain GPO > OU GPO.
                                              ← Precedence|
```

- **Local policies**: They are local settings, which are set in the local group policy of the system on which the user is logging
- **Citrix Policies**: These are also a set of settings and rules, which is applied at the site level in the Citrix Studio
- **Site GPO**: These are a set of settings, which is applied in the active directory at the site level
- **Domain GPO**: These are a set of settings, which is applied in the active directory at the domain level
- **OU GPO**: These are a set of settings, which is applied in the active directory at the organizational unit level

If you have worked on the older version of XenApp, Citrix integrated the policies with the active directory. Due to this, we have the flexibility to manage the group policy from Citrix Studio or group policy management console, but it is not recommended to use both(Citrix Studio and group policy management console) to manage the Citrix polices.

If we are using Citrix Studio to creating and manage the policies, these settings will get saved in the site database, while if we are using group policy management console to do so, these settings will be saved in the active directory.

We create a number of policy for the different set of users, based on the connection type and other things to make sure there is no policy conflict with each other and at the end, the policies are getting applied to the required user group. There is a feature of Citrix group policy modeling with the help of which system administrator tests the policies based on the users and computer and makes sure there is no conflict and no failure.

Policies get applied in the following manner:

1. The user logs in to the endpoint device using the domain ID and password.
2. Domain ID and password get transferred to the domain controller for the authentication.

3. Once authenticated, active directory applies the group policies based on endpoint, active directory site, active directory domain, and the organizational unit the user belongs to.
4. The user launches the Citrix Receiver to access the assigned applications and shared desktop.
5. At this point, Citrix and Microsoft policies get applied to the endpoint and machine hosting the user session. These policies gets applied based on the filtering and priority of precedence, and these settings get applied to the registry of the endpoint device and machine hosting the user session.
6. If the user logs off from the Citrix application, the Citrix policy settings get unloaded from the registry.
7. If the user logs off from the endpoint, it unloads the active directory group policy.
8. If the user powers off the endpoint, this action releases the active directory group policy setting meant for that machine.

# Creating a policy

In earlier versions, we used to have the policies separated, based on the computer and user, but when you will go to the Citrix Studio console in the policies node, you will notice that they are not separated anymore:

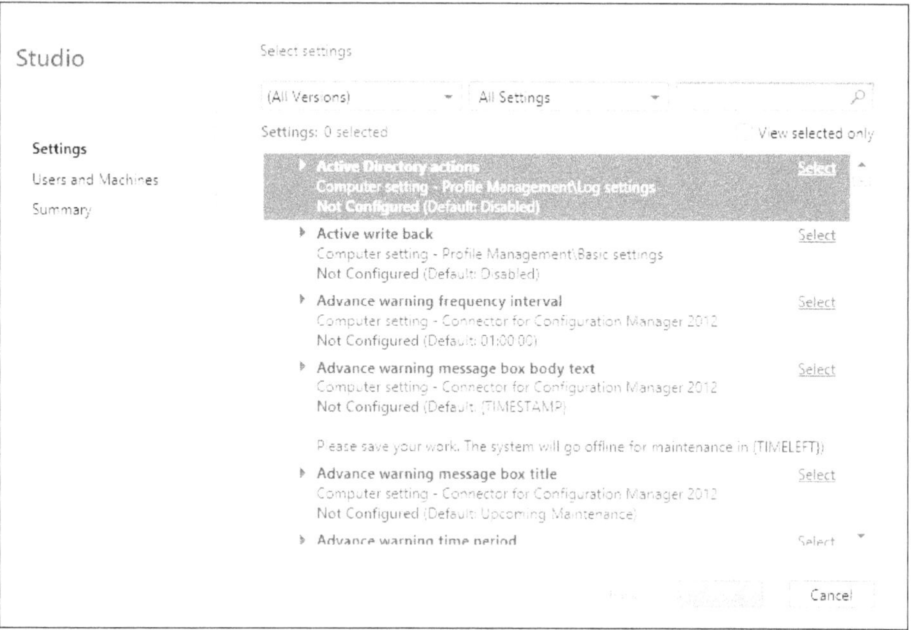

Before you actually start creating the policies, the administrator has to identify the group of users or device he is targeting for the policies he will be creating. In case if there is a pre-existing policy for the identified group, it is always recommended to edit the policy to add new setting or to modify the existing setting rather than creating a new policy.

When you are creating a new policy, you can use the pre-existing policy templates, and based on that, you can customize them as per the requirement. There is an option to create your own template as a base line policy as well:

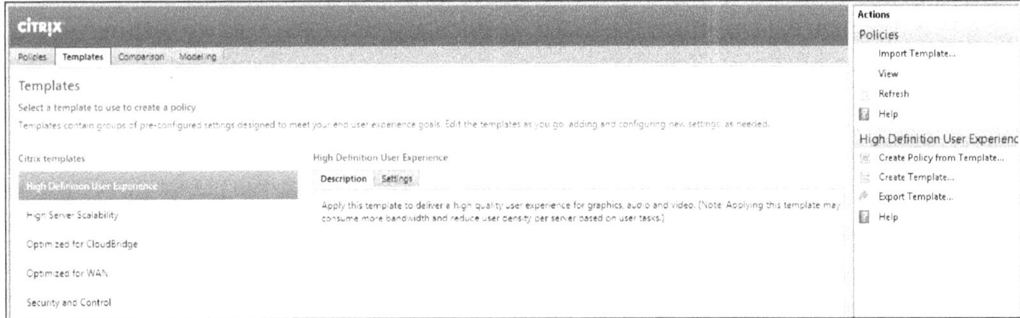


Generally, the first policy that we create in the XenApp deployment is the unfiltered policy. This is one of the most critical policies, which contains the setting that you want to apply to any object of the site:

It is not recommended to configure this if you want settings to be filtered, based on device or the user group. In these cases, you can go ahead and use the templates or create a new one.

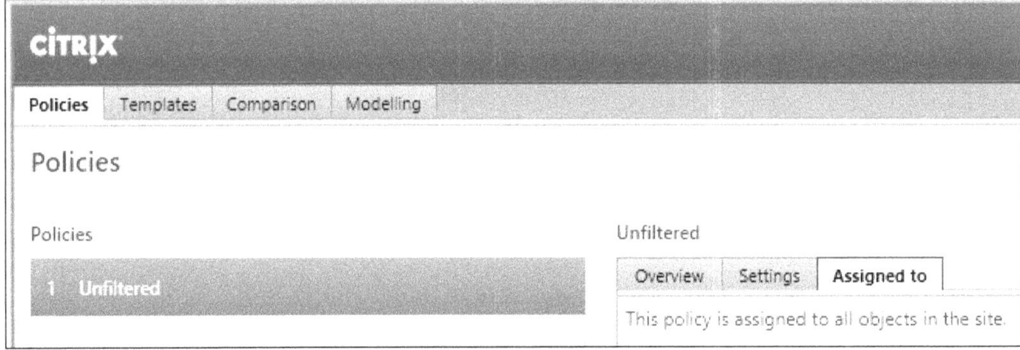

If you go into the **Edit** section of policies, you will be able to see that there are more than 100 settings listed there. You can filter them based on the version of virtual delivery agent or based on the setting categories such as ICA settings where most of the setting reside, then load management where you can configure load evaluators, profile management where you can configure the profile setting, receiver setting, and virtual delivery agent settings for the device.

All of these settings can be added to any existing policy, or you can create a new policy and configure them:

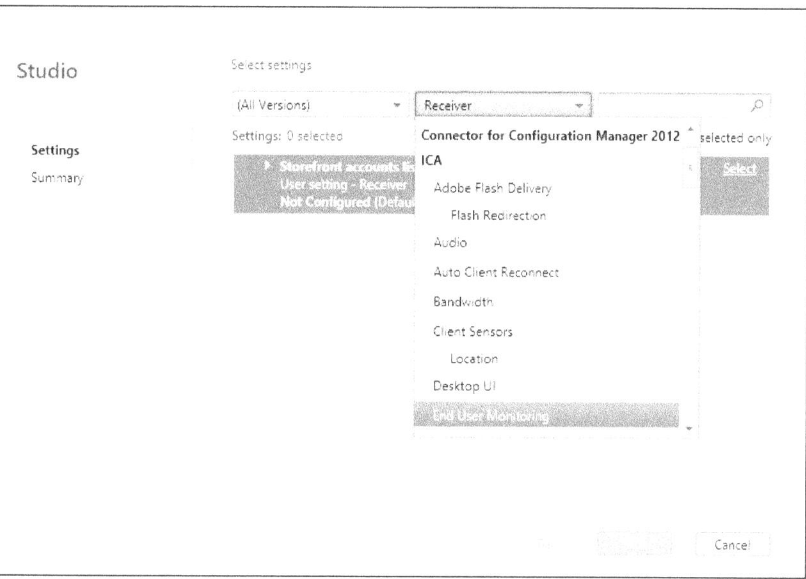

# Creating a new policy template from Citrix® Studio console

Launch Citrix Studio console from the Citrix Delivery Controller and follow these steps:

1. Inside the Citrix Studio, navigate to the **Policies** node:

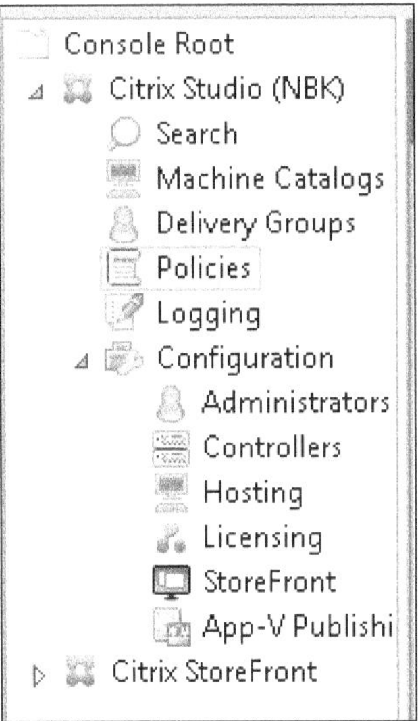


2. Inside **Polices**, select the **Templates** tab:

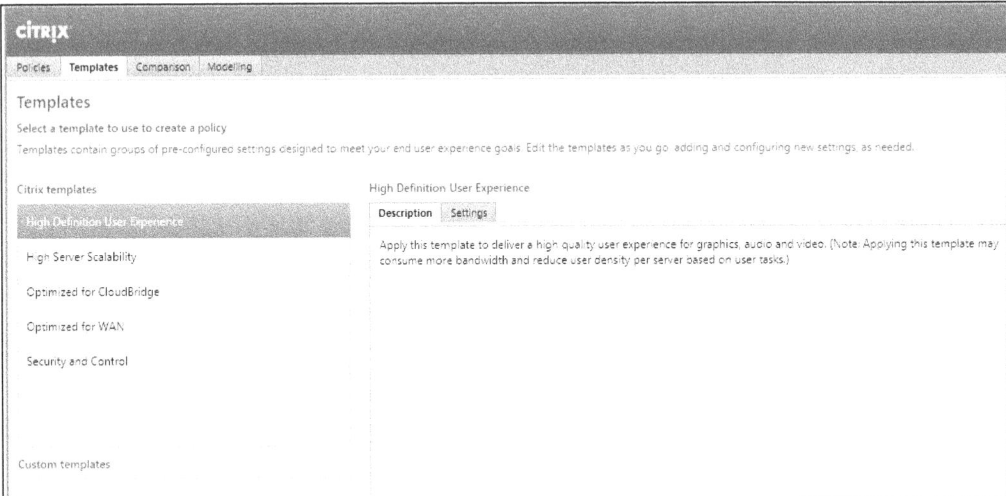

3. First, select the policy template and then from the right pane, click on **Create Policy from Template...**. In this case, I have made the selection for **High Definition User Experience**:

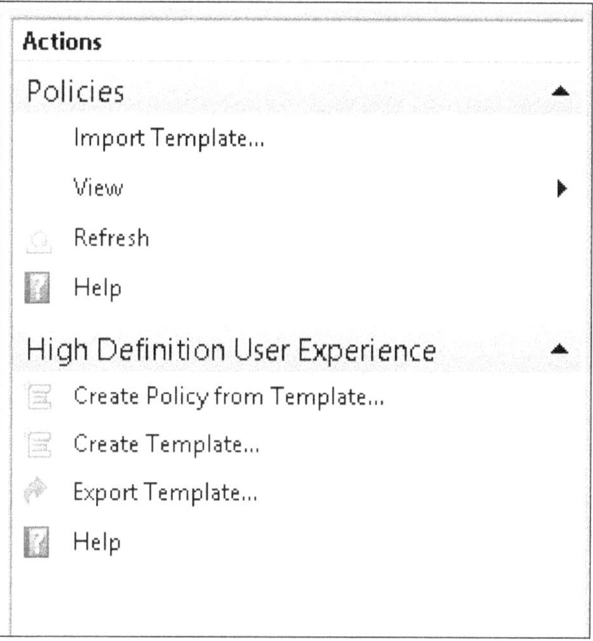

4. It will launch the create policy wizard and you will have options to either use **Template default setting (recommended)** or **Modify default settings and add more**. In our scenario, we will make the selection to **Modify default settings and add more**. At the moment, we will not make any changes and click on **Next**:

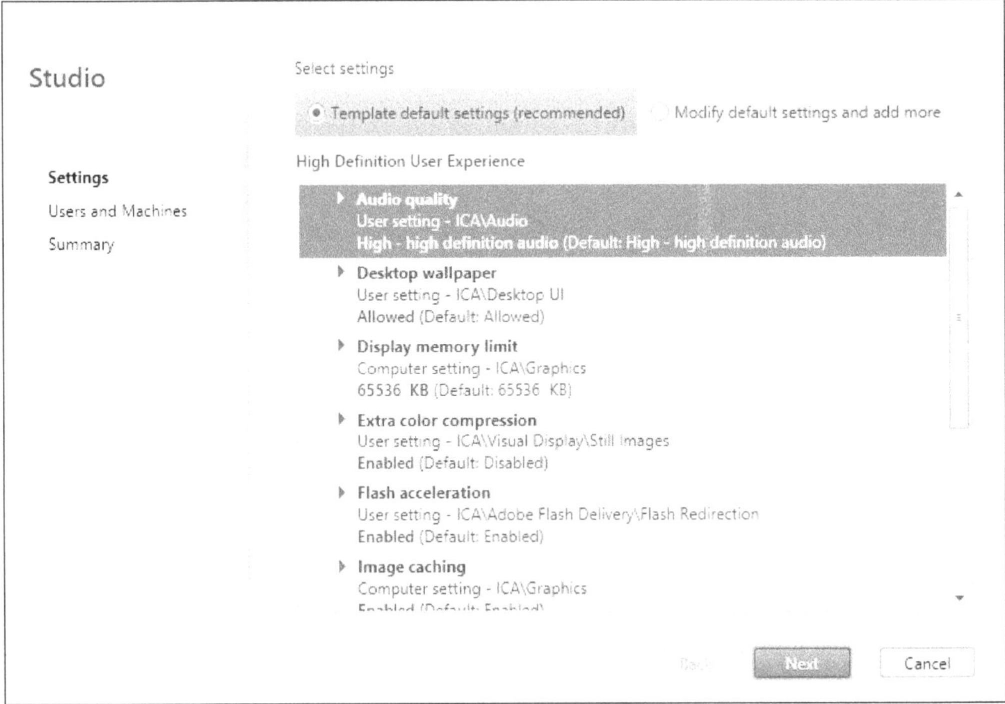


5. The next screen will ask about the filters, which will be based on the users and machines. On this wizard, we will have two options:
    - **Assign to selected user and machine objects**
    - **Assign to all objects in a site**

6. I want to assign this policy to delivery group, so I will choose the **Delivery Group** option and click on **Assign**:

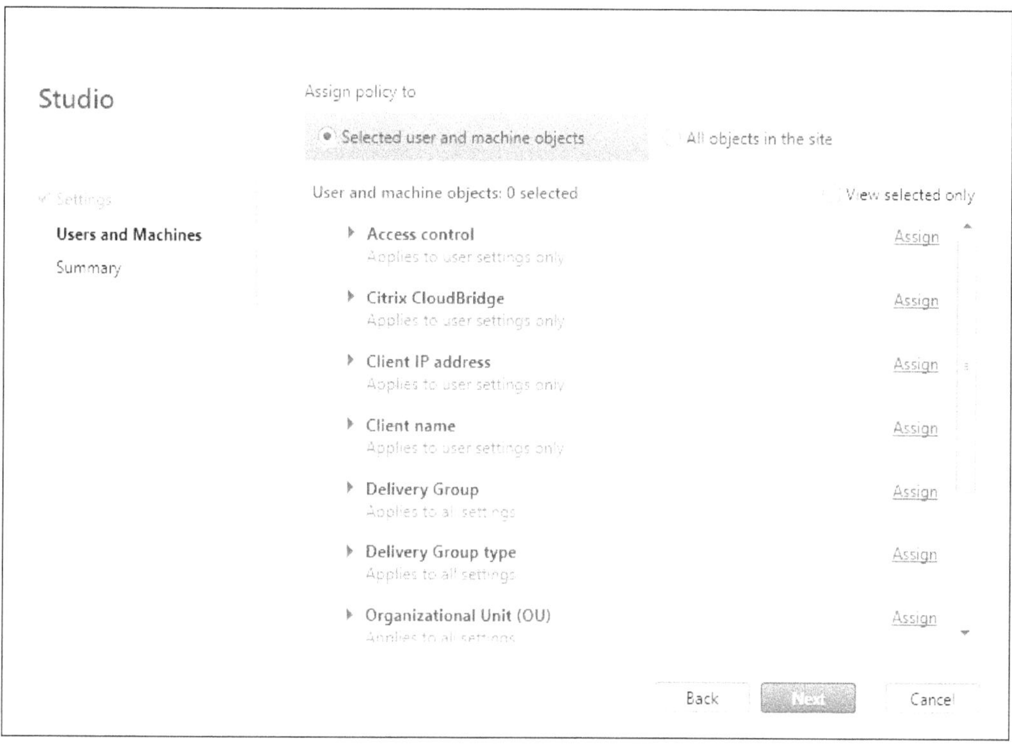

7. Choose **Notepad** and click on **OK** and then click on **Next**:

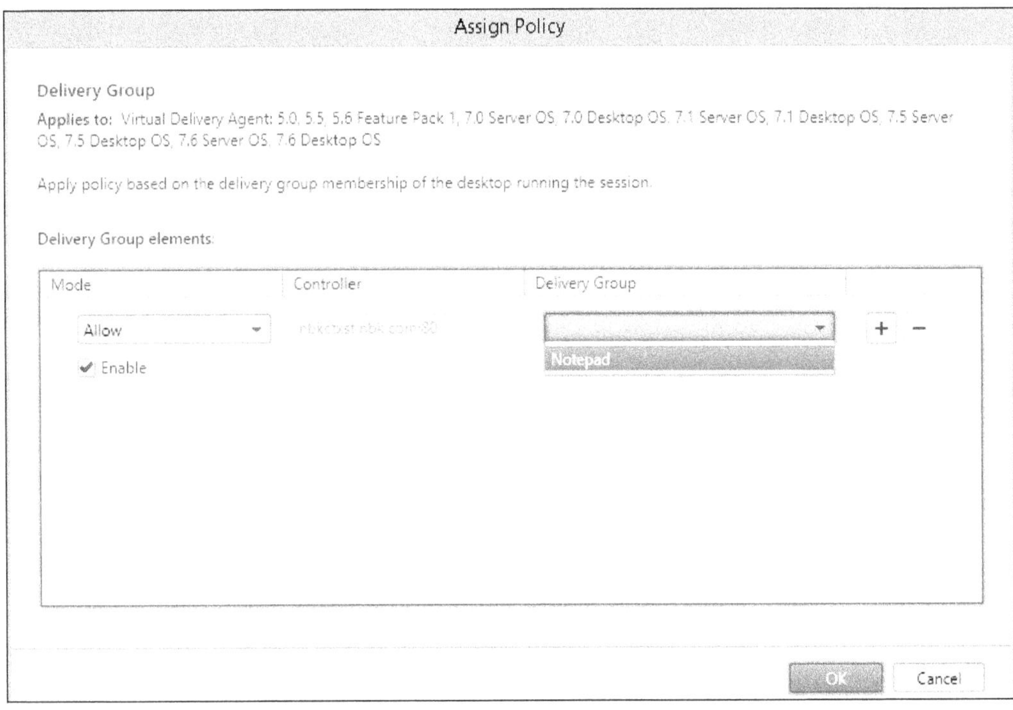

8. The last step will be the summary wizard where you can name your policy, enable or disable it, and add the custom description. Once you are done with the review, click on **Finish**:

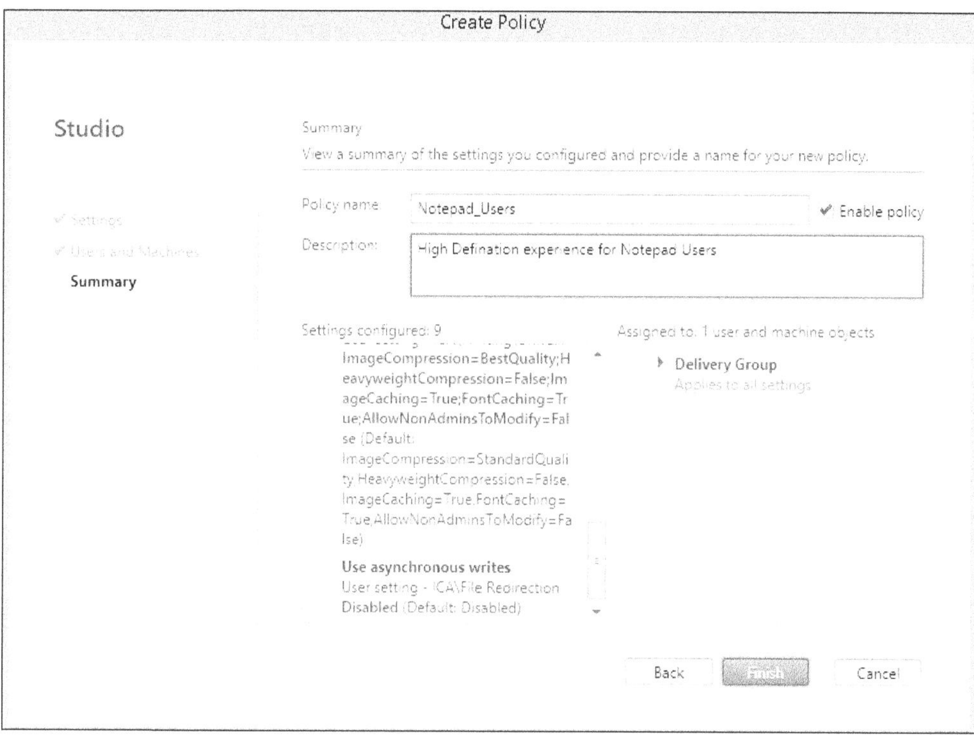

9. Once done, you can change tab to **Policies**, and you will be able to see the new policy that you created:

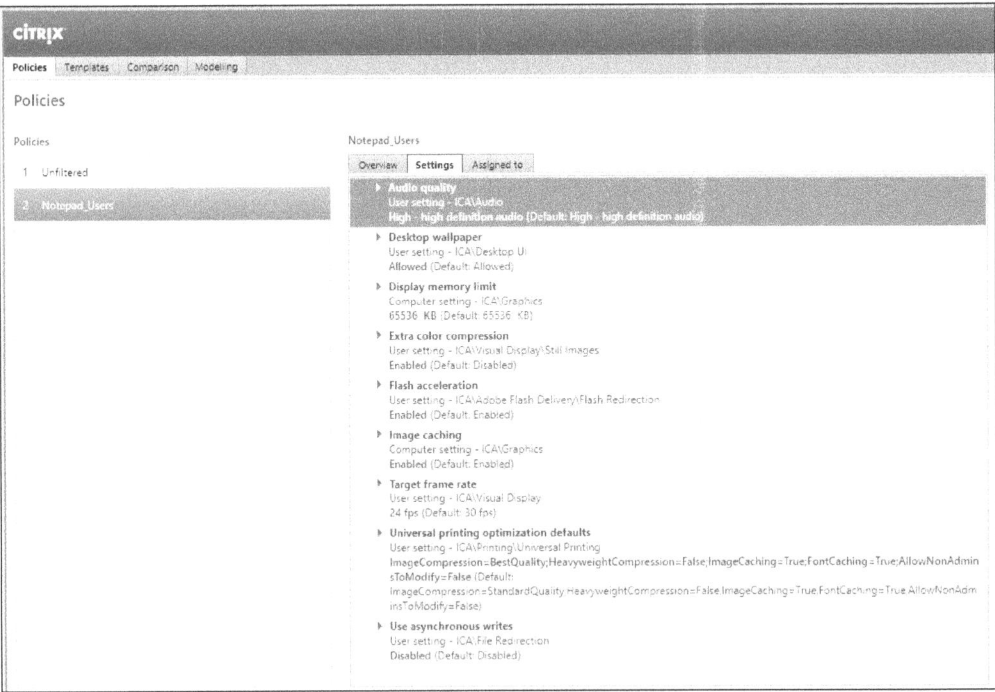

## Creating a new Citrix® policy using the Citrix® Studio console

Select the Policies node in the Citrix Studio console and follow these steps:

1. Click on the **Policies** tab:

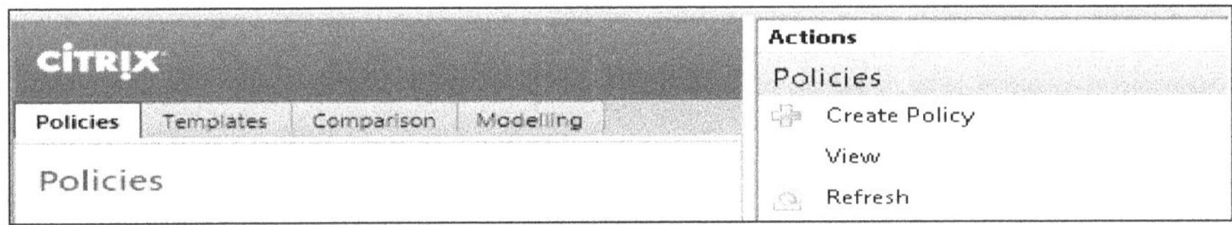


2. Click on the **Create Policy** option in the **Actions** pane:

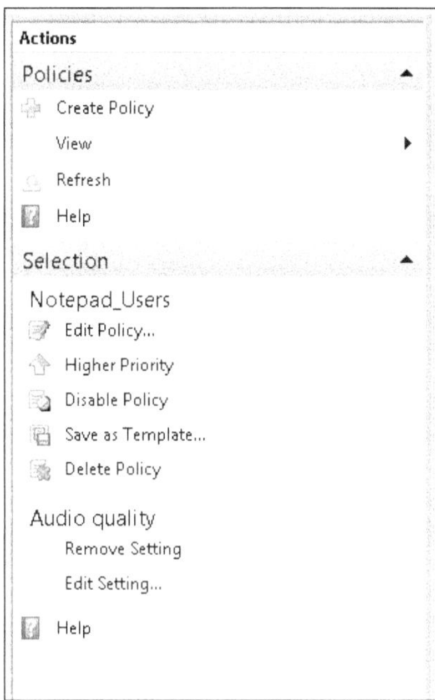


3. It will launch the **Create policy** wizard, which contains settings, and you can filter them based on the virtual delivery agent version and settings, or you can do a quick look up from the search box:

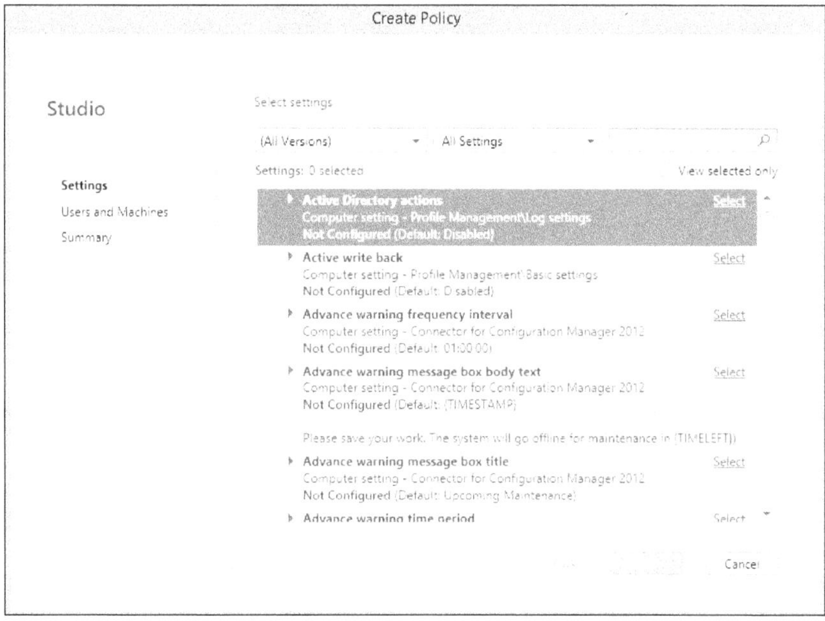

4. You can add all the setting you want to add here. I have enabled the keep alive settings, session limits and then clicked on **Next**.
5. On the next screen, you have to choose the filters based on the users and machines. In this case, I will choose the security group for the Citrix users:

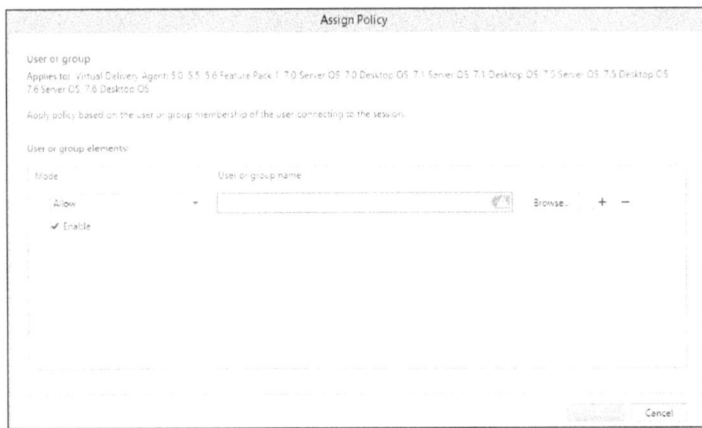


6. Click on **Browse...** and search for the security group and then click on **OK**. It will show up in the **Assign Policy** wizard:

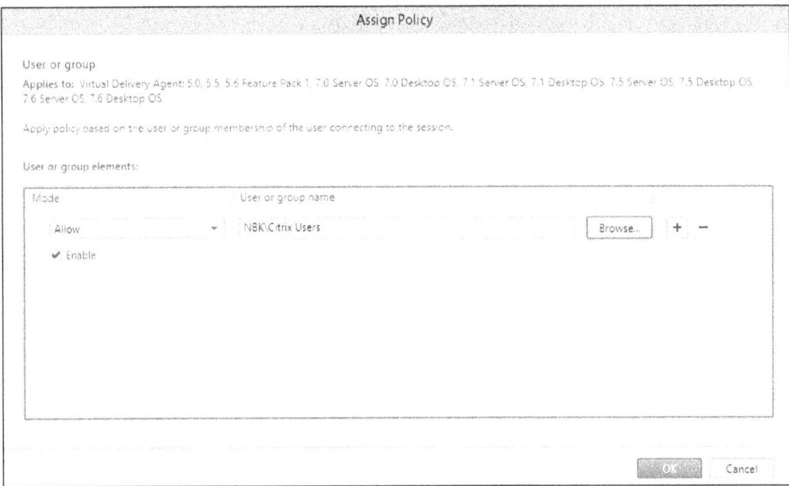


7. Click on **OK** and then **Next**.
8. The next screen is the summary screen where you can name your policy, enable or disable it, and add the custom description. Once you are done with the reviewing, click on **Finish**:

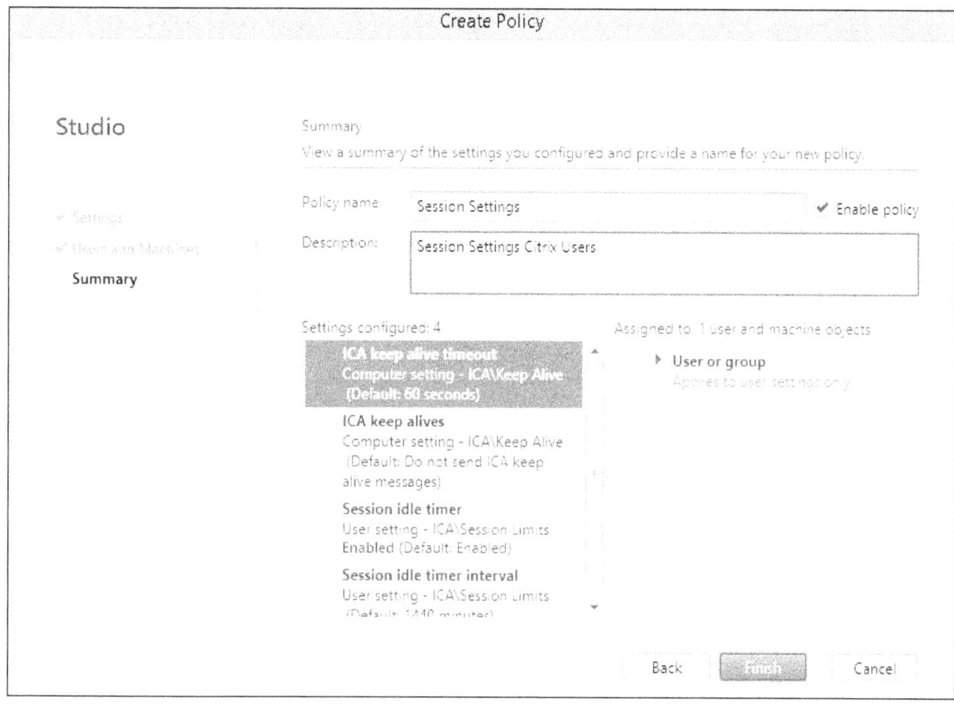


9. It will take a moment to create a policy and save the setting for the site database. Then, it will appear in the **Policies** tab:

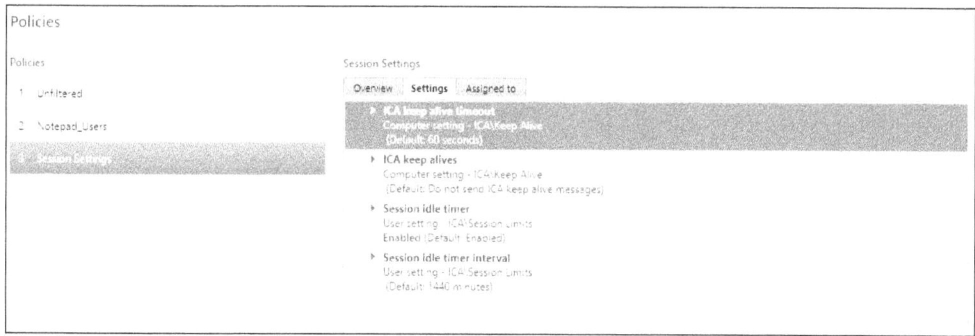


This is how we set up the Citrix policies from the Citrix Studio console.

# Installing the group policy management feature

It is recommend that you use the group policy management console for applying the Citrix policy because it is central control panel from where active directory group policy is also applied. As you are aware, the sequence active directory OU GPO always wins when it comes to group policy applying to user or computer and it also avoids any potential conflicts between the policies, which means no issues in the environment. If you have worked on the group policy, you must be aware of the fact that how difficult it is to troubleshoot the conflicts.

In order to manage the Citrix policies via group policy management console, let's go through the steps to install the group policy management console feature on the existing Citrix Delivery Controller:

1. Open **Server Manager** on the Citrix Delivery Controller.
2. In the **Server Manager** dashboard, click on **Add roles and features**:

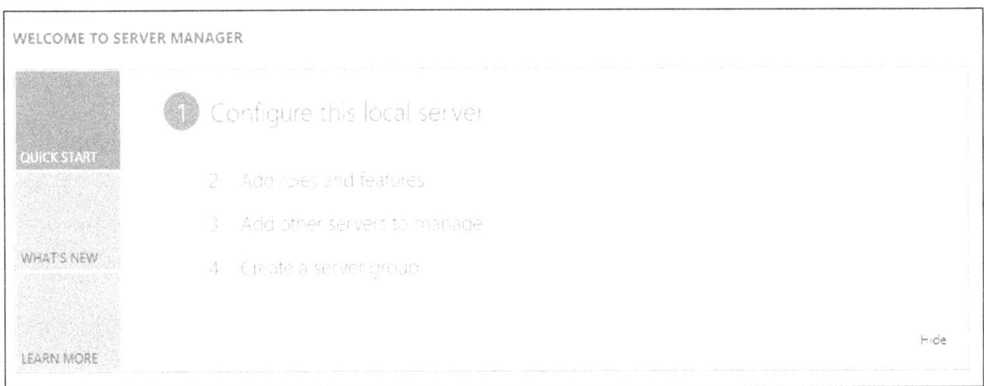


3. It will bring up the **Add roles and features** wizard where the first step is **Installation Type**:

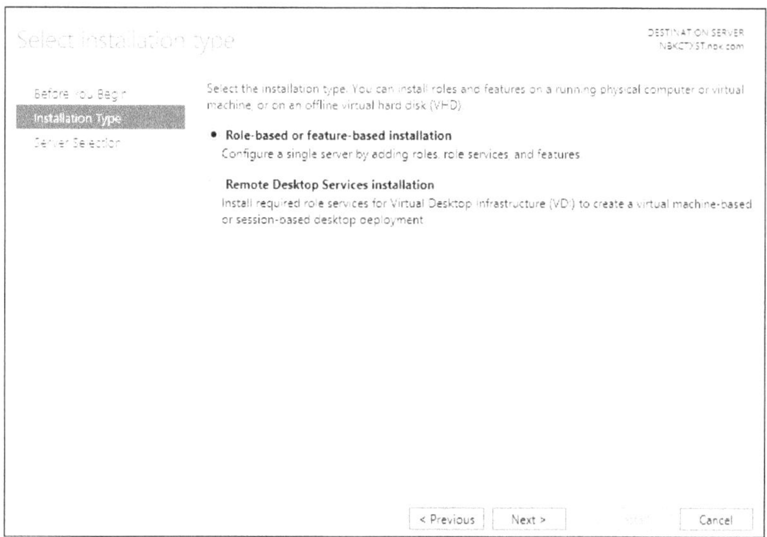


4. Select **Role-based or feature-based installation** and click on **Next**.
5. On the next screen, select the server from the pool and click on **Next**:

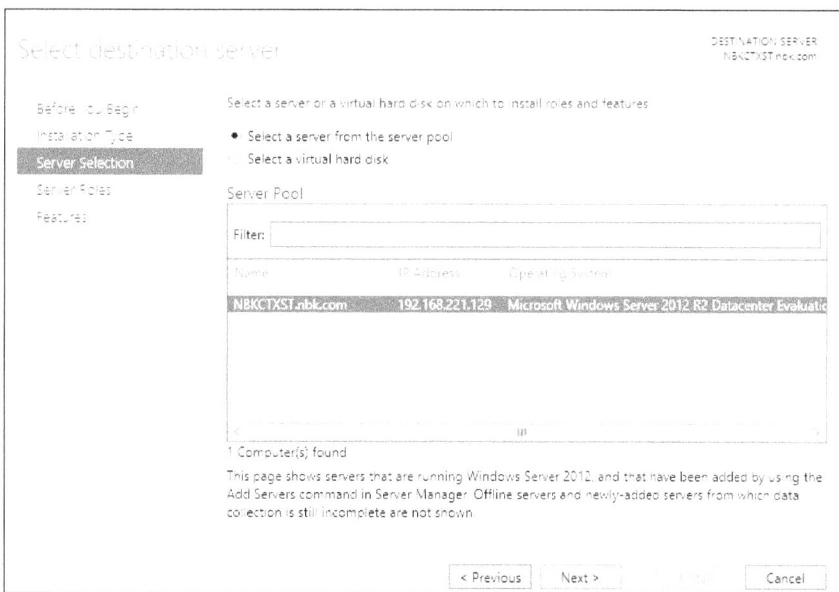


6. The next step will be to choose the role. We will skip this step by clicking on **Next**.

7. The next step will be to choose the feature that you want to install. Select **Group Policy Management** and click on **Next**:

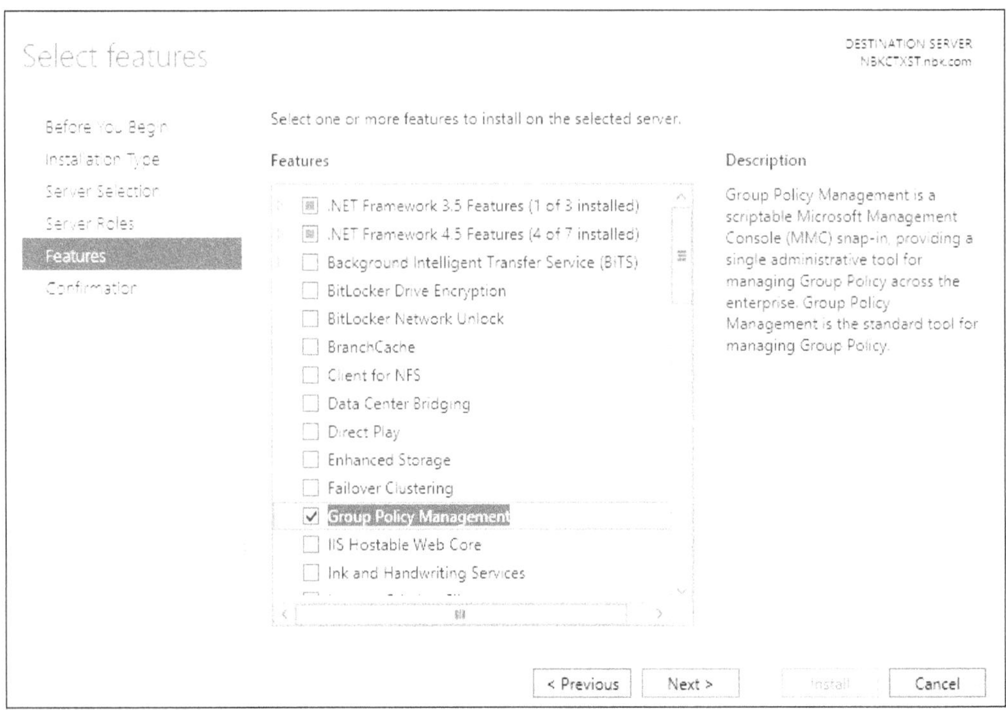

8. The next step will let you confirm your selection. Click on **Install**:

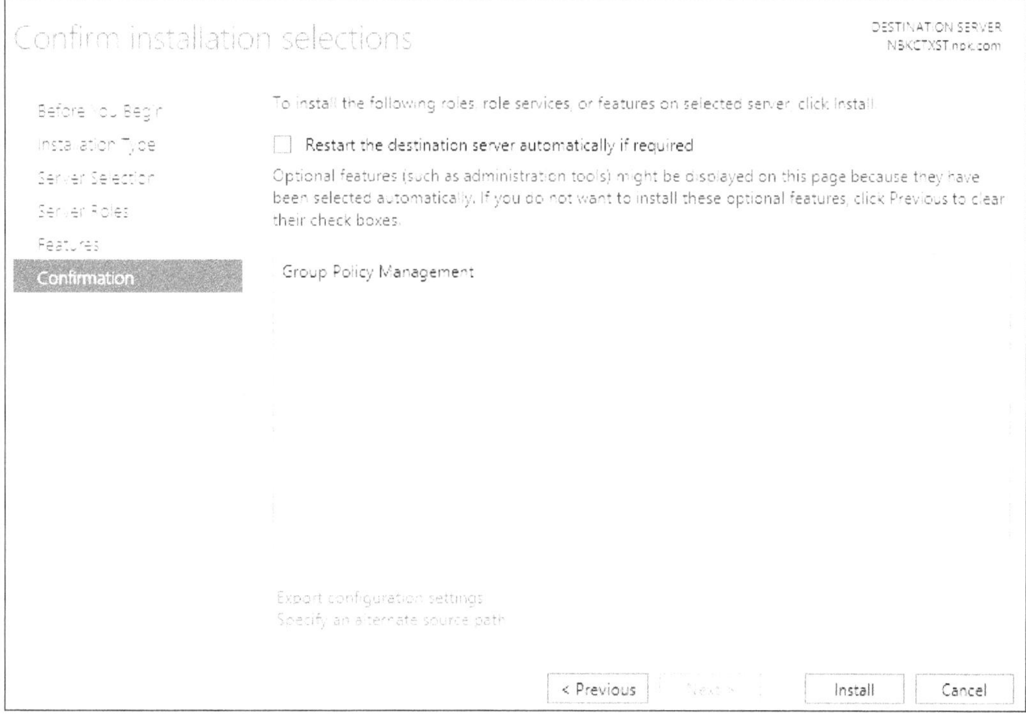

9. It will take a while to install the group policy management feature on the Citrix Delivery Controller. Once done, you can click on **Close**:

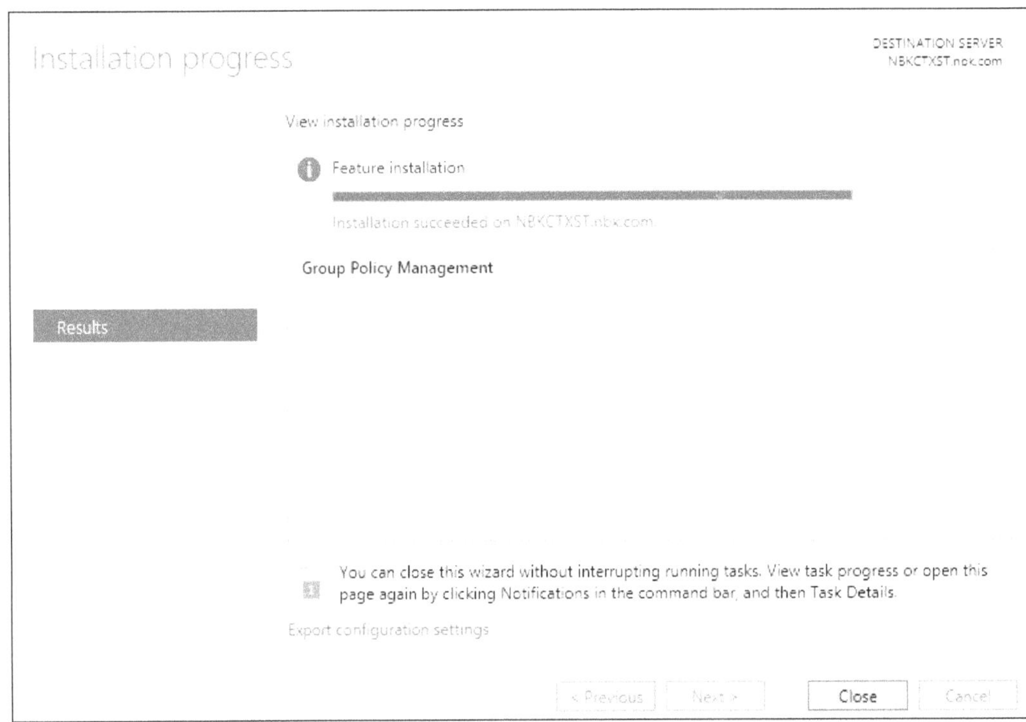


This will complete the installation of the group policy management console on the Citrix Delivery Controller.

# Creating and managing policies inside the group policy management console

In order to manage the Citrix group policy from the group policy management console, follow these instructions:

1. Launch the group policy management console on the Citrix Delivery Controller by going to **Start | Administrative tools | Group policy management**, and it will open the following window:

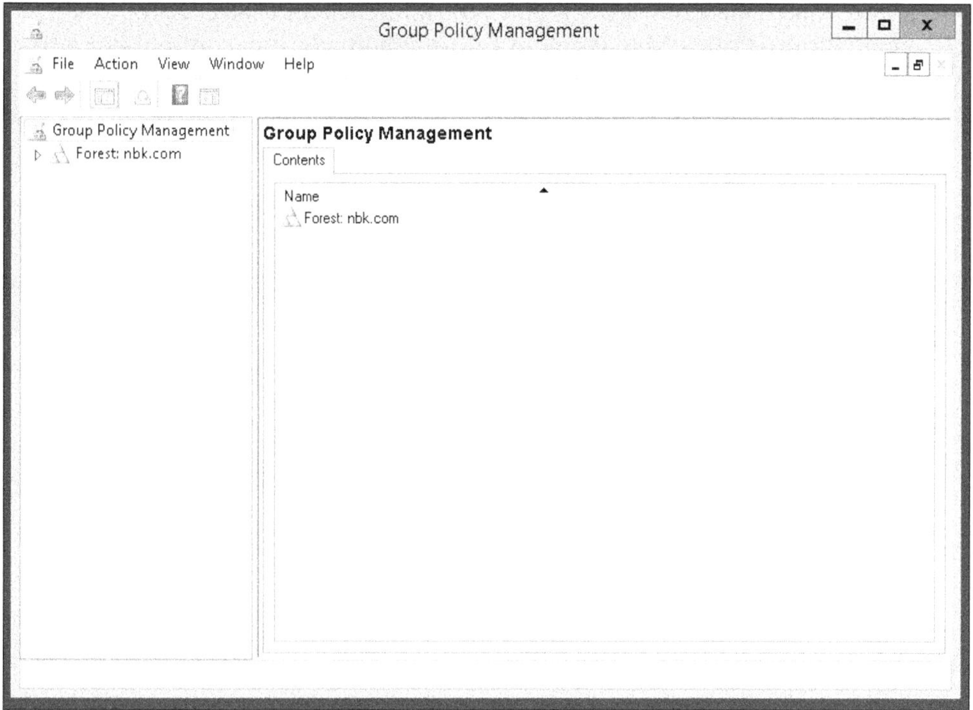


2. Expand `Forest: nbk.com`, and you will be able to see this:

3. Further, you have to expand the domain and then the name of the domain. You can start creating your group policy object inside the Group policy object.

4. Once you create a new object, you can right-click and select **edit**. It will open **Group Policy Management Editor** where you can configure or edit the settings. Here, settings are divided into **Computer Configuration** and **User Configuration**, which is unlike Citrix Studio, where all the settings are grouped in one:

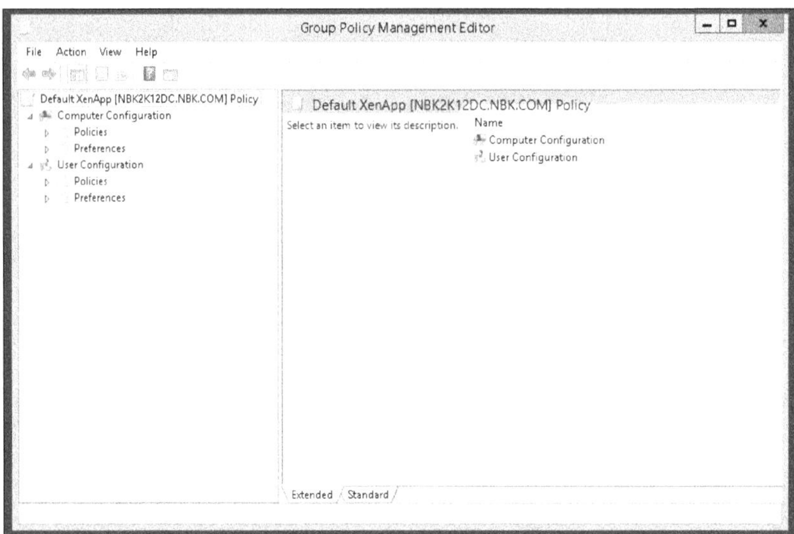


5. You can apply the Citrix policies to user and computer, and in order to do that, you have to expand the **Policies** node, and you will be able to see the **Citrix Policies** node for user and computer:

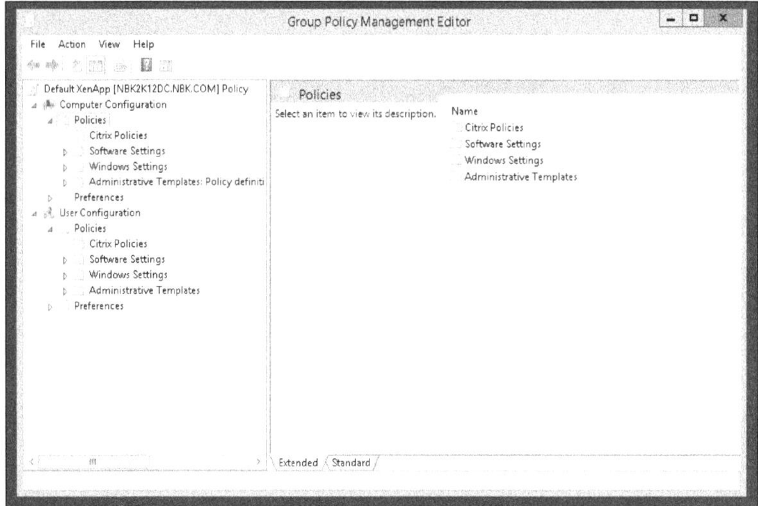

6. Even here, the interface to create the policies for Citrix looks almost similar. You can create a new policy from **Template** or just create a new policy by clicking on **New** and selecting the desired setting and assigning them to the group of user and other filters available to choose from:

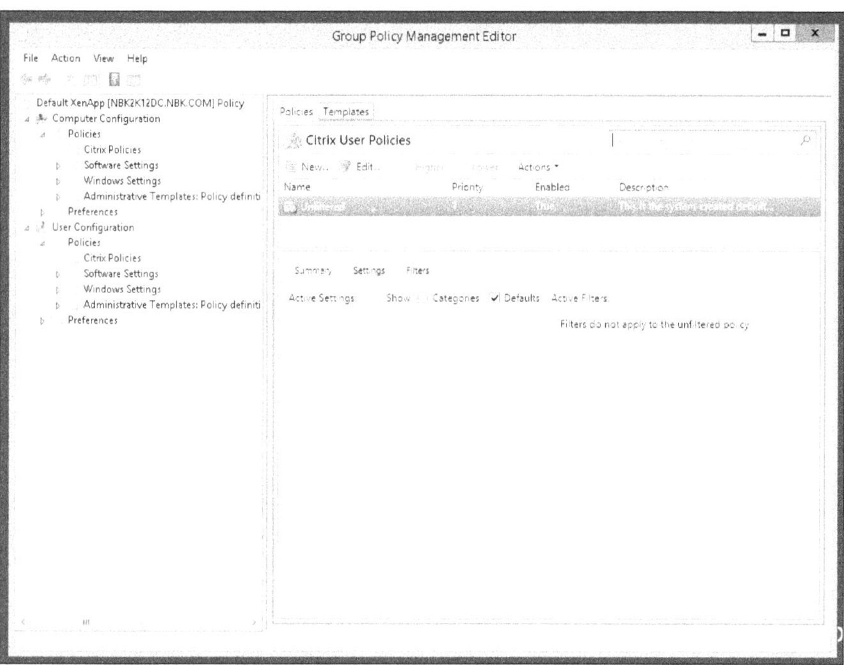

# Printing policies

Over the years, printing in Citrix gave nightmares to the Citrix administrator, but at the same time, Citrix never gave up and continued their effort to provide the better user experience when it came to printing.

With the release of Citrix XenApp 7.6, it also released the new version of Citrix Universal Print Server 7.6 and after regressive testing, the Citrix experts found that:

- Citrix UPS is able to take 50 print jobs per minute.
- It showed better efficiency and recovery during the high load.
- It has got better performance when it comes to WAN printing. Users were able to interact with the print dialog box six times faster.

As you are aware, printing put a high load on the network bandwidth and with the help of, the HDX protocol did some compression between Universal Print Server and client that helped in the WAN performance.

# Implementing Universal Print Server 7.6

Universal Print Server enables the IT administrator to use the single driver on server operating system, which allows users to print from almost any printer available. It is always recommended to use the universal printing when it comes to Citrix and network printing. Whenever a user prints any document with the help of Citrix, the universal print job gets transferred to network in a compressed format, which improves the network performance, providing a better printing experience to the user.

Let's talk about how we can implement Universal Print Server. Citrix Universal Printer Server contains a couple of components, which are as follows:

- Server component: This is the installer, which needs to be installed on the print server from where session printers are provisioned. The driver used is the universal print driver.
- Client component: This is another installer, which needs to be installed on the server where user's session are hosted and from where user will send all the printing command.

The following image shows how the network printing work when you are using Universal Print Server:

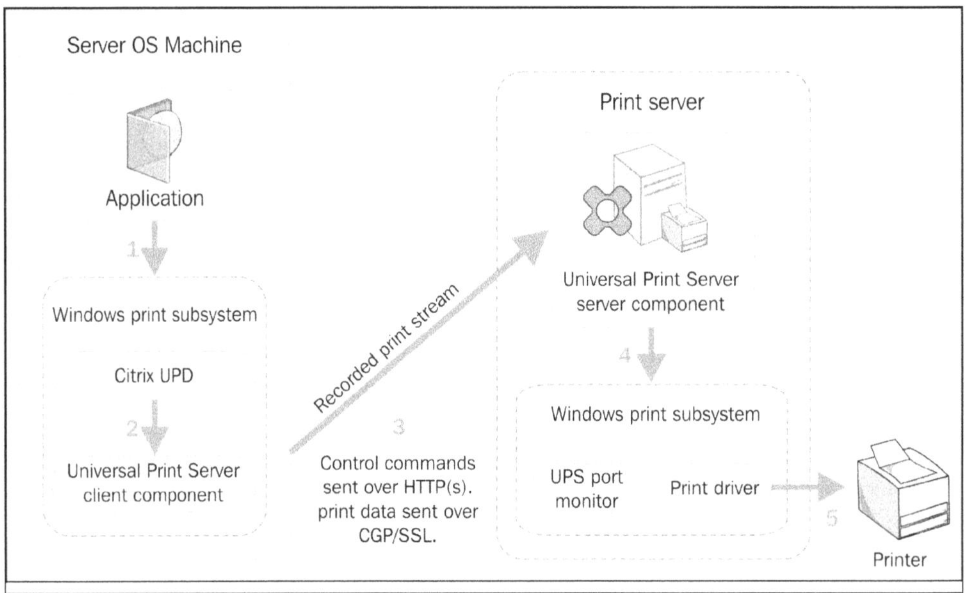


Image reference:docs.citrix.com/en-us/xenapp-and-xendesktop/7-6/xad-print-landing.html

# Citrix® printing policies

Once you have the universal printer set up, you can use the Citrix policies to optimize the better experience for users when it comes to printing. When defining the policies, you have to keep a few things in mind:

- Which printers are required by the user in there Citrix session
- How to route the print jobs given by the users
- How to manage the drivers for printer

Let's see what all things can be optimized via Citrix policies:

Citrix has the following set of policies when it comes to printing:

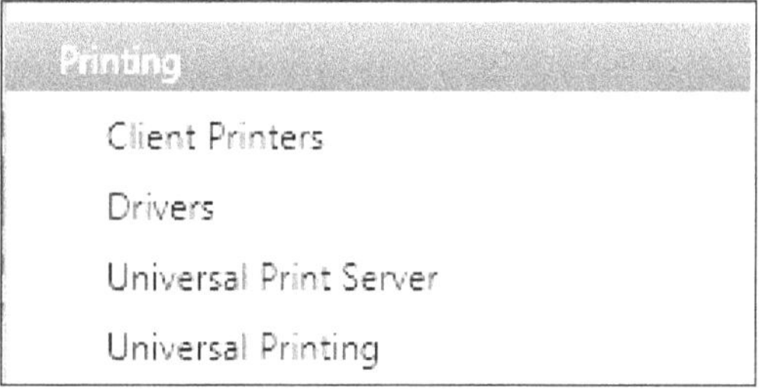


To start with, let's discuss what client printers are and what all policies can be configured inside the client printers.

**Client printers** are basically those printers that are already installed on the local computer from where users can access the Citrix-hosted application. The first policy for client printer is:

- **Auto-create all client printers**: When you will select this policy, you will have four options:

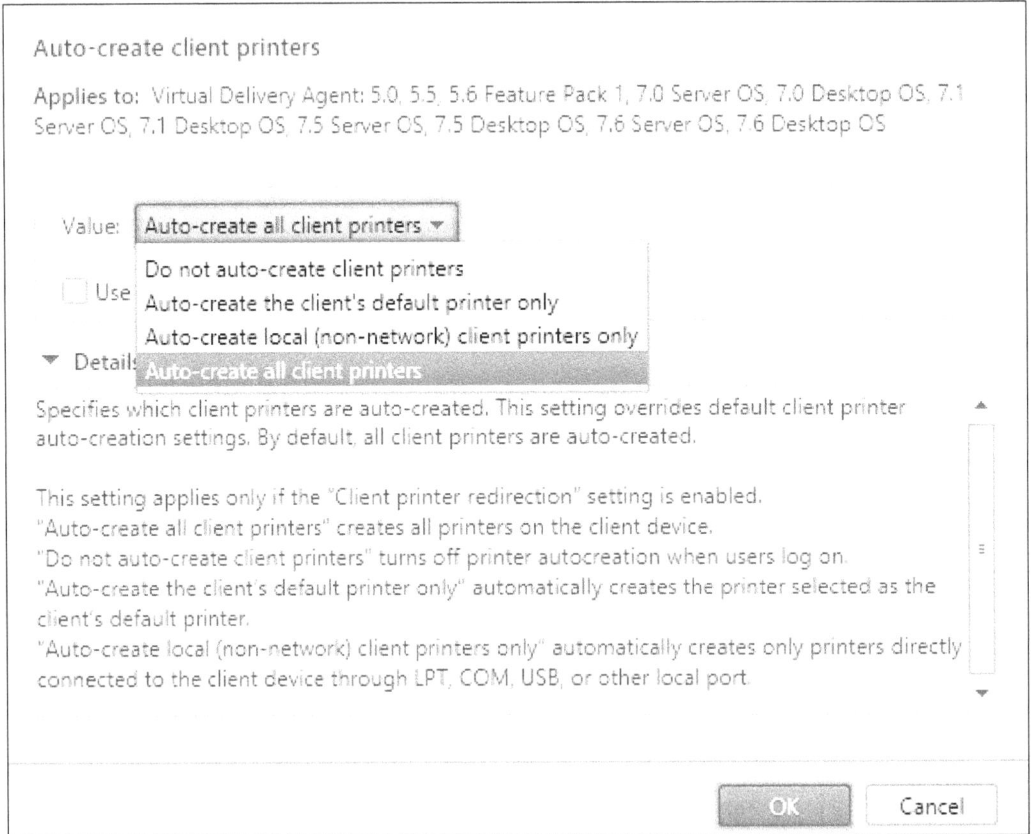
Auto-create client printers
Applies to: Virtual Delivery Agent: 5.0, 5.5, 5.6 Feature Pack 1, 7.0 Server OS, 7.0 Desktop OS, 7.1 Server OS, 7.1 Desktop OS, 7.5 Server OS, 7.5 Desktop OS, 7.6 Server OS, 7.6 Desktop OS
Value: Auto-create all client printers
Do not auto-create client printers
Auto-create the client's default printer only
Auto-create local (non-network) client printers only
Auto-create all client printers
Use
Details
Specifies which client printers are auto-created. This setting overrides default client printer auto-creation settings. By default, all client printers are auto-created.
This setting applies only if the "Client printer redirection" setting is enabled.
"Auto-create all client printers" creates all printers on the client device.
"Do not auto-create client printers" turns off printer autocreation when users log on.
"Auto-create the client's default printer only" automatically creates the printer selected as the client's default printer.
"Auto-create local (non-network) client printers only" automatically creates only printers directly connected to the client device through LPT, COM, USB, or other local port.
OK
Cancel

    - **Do not auto-create client printers**: Choose this when you don't want users to use their local printers
    - **Auto-create the client's default printer only**: This allows only local default printer to be created in the Citrix session
    - **Auto-create local (non-network) client printers only**: If you are going to select this, only non-network printers will be created in the Citrix session
    - **Auto-create all client printers**: This will make all the client printers visible in the Citrix session

In most of the scenarios, if the printing is allowed from the client computer, then it is recommended to use the **Auto-create the client's default printer only** option as the default is the frequently used printer.

- **Auto-create generic universal printer**: This will enable the Citrix universal printer to be created in the session and when a user gives the command, it will send the job to the default printer on the local client computer from where the user is accessing the session:

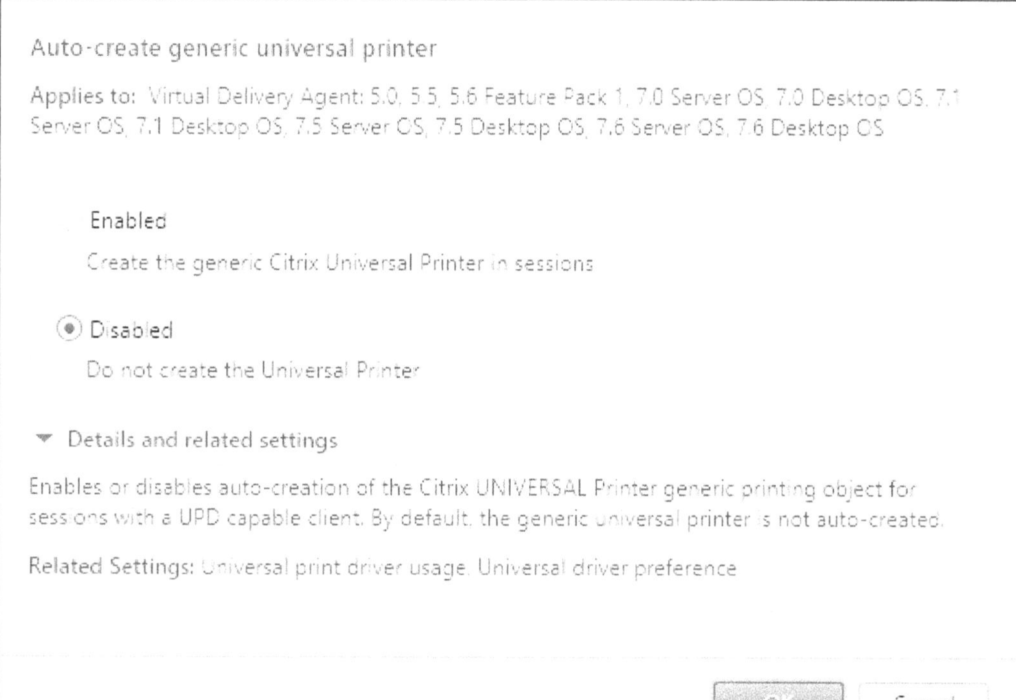

Auto-create generic universal printer
Applies to: Virtual Delivery Agent: 5.0, 5.5, 5.6 Feature Pack 1, 7.0 Server OS, 7.0 Desktop OS, 7.1 Server OS, 7.1 Desktop OS, 7.5 Server OS, 7.5 Desktop OS, 7.6 Server OS, 7.6 Desktop OS
Enabled
Create the generic Citrix Universal Printer in sessions
Disabled
Do not create the Universal Printer
Details and related settings
Enables or disables auto-creation of the Citrix UNIVERSAL Printer generic printing object for sessions with a UPD capable client. By default, the generic universal printer is not auto-created.
Related Settings: Universal print driver usage, Universal driver preference
OK
Cancel

- **Auto-create PDF Universal Printer**: This enables the users to print from Chrome book or when users are accessing the application via Citrix HTML client:

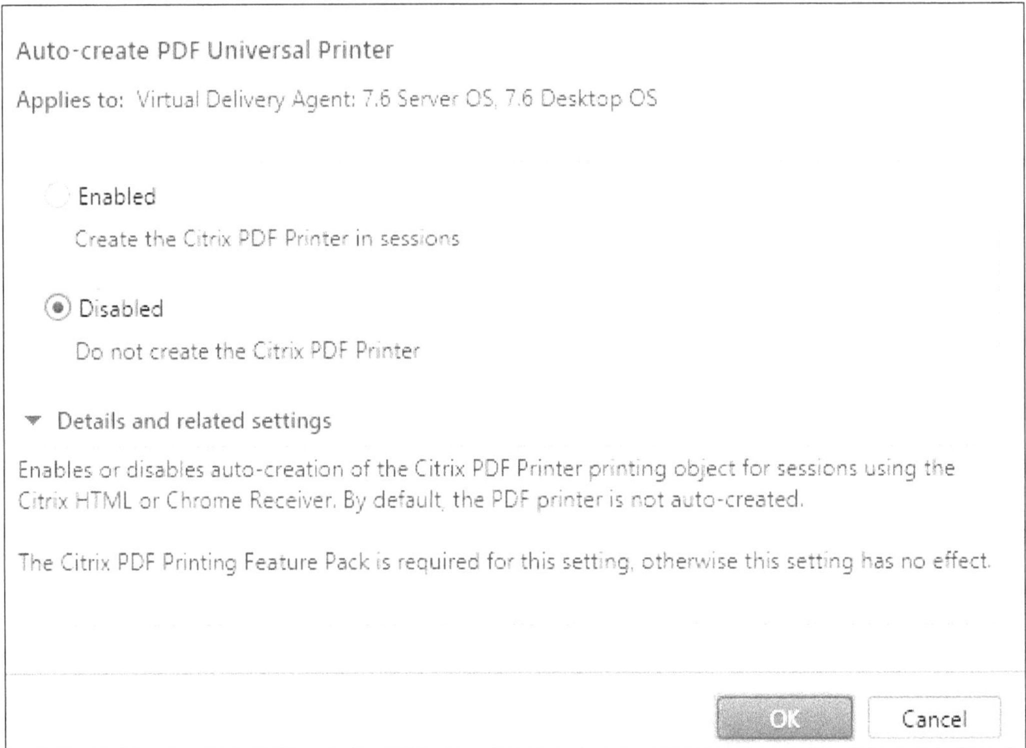

Auto-create PDF Universal Printer
Applies to: Virtual Delivery Agent: 7.6 Server OS, 7.6 Desktop OS
Enabled
Create the Citrix PDF Printer in sessions
Disabled
Do not create the Citrix PDF Printer
Details and related settings
Enables or disables auto-creation of the Citrix PDF Printer printing object for sessions using the Citrix HTML or Chrome Receiver. By default, the PDF printer is not auto-created.
The Citrix PDF Printing Feature Pack is required for this setting, otherwise this setting has no effect.
OK
Cancel

Then there are other policies as well that can be configured for naming the printer, how the print jobs need to be routed, whether users' preferences need to be retained, and so on. Here is a screenshot for your reference:

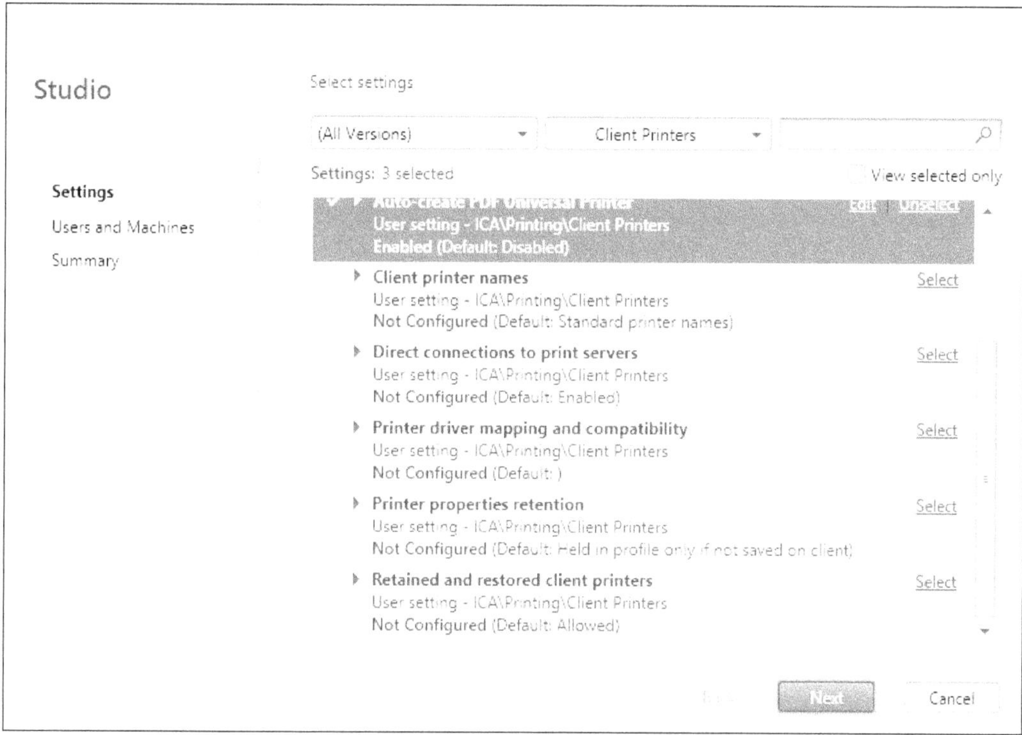

After the client printers, it is time to discuss about the print drivers. Under the driver settings, we have three settings, as shown in the following screenshot:

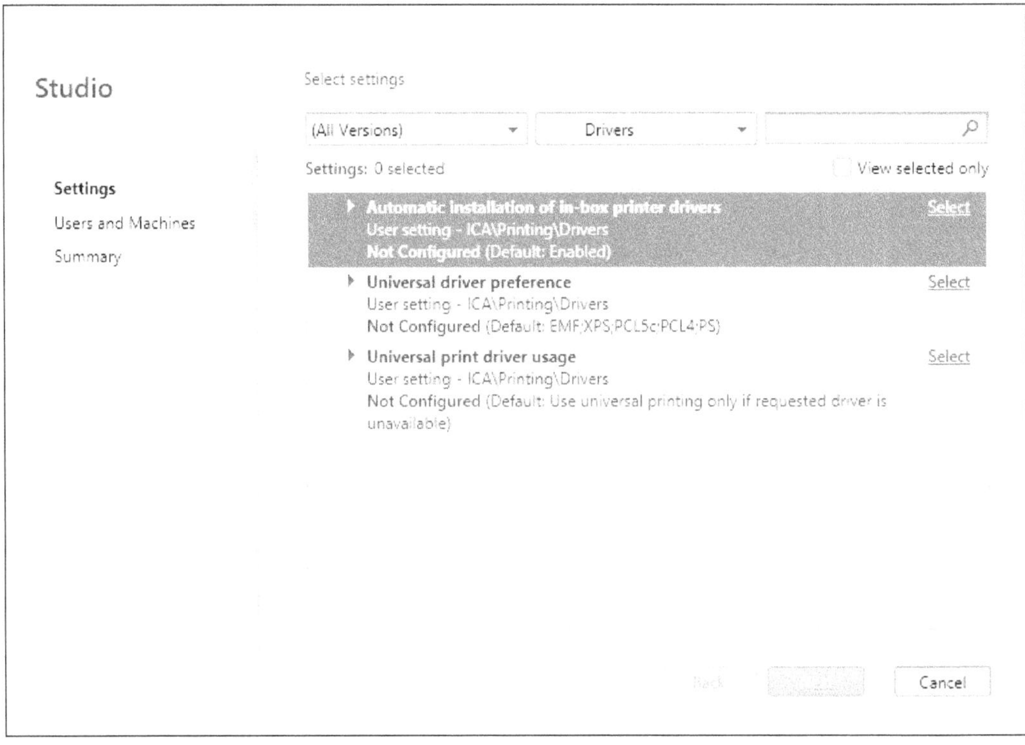


- **Automatic installation of in-box printer drivers**: This allows the printer drivers to be installed automatically. It is not recommended to disable this to avoid the unwanted print drivers to be installed. It is always recommended that you use the Microsoft native drivers, which come with the operating system.
- **Universal driver preference**: In the policy setting, you can define the preference in which XenApp is going to use the universal driver. The options of drivers are:
    - EMF
    - XPS
    - PCL5c
    - PCL4
    - PS

  You can set the priority and delete the drivers if you want to.

- **Universal print driver usage**: In this setting, you have four options to select from:
    - **Use only printer model specific drivers**: Choose this when you have printer driver installed on your servers hosting the session.
    - **Use universal printing only**: Choose this when you want to use the generic driver for the printer, which reduces the headache of driver management on the host machine.
    - **Use universal printer only if requested driver is unavailable**: You can choose this option when you have installed the specific printer model driver on the computer. When the user tries to print from an unknown printer and the driver is not available on the server, it will fail over to universal print driver for successful printing.
    - **Use printer model specific drivers only if universal printing is unavailable**: Well, there are printers that are not compatible with universal printer driver; in those cases, we can use this option to deal with such printers.

Then, we have the policy setting group on the basis of **Universal Print Server**, in which you can enable the Universal Print Server and if it is not available, it will fall back to native remote printing from Windows or with no fallback to Windows native remote printing.

It also has the setting where you can define the TCP port via which the bulk print data stream needs to be delivered to the print server. By default, the port for this is `7229`.

Another setting is where you can define the print stream bandwidth to be used; you can limit the bandwidth in the kbps unit.

The last setting under Universal Print Server is Universal Print Server web service (HTTPS/SOAP) port:

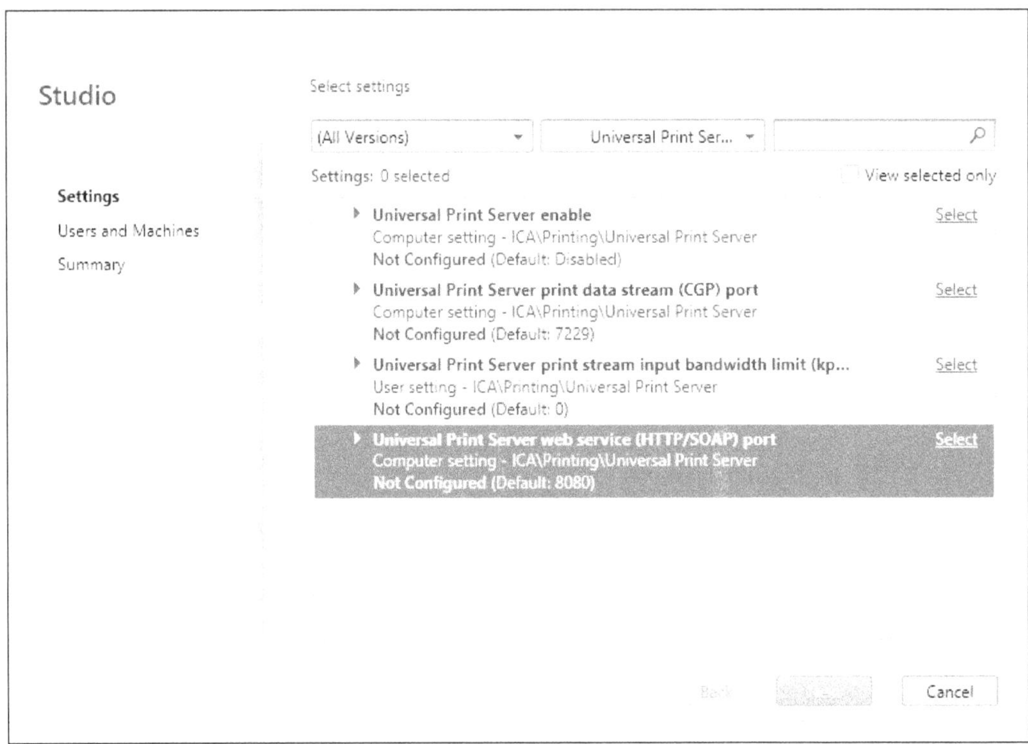


When using the Universal Printer Server, all the printing command are sent from XenApp host to Universal Printer Server via SOAP over the HTTP. By default, the port used for this is `8080`, but you can change the port if you want the different port to be used for this.

In **Universal Printing** group of printing policies, you can configure most critical settings, which is how the print jobs need to be processed, compressed, and cached, and last but not least, how the print quality would be. The following is the list of setting that can help you configuring these:

- Universal printing EMF processing mode
- Universal printing image compression limit
- Universal printing optimization defaults
- Universal printing preview preferences
- Universal printing print quality limit

# Configuring remote assistance

Remote assistance is used when you want to troubleshoot the issues reported by the user. As you are aware that Citrix enables the user to work from anywhere, it is difficult for the administrator to go to user computer to see the issue and know the steps that users are doing.

With the help of Citrix Director, an IT administrator can shadow the user's session as this administrator can quickly connect to the remote user's session and diagnose the issue.

In order to enable this feature, the server hosting the session must have the windows remote desktop assistance feature enabled.

Let's have a look at the steps on how to enable the Windows remote desktop assistance on the XenApp servers. We can enable this feature when we install the VDA:

1. Click on the **Start** button for **XenApp Deliver applications**:

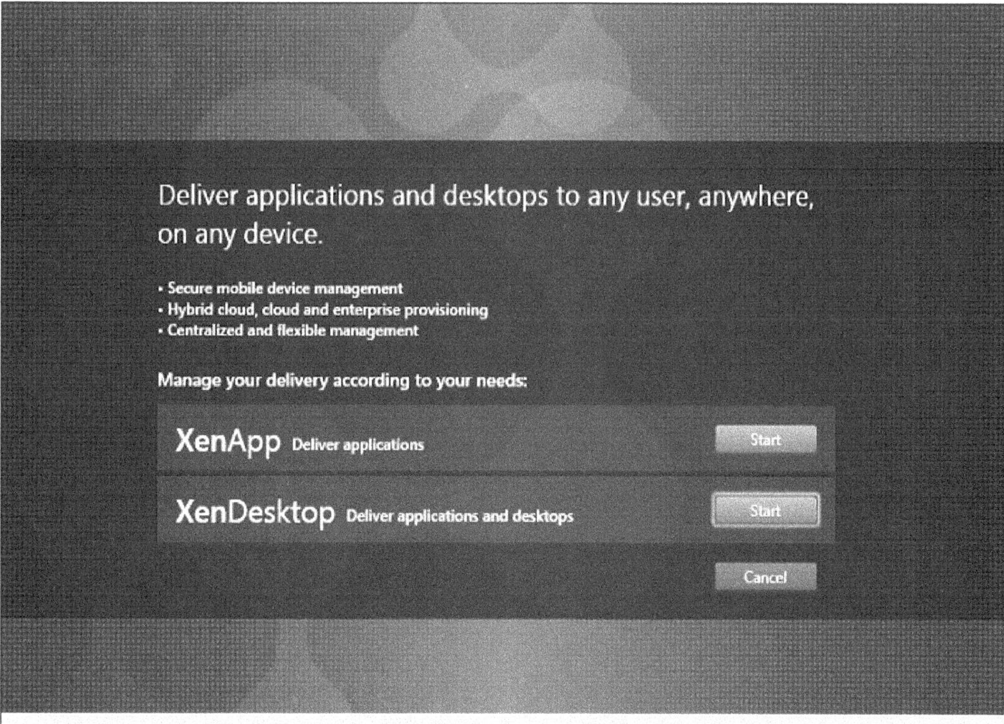

2. It will open a wizard in which you need to choose **Virtual Delivery Agent for Windows Server OS**:

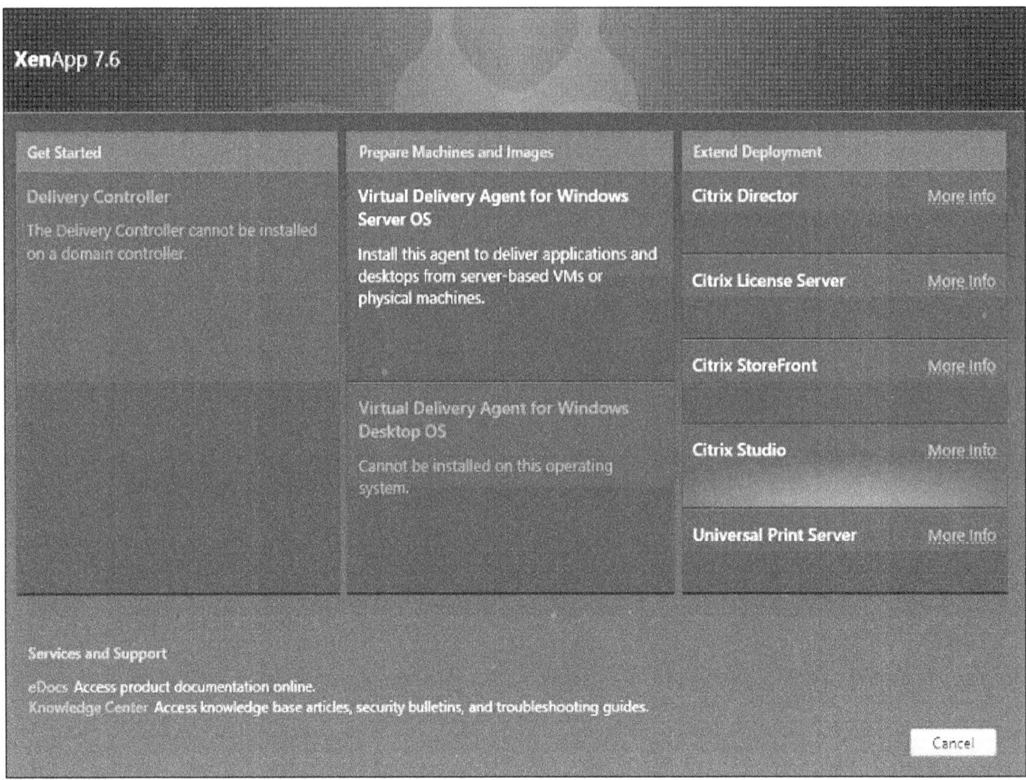

3. In the **Environment** section of the virtual delivery agent installation wizard, click on **Enable connections to a server machine**. You can also choose **Create a Master Image** if you are creating the template or using MCS or PVS to create the other servers. Click on **Next**:

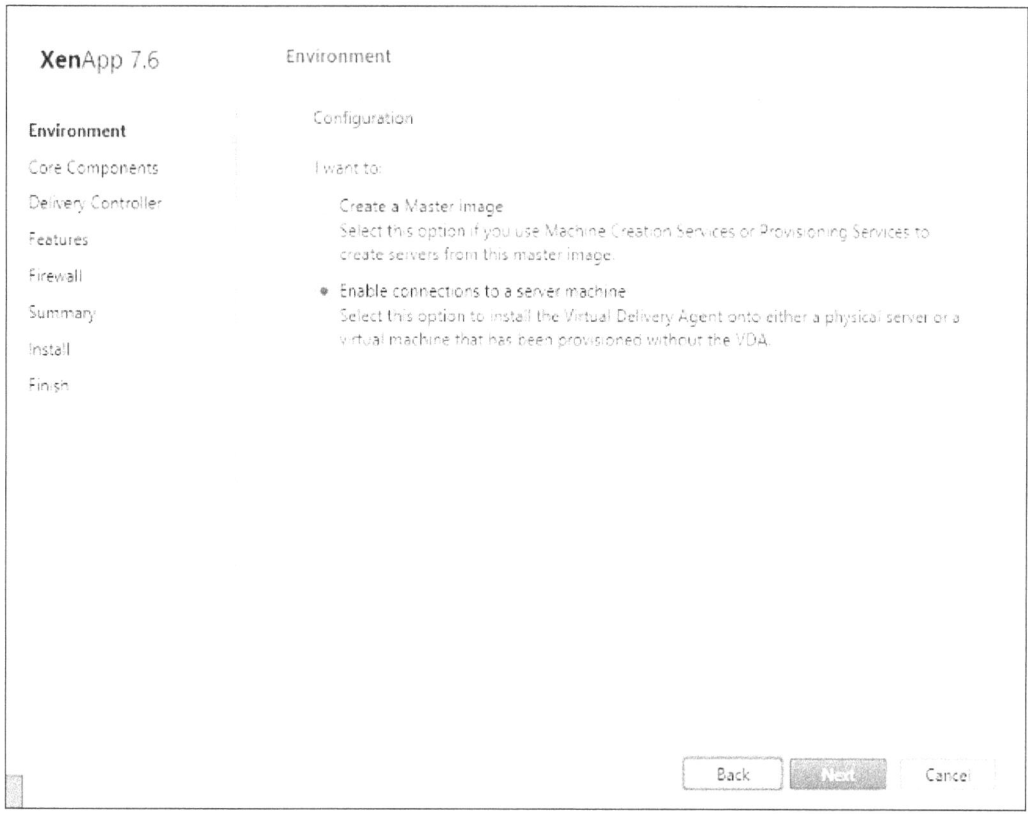


4. On the next screen, virtual delivery agent will be mandatory in this installation and if you want, you can choose Citrix Receiver and proceed to the next screen where you have to mention your Delivery Controller. Once done, click on **Next**.

5. It will take you to the feature selection wizard where you will get the option to enable the remote assistance. By default, remote assistance works on the TCP port `3389`. Make the selection and click on **Next**:

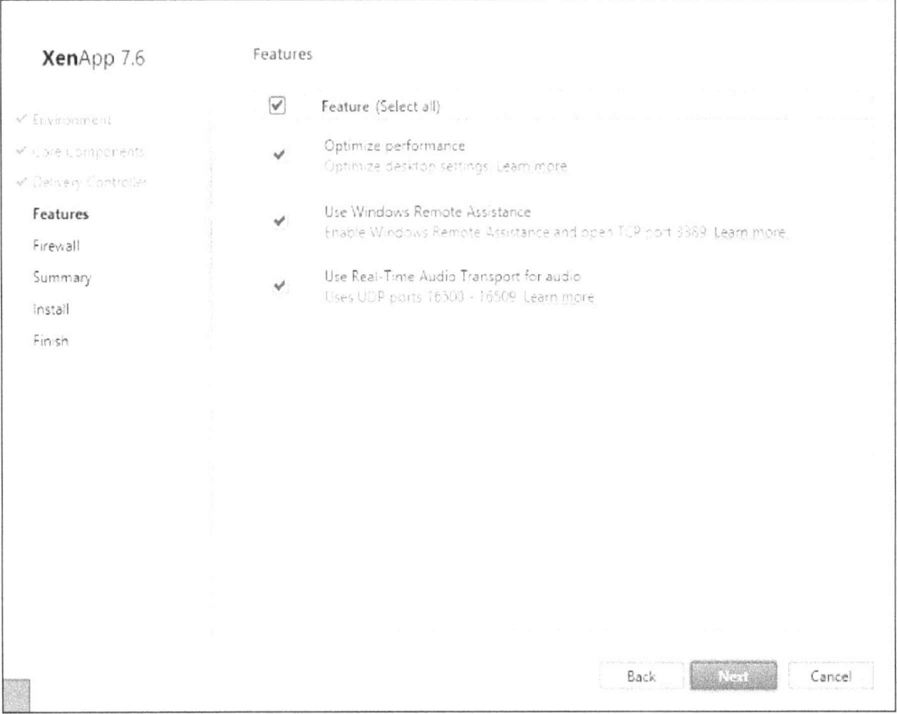


6. Follow the installation wizard and allow the auto configuration of the ports and review it. Then, click on **Install**. Once done, it will install the virtual delivery agent and also enable the remote assistance on the server.

After completing the above steps, IT administrator can shadow the user's session from the Citrix Director.

# Citrix® profile management

To start with, let's try to understand why we use the profile. Profiles are basically created when user logs in to any computer and all the personal preferences and settings are saved in it. Each time you log in, it will give you the same consistent experience. When we say preferences and settings, it means how your computer look and work when you log in to it, such as your desktop wallpaper, mouse pointer preferences, volume settings, and others.

We have different types of profile that can be used on different use case scenarios:

- **Local profiles**: Local profile gets created when you log in to any computer for the first time. It is created on local hard drive of the computer. Local profile is a profile that stays specific to a computer.
- **Roaming user profile**: This is created by IT administrator and all the profiles for the user is saved on the central network storage. Each time a user logs in to any computer, this profile gets loaded from the network share and when user logs off from the computer, all the changes in the profile made by user get written back to the network share. This profile provide the consistent user experience in terms of preferences and setting on every computer.
- **Mandatory user profile**: This is also created by the IT administrator and stored on the shared network location, but in case of this profile, user changes cannot be updated to the central network share at the time of log off. This means when a user will log in, he will receive the same setting created by the administrator for the user. In case mandatory profile fails to load, the user will not be able to log on to the computer.

We also have other options for profile solution when we are planning to deploy it for the Citrix XenApp:

- **Multiple profiles**: It is the combination of two or more profiles, for example, local and mandatory, local and roaming, or other possible combinations. This is useful in the cases where applications are hosted on small set of servers and users are using multiple app hosted on them. In those cases, mandatory profiles can be used where users are logging on to their local computer and when they are logging on to other computer, it will be a roaming profile.
- **Citrix user profile management**: This is almost similar to roaming profile, but at the same time, it eliminates the drawback of the last write. The reason behind it is this profile management have the feature of active write back, whereas roaming profile changes get updated when the user logs off.

So, before selecting the profile solution, you have to work with the users and understand their needs and then select the profile based on these things.

In most of the use cases for Citrix XenApp, Citrix user profile management is more suitable as users are accessing multiple application hosted on the different servers. It also gives them a consistent experience, making sure that their setting are getting saved in the central repository.

Citrix user profile management get installed on the servers silently when you install virtual delivery agent, and it is recommend to do the profile management settings via group policy.

If you have checked the Citrix Policies node, it contains a number of settings for the profile management. Let's have a look at them in detail:

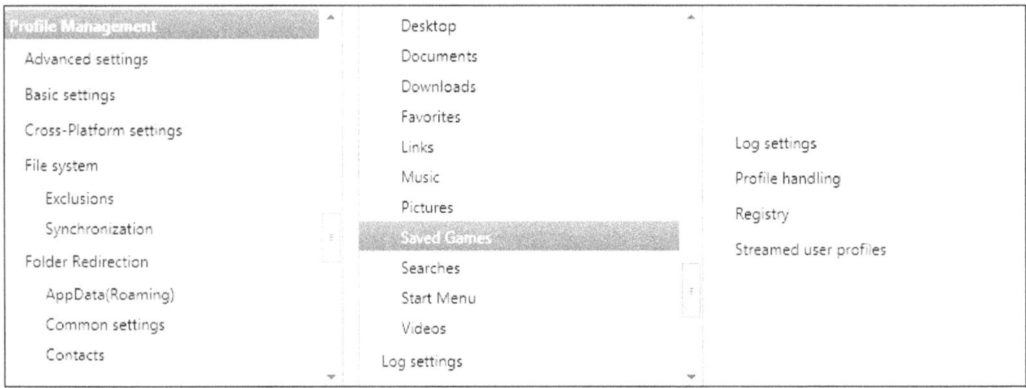


**Advanced settings** lets you define the following settings related to the automatic configuration based on the environment in use, log off in case of issues with profile, number to retires for the locked file, and how to deal with Internet cookies at the time of log off:

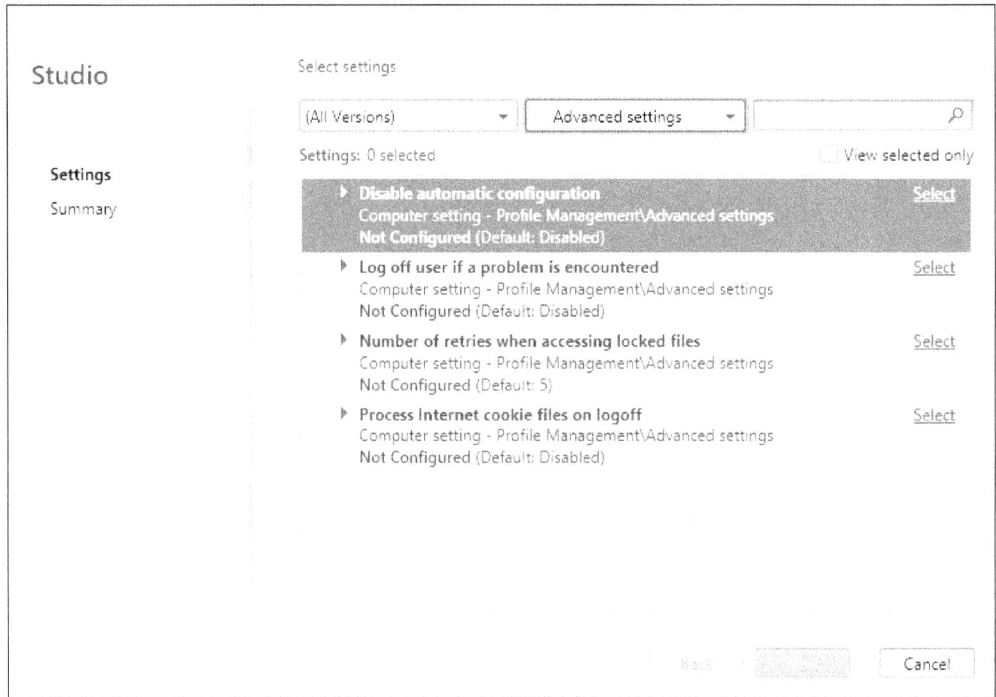

**Basic settings** lets you define settings such as when you want to enable the active write back, specify the profile store, and mention the active directory or local groups for which you want to manage the profiles:

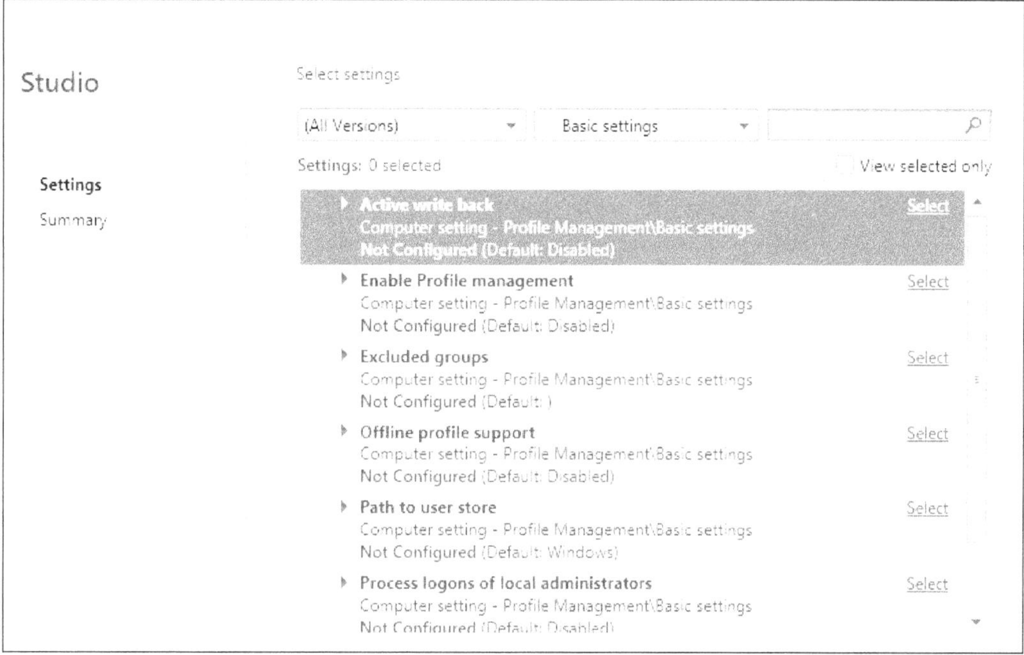

**File System** lets you include the folders that you want to synchronize; you can exclude the folders to be ignored during the sync, choose any specific file that you don't want to be synchronized, and so on:

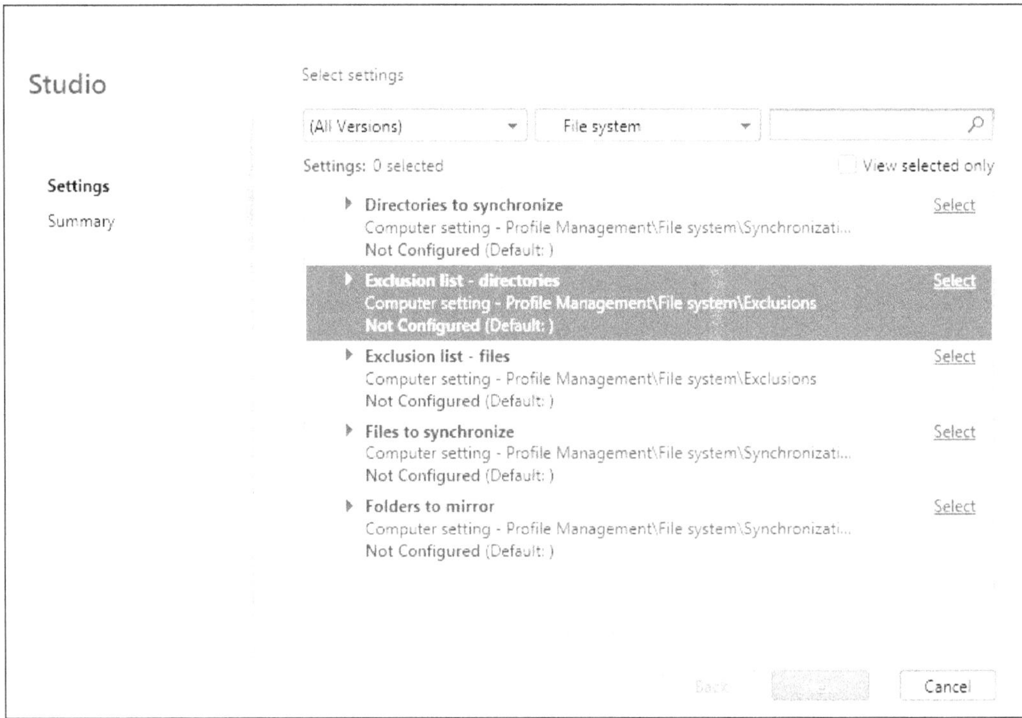

**Log settings** lets you enable the detailed logging, which comes handy at the time of profile issues. You can enable the loggings based on information, warning, notification, when to log the information, and what should be the file size of log file:

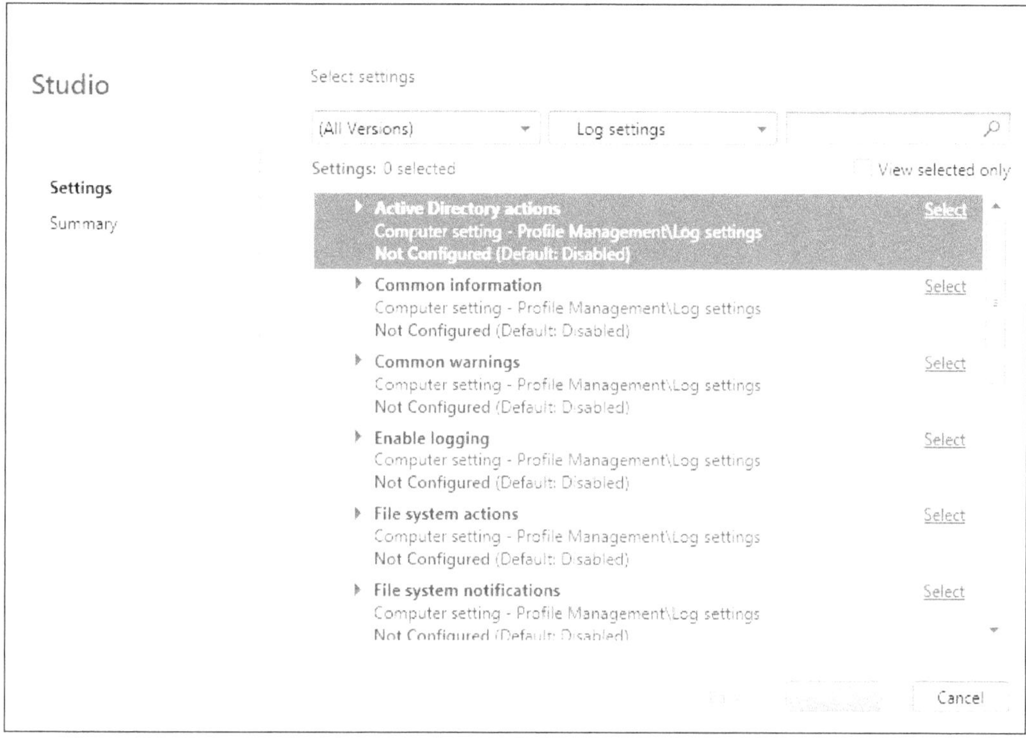

**Profile handling** are a set of settings that defines how the profile is going to load, for example, here you can configure if you want to keep the cache profile, what to do in the situation of local and user profile conflict, and specify the template from which the profiles will be created for new users:

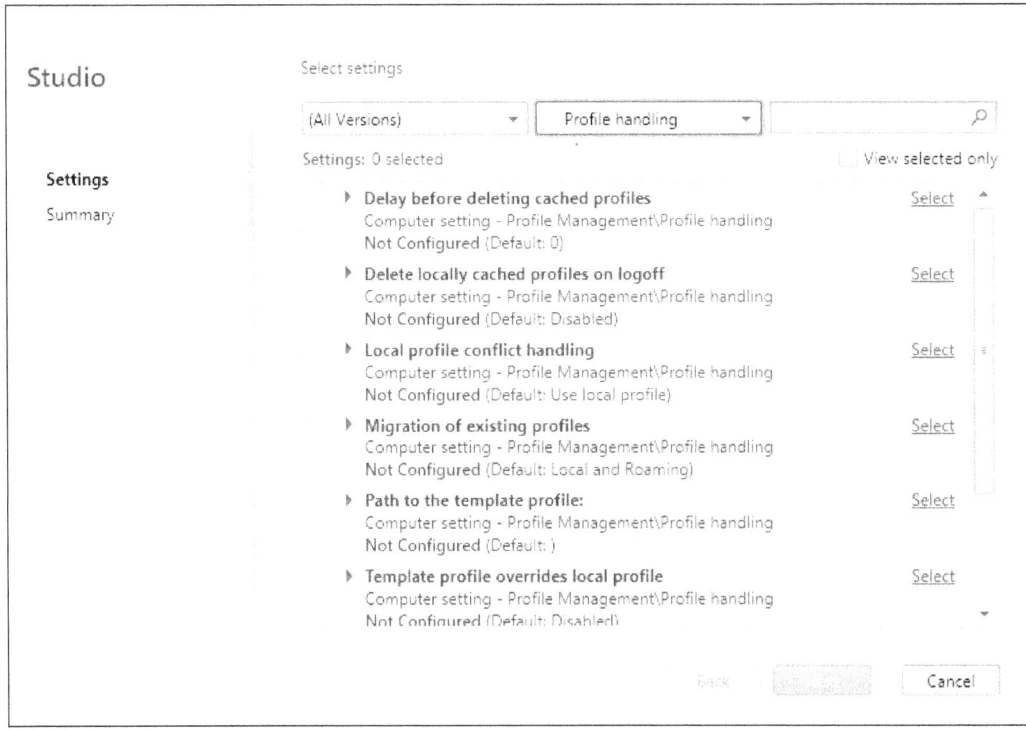

**Registry** is where you can specify which registry to be ignored at the time of log off. You can also specify the specific registry hives that need to be processed at the time of log off. If the inclusion is disabled, by default, all the HKCU hive will be processed at the time of log off:

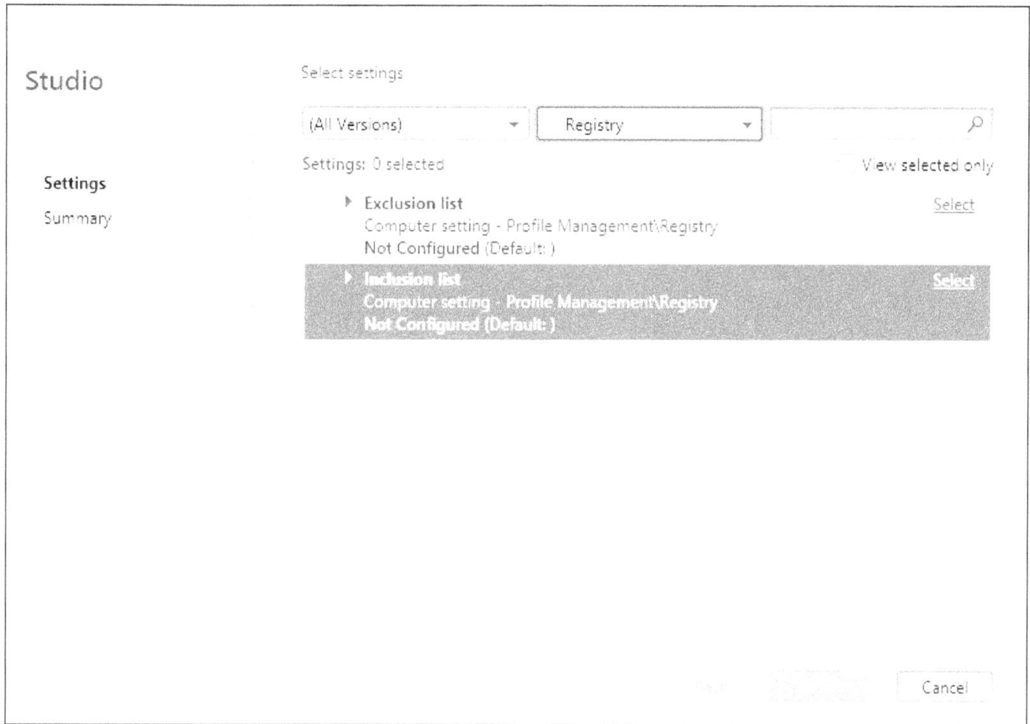


# Summary

In this chapter, you learned about the policies that can be applied to servers and users to make the user experience better, keeping the enterprise security in mind. You learned how to create the policy and policy template, install the group policy management console for the Citrix policy management, and set up remote assistance. You also learned about the printing policy setting that are available and can be configured for XenApp 7.6 and the Citrix user profile management policy setting that is available and can be configured for XenApp 7.6.

In the next chapter, we will be working with Citrix Provisioning Services to set them up for the provisioning of vDisk and to have disk-less environment for Citrix XenApp 7.6.

# 7
# Setting Up Citrix Provisioning Services™

In this chapter, we are going to set up the infrastructure of the Citrix Provisioning Services to create the disk-less infrastructure for the Citrix XenApp 7.6 solution. This will help in the management of a high number of virtual machines via a few virtual disk images. It also has other key benefits, which will be discussed during the chapter.

The things we will be covering in this chapter are as follows:

- The Citrix Provisioning Services architecture
- Setting up the Citrix Provisioning Services server and configuring it
- Installing the Citrix Provisioning Services console
- Configuring the boot from network
- Configuring the Bootstrap for high availability
- Configuring the Master Target Device
- Creating a vDisk
- Assigning a vDisk to a target device

## Citrix Provisioning Services™

In this chapter, we will be working on the latest version of the Citrix Provisioning Services, which is 7.6, and before we get into the details, let's try to understand what Citrix Provisioning Services is.

Provisioning Service is one of the best solution in the market when it comes to vDisk streaming to virtual or physical machine. This solution was developed by a company called Ardence, which was later acquired by Citrix and now it is known as the Citrix Provisioning Services. With this technology, you can create virtual disks and then stream those to virtual or physical machines via a network.

It eliminates the need for single virtual or physical machine management and all the management tasks, such as patching and updating the installed software, can be done on the single vDisk and then it can be streamed back to virtual or physical machine.

It also helps IT organizations to save the cost related to the procurement and management of storage and server devices, and if we talk about the storage cost, it has been found that it reduces the storage cost by 90 percent.

Now the Citrix Provisioning Services is not available as a separate version, so in order to use the Citrix Provisioning Services, you need to have a valid XenApp or XenDesktop license.

What's new in Citrix Provisioning Services 7.6:

- Citrix has added the support for the HP moonshot system
- In this version, Citrix added the test mode for personal vDisk, and we can use this mode to test the new updates and to make sure that there is no issue caused due to the updates applied on the vDisk
- This version of the Citrix Provisioning Services supports the SQL server 2014 and SQL AlwaysOn for SQL server 2012 and 2014
- Citrix added the support for Hypervisor XenServer 6.2

# The Citrix Provisioning Services™ architecture

In order to implement the Citrix Provisioning Services solution, you need multiple infrastructure components to work together to deliver the vDisk to the machine, either it is physical or virtual.

I have created a simple diagram that shows the provisioning architecture:

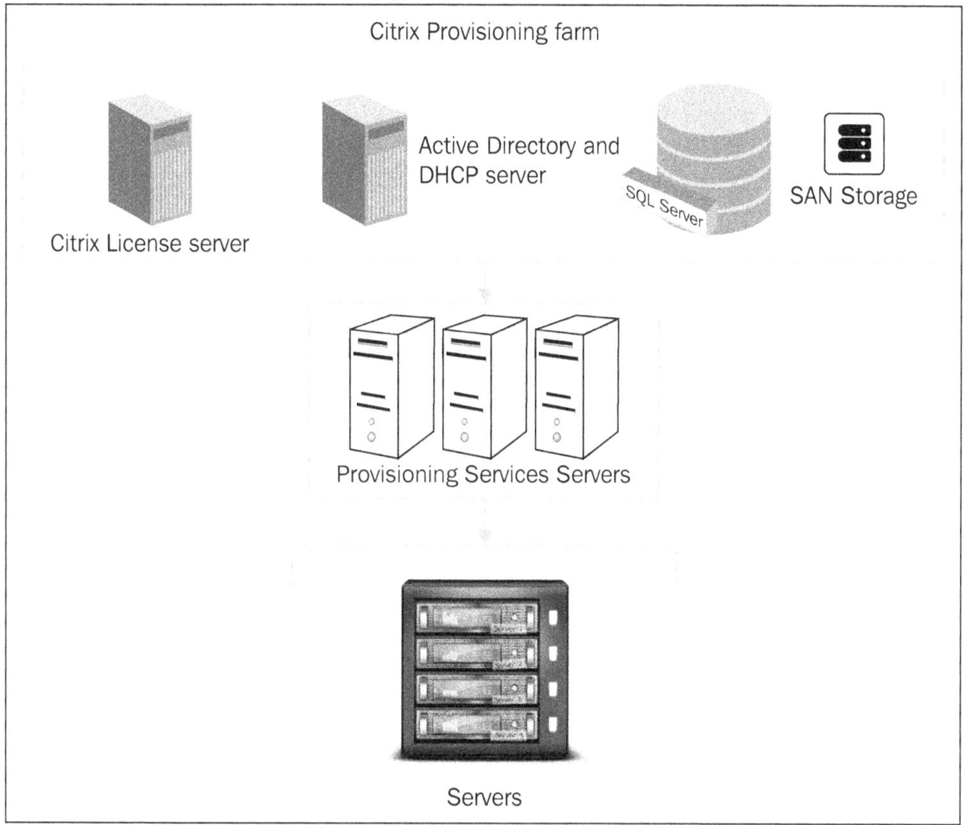


This architecture include the following components:

- **Citrix License server**: This will be holding and delivering the product license requirement to the provisioning server.
- **Provisioning Services Database server**: This server will be holding all the system and configuration-related information for the Citrix provisioning server farm. In a single Citrix provisioning server farm, we can only have one database and all the provisioning should be able to communicate to the farm.
- **DHCP Server**: This server will help in the network boot of the virtual and physical machine as it will hold the PXE service, which will help providing the IP information and downloading the boot program information from the Citrix provisioning server to the target virtual or physical machine.

- **SAN Storage**: SAN storage will hold the stores, which will contain the virtual or physical vDisk. We can create the store on the local provisioning server or on the shared network storage.
- **Provisioning Services Servers**: These are the servers on which you will install the Citrix Provisioning Services and from here, vDisk will be streamed to the virtual or physical machine, also known as a target device. This server will also have the management console to manage the Citrix provisioning farm.
- **Servers**: These are the servers that will not have any physical or network disk allocated to them. When these servers will be powered on, they will boot from the network and the assigned vDisk will be streamed to the servers, based on the configuration and provisioned vDisk.

Let's try to understand how the boot process works with the Citrix Provisioning Services:

1. When the target device will be powered on, it will look for the DHCP.
2. Once the DHCP server will be discovered, it will allocate the IP configuration and send the boot server hostname and boot file name, which will be configured as a PXE service on the DHCP server.
3. The IP, boot server hostname, and boot file name will be loaded to the target server. After that, the target server will contact the provisioning server, which will be written in the boot server hostname.
4. The provisioning server will then match the MAC address of the device from the provisioning database, and based on the match, the configured vDisk will be streamed to the target device. The resulting vDisk will boot and Windows will start, and it will be available for use by the users or the server administrators.

# Setting up a Citrix Provisioning Services™ server and configuring it

In this section, we will be installing the provisioning server along with the provisioning server console. Follow these steps:

1. I am going to install the provisioning server on a Microsoft Windows 2012 R2 server. You need to download Citrix Provisioning Services 7.6 from `http://www.mycitrix.com`, and once downloaded, you can mount the ISO to the server. Once mounted, it will bring up the autorun wizard:

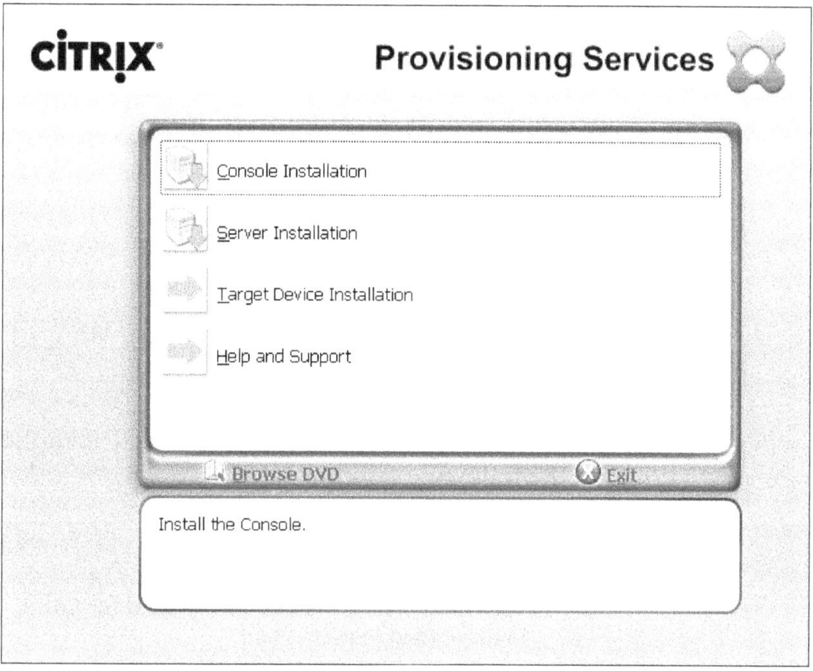


2. From the available options, we will select **Server Installation**. This will bring up the following screen:

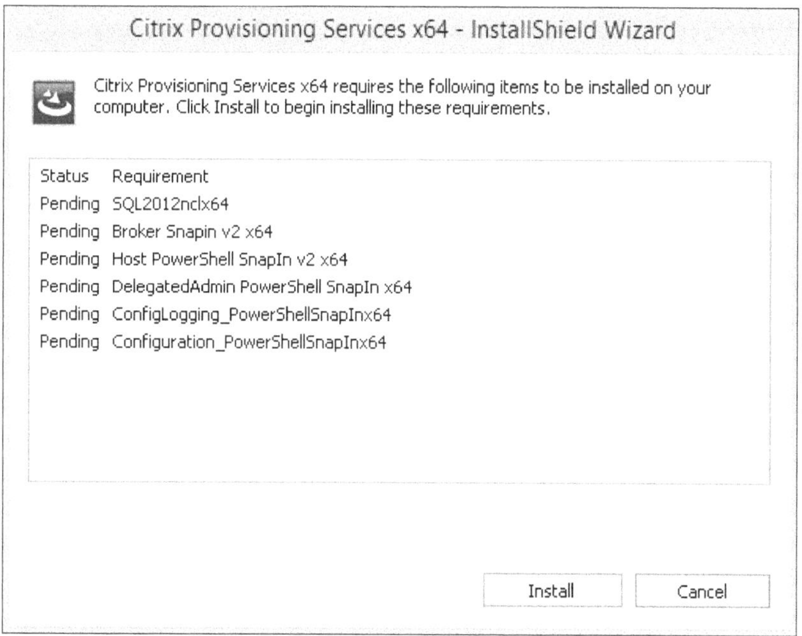

3. It will ask you to install the SQL 2012 client. In my case, I will choose **No** as I already have the client installed on the different server:

4. It will go through the installation, which will take a while to complete. Once done, it will bring up the following window:

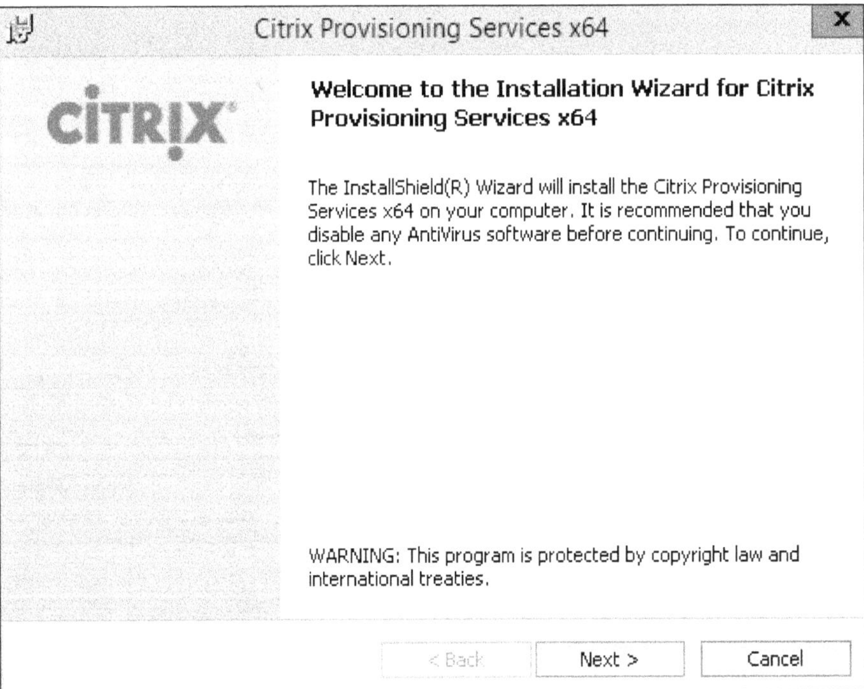

5. Click on **Next** to continue and accept the license agreement. Again click on **Next**. It will bring up a window where you have to enter **User Name** and **Organization**:

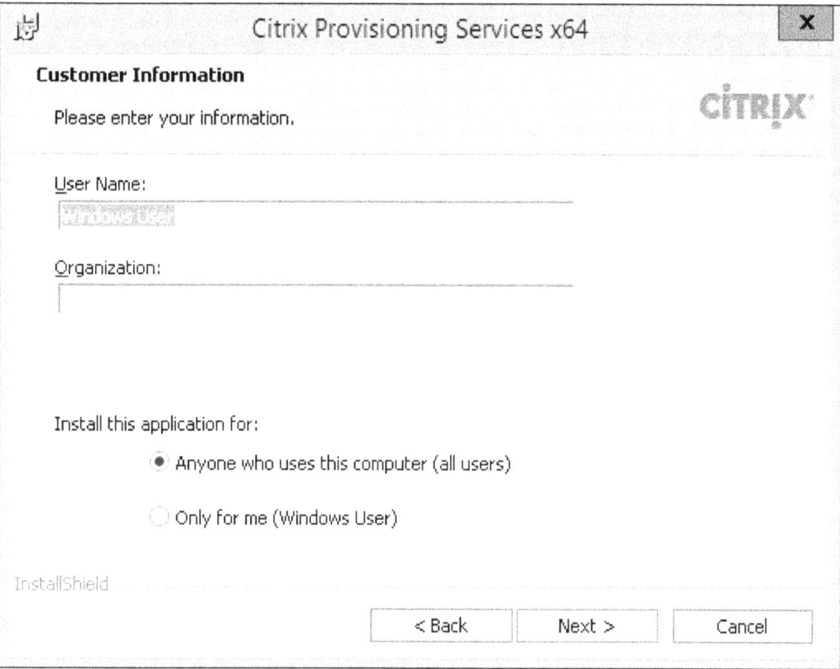

6. Enter the details and click on **Next**. Select the install path; in our case, I will keep it as default and click on **Next**:

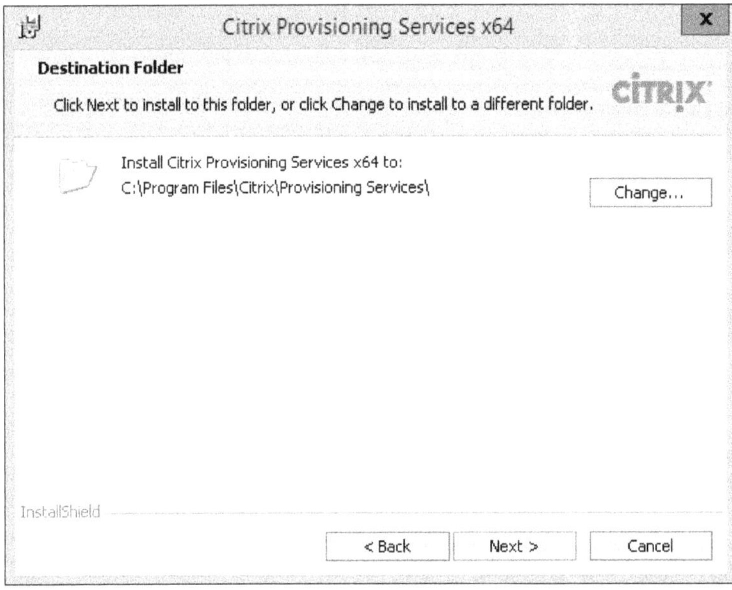


7. It will bring up the ready installation wizard. Click on **Install** to begin the installation of the provisioning server to the MS Windows 2012 R2 server:

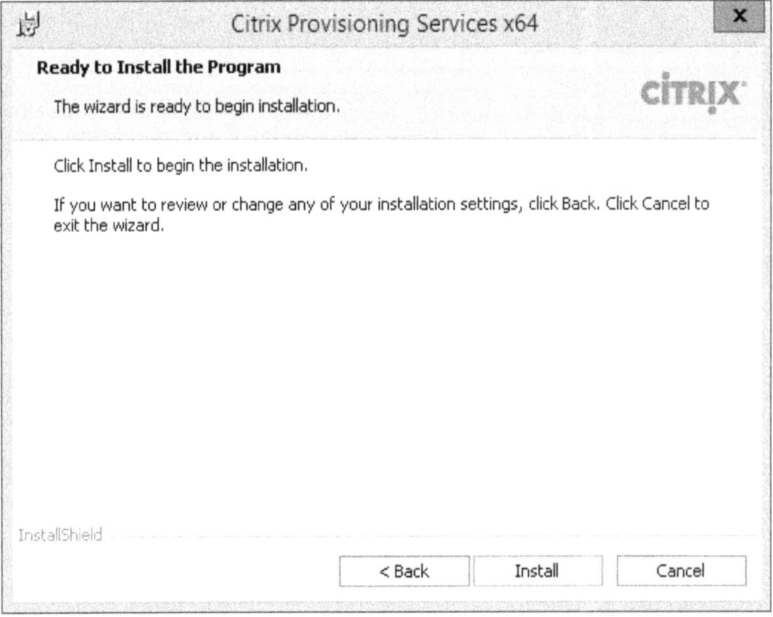

8. It is again going to take a while to complete the installation. Once installed, click on **Finish**. After that, you will get the prompt that **The PVS Console is not detected**, and it will also ask you to install the same by clicking on **OK**:

9. It will bring up the PVS configuration wizard. Click on **Next**, and it will ask you for the DHCP services and give you the options, as shown in the following screenshot:

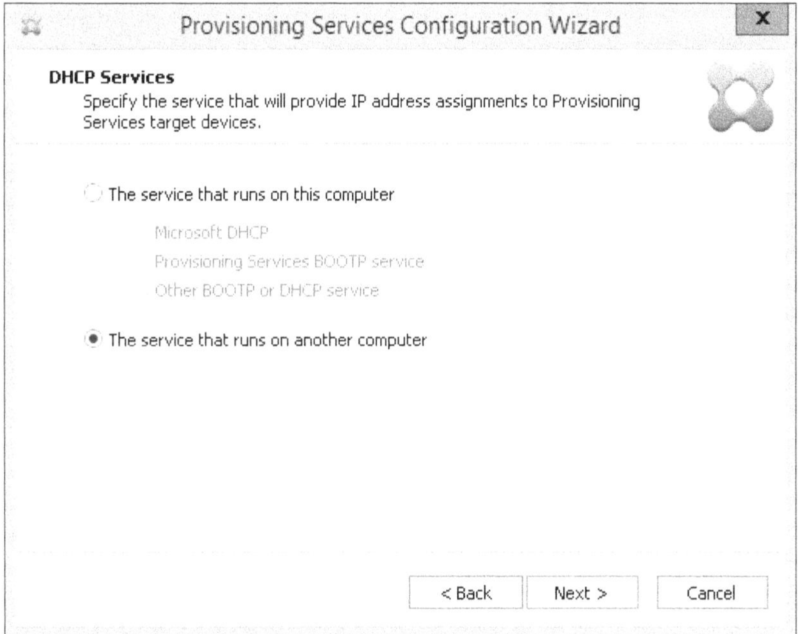

10. In our case, I already have the server which has the role of DHCP on it, so I have selected **The service that runs on another computer** Click on **Next** to continue. On the next screen, it will ask about the PXE services. Even in this case, I will choose **The service that runs on another computer** and click on **Next**:

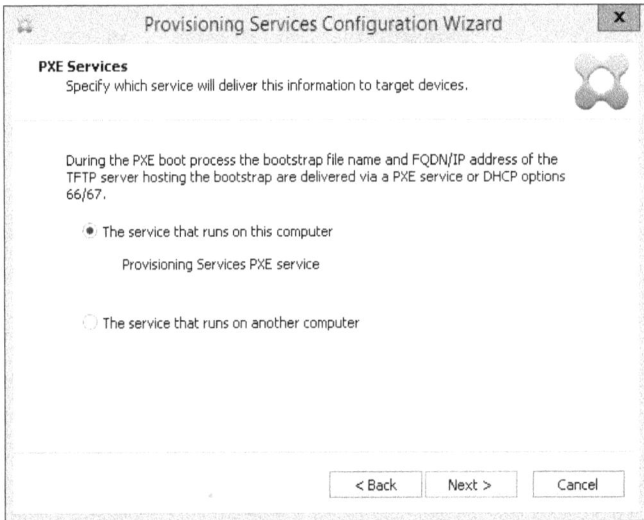


11. The next screen will ask whether you want to create a farm or join the server to any existing farm. As this is a fresh installation, select **Create farm** and then click on **Next**:

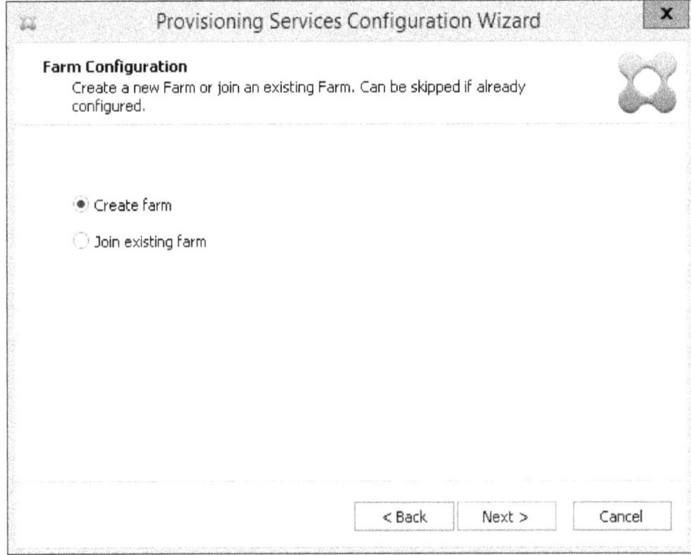

12. The next screen will ask you for the database server information. Enter the required information and click on **Next**:

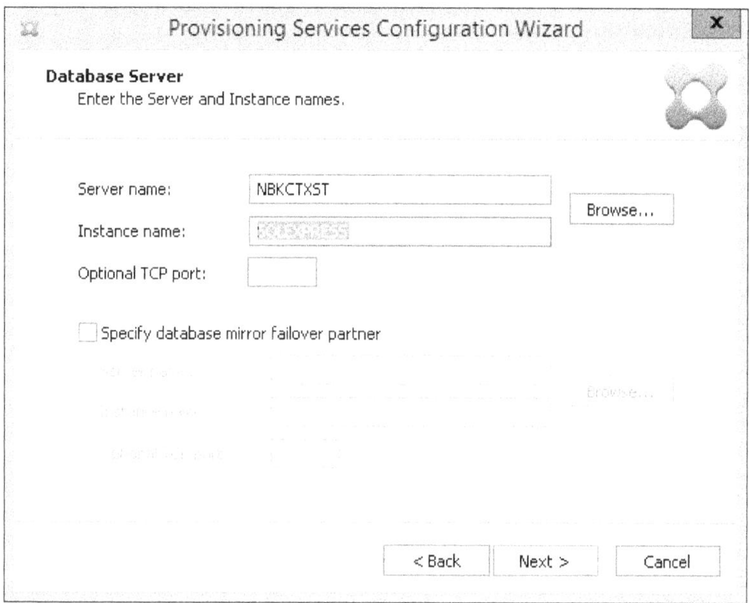


13. On the next screen, it will ask you for **Database name**, **Farm name**, **Site name**, **Collection name**, and **Farm Administrator group** for security. Enter the information and click on **Next**:

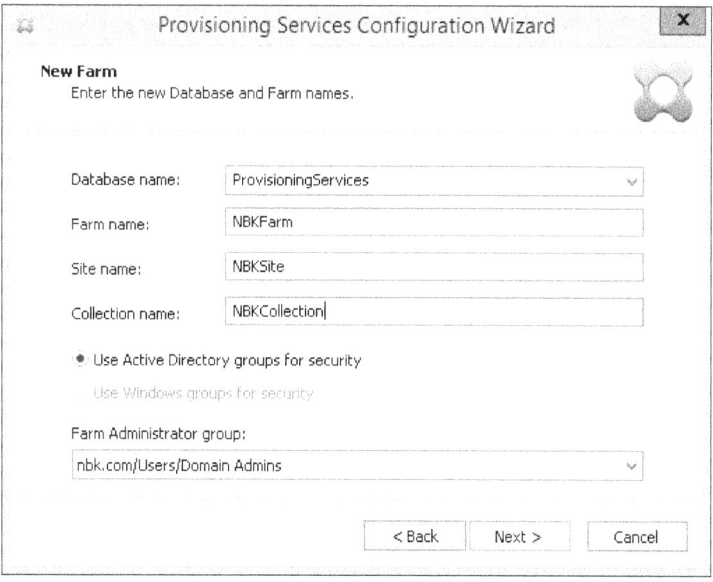

14. On the next screen, it will ask you for the store information where it will store the vDisk of the PVS farm, which can be allocated to the physical or virtual machine. As this is a test environment, I will use the local hard disk for the store, but it is recommended to have the shared network location for the store to keep your vDisk:

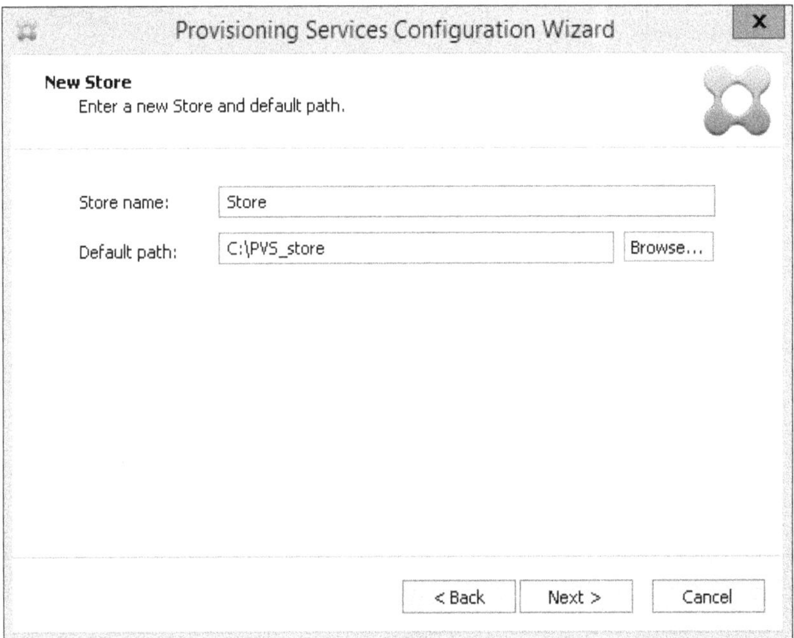

15. On the next screen, you have to enter **License server name** and **License server port**, and you can also validate the version to meet the requirement of PVS configuration. Once done, click on **Next**:

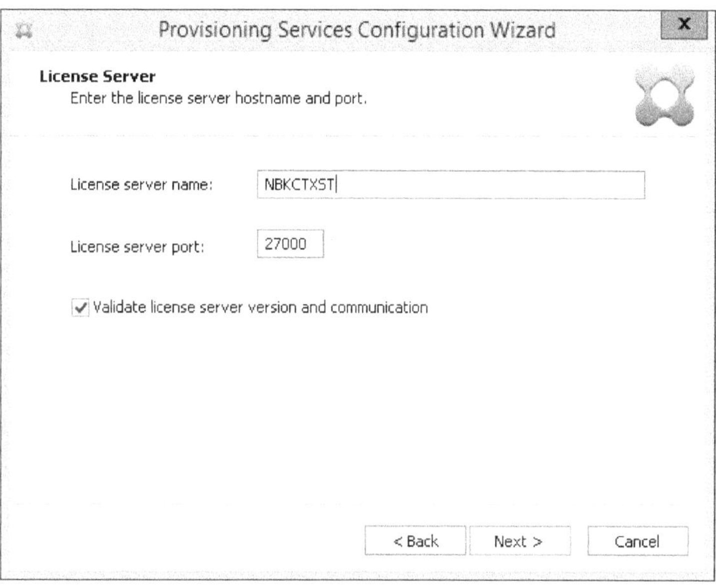


16. On the next screen, you will be asked about the user account, which will be used to run the most critical services of PVS known as stream and soap services. Enter the service account details and click on **Next**:

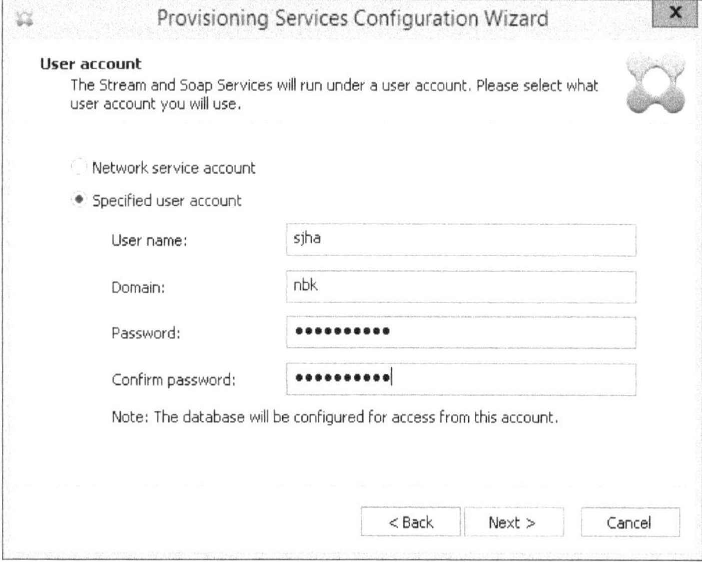

17. The next screen will ask you for the active directory computer account password updates. You can automate the password update using the wizard and also set the number of days between the password update. This is based on the environment requirement; I will leave the defaults and click on **Next**:

18. On the next screen, you will be asked for **Streaming network cards** and **Management network card** and port information for **First communications port** and **Console port**. Leave the defaults and click on **Next**:

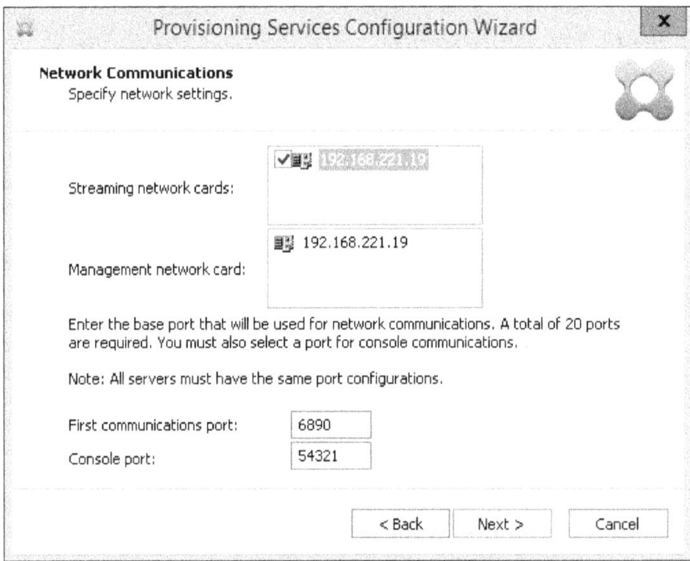

As we are doing this in the POC environment, that's the reason we are seeing the similar NIC, but in production, you should have different NIC.

19. On the next screen, you will be asked for **TFTP Option and Bootstrap Location**. Select **Use the Provisioning Services TFTP service** and click on **Next**:

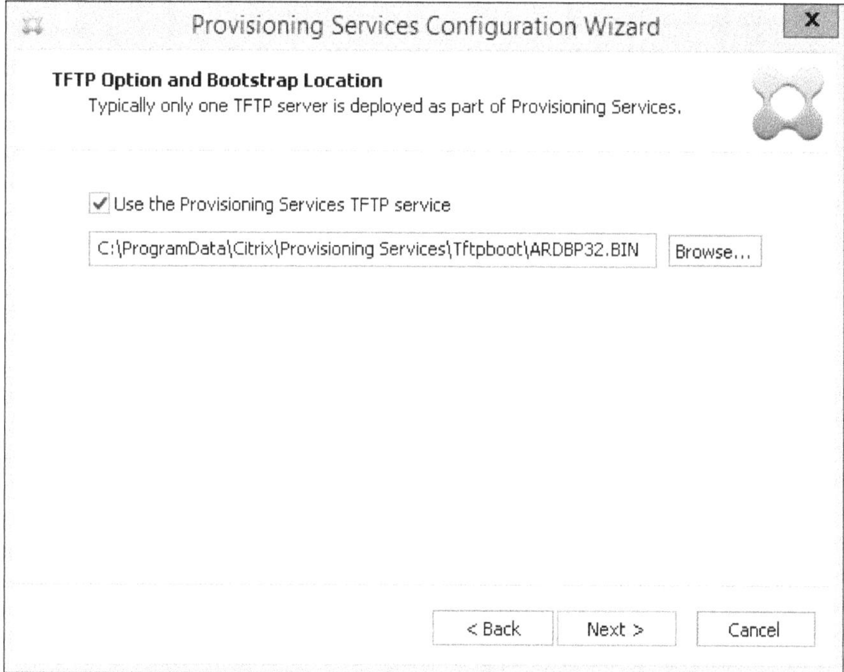

20. On the next screen, you will be asked for the **Stream Servers Boot List**. Enter the details and click on **Next**:

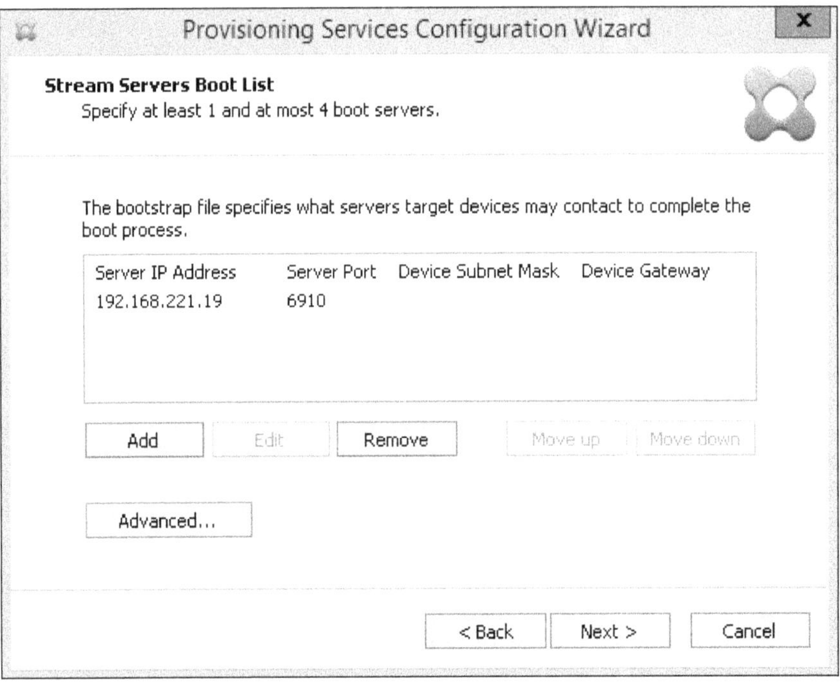


21. On the last window, it will show you the summary of the configuration information you have selected and entered in the wizard. You can review the information, and click on **Finish** to complete the installation and configuration of the PVS farm.

22. Once completed, it will show you the following window:

# Installing the Citrix Provisioning Services™ console

We will be using the Citrix Provisioning Services console to manage the PVS farm, and this console can be installed on the client computer or any other server as well. The only thing which is needed is that the PVS console should be able to communicate to the PVS server on port `54321`. The following are the steps:

1. I will be installing the PVS console on the PVS server itself, which already has the PVS ISO mounted, and I will click on the `autorun.exe` to get the installation option as shown here. I will choose **Console Installation**:

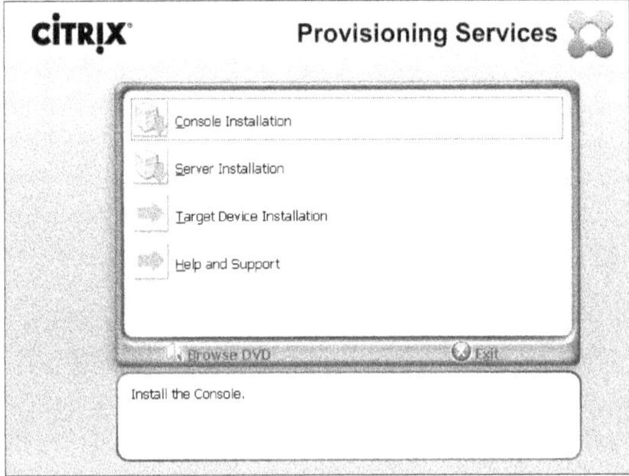


2. Post clicking on **Console Installation**, it will go through the prerequisite check and installation and will bring up the following window:

3. Click on **Next** to continue the installation of the PVS console and accept the agreement. You will be asked for **User Name** and **Organization**:

4. Select the install directory and click on **Next**. Then, select the **Complete** installation. Please note that you can do the selective installation by clicking on **Custom**.

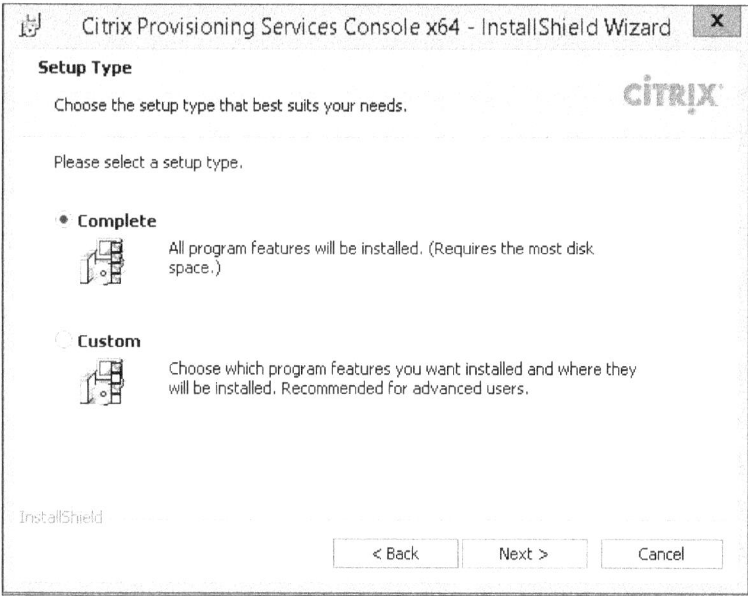

5. After that, click on **Install** to begin the installation of the PVS console, and it will take a few moments to complete:

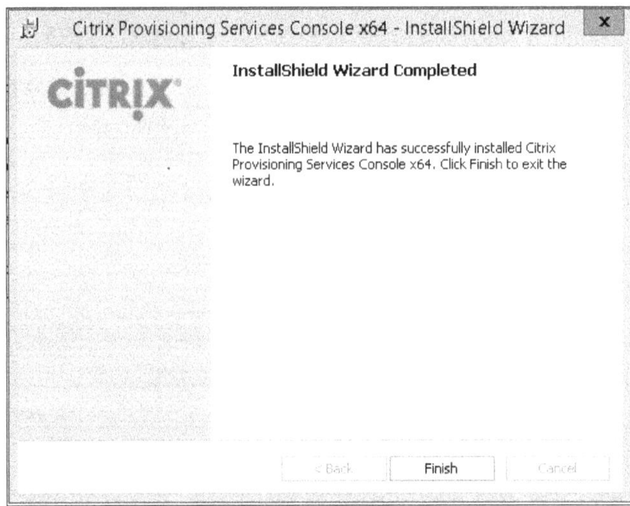


# Connecting the Citrix Provisioning Services™ console to the farm

Post installation, when you will launch the PVS console, it will show you the following window. You need to connect your PVS to the farm by using the connect to farm wizard:

1. Launch the console by going to **Start** | **All programs** | **Provisioning Service Console**, and it will launch the PVS console:

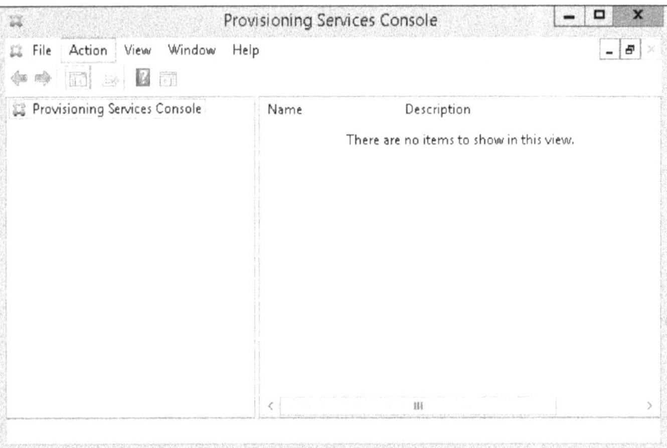

2. Once you have the console launched, right-click on **Provisioning Services Console** from the left-hand side pane and click on **Connect to Farm...**:

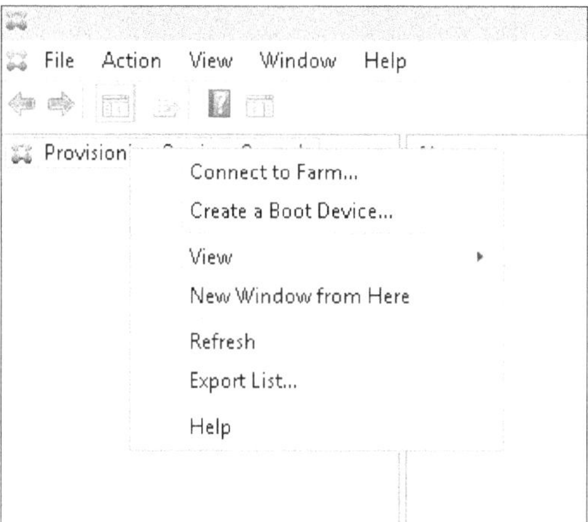


3. It will bring up the **Connect to Farm** wizard, where you have to mention farm **Name** and **Port** to connect. Also, you can specify different credentials or use your local Windows login and enable the option of **Auto-login on application start or reconnect** so that you don't have to do this again and again:

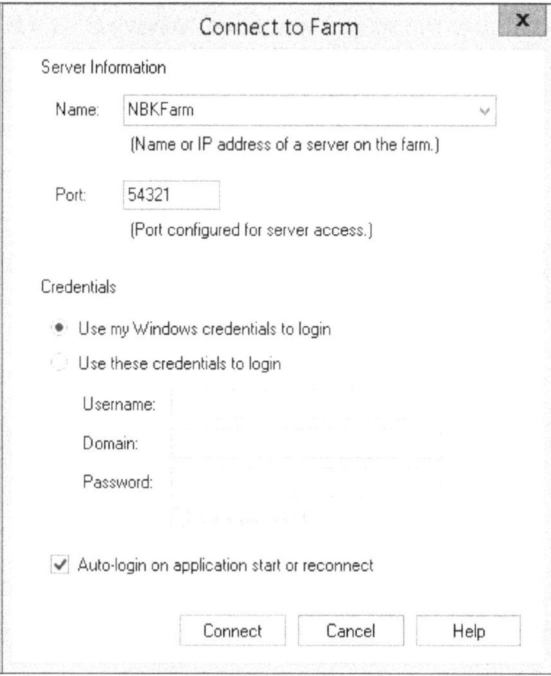

4. Post making the connection to the PVS farm, you will be able to see your farm's first look:

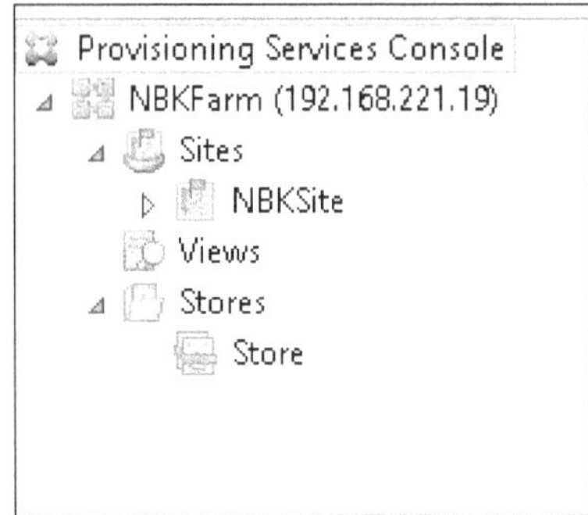


# Configuring the boot from network

In this section, we will configure our environment network configuration to support the boot from network. We will add scope to the DHCP scope option. In order to do that, we have to configure the scope of 66 and 67 in our DHCP scope, which will help the incoming client/server to boot from the network.

Let's configure the DHCP 66, 67 scope by following these steps:

1. In order to configure the scope, you need to have the DHCP server. If you can recall, in the previous section, we mentioned that our DHCP server is on another server, so log in to your DHCP server and the DHCP management console. Choose the scope that you will be using for the servers, which will be booting over the network with PVS vHD:

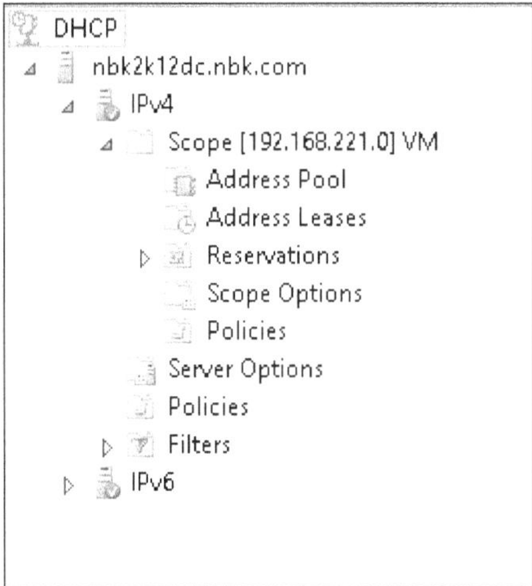

2. From the left-hand side pane, choose the **Scope** option and right-click on configure options, which will bring up the window with the list of all the DHCP scope options. You have to scroll down and configure scope options **066** and **067**, which will be **Boot Server Host Name** and **Bootfile Name**, respectively:

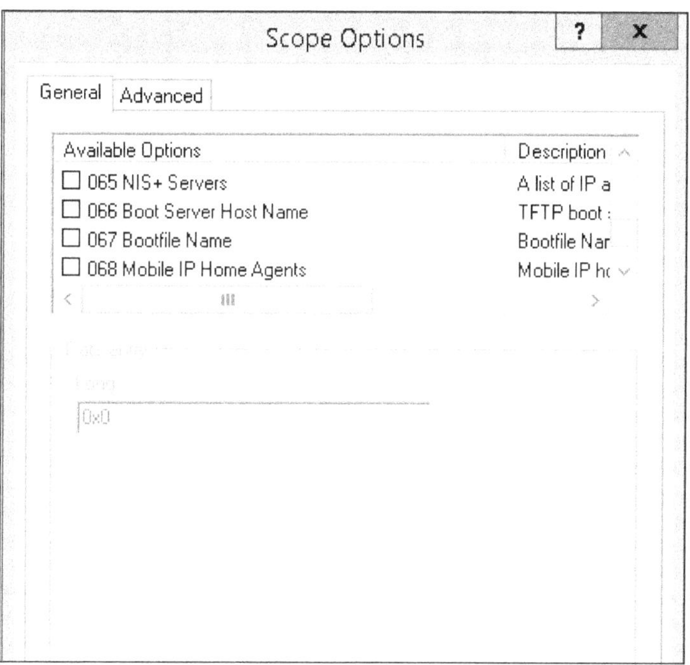


3. In **Boot Server Host Name**, you have to mention the host name of the provisioning server and in **Bootfile Name**, you have to enter the name of the Bootstrap, which contains the necessary information to boot the server. Post configuring the scope, you will be able to see them in **Scope Options**:

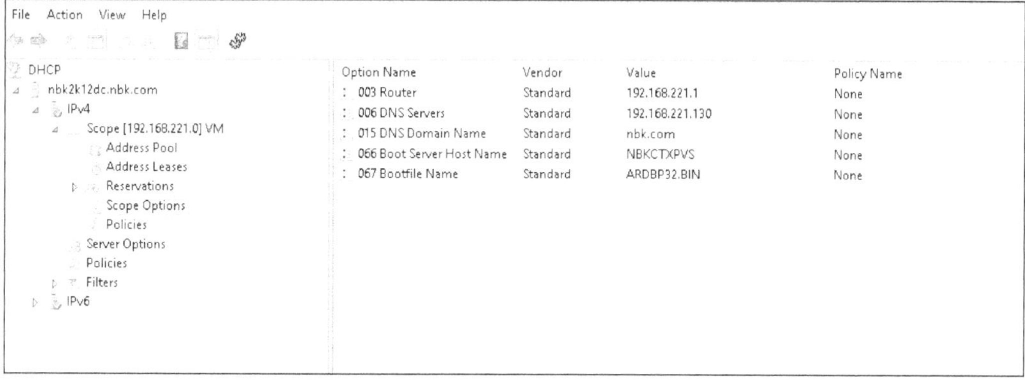

This DHCP scope is specific to the PXE service to boot the clients from network.

## Configuring the Bootstrap for high availability

In this section, I will walk you through how to configure your Bootstrap for high availability. We generally do this in the scenario where we have multiple PVS server.

The best way to load balance and to have the high availability is to configure the Bootstrap and add the other PVS server IP details in the following window by clicking on **Add...**:

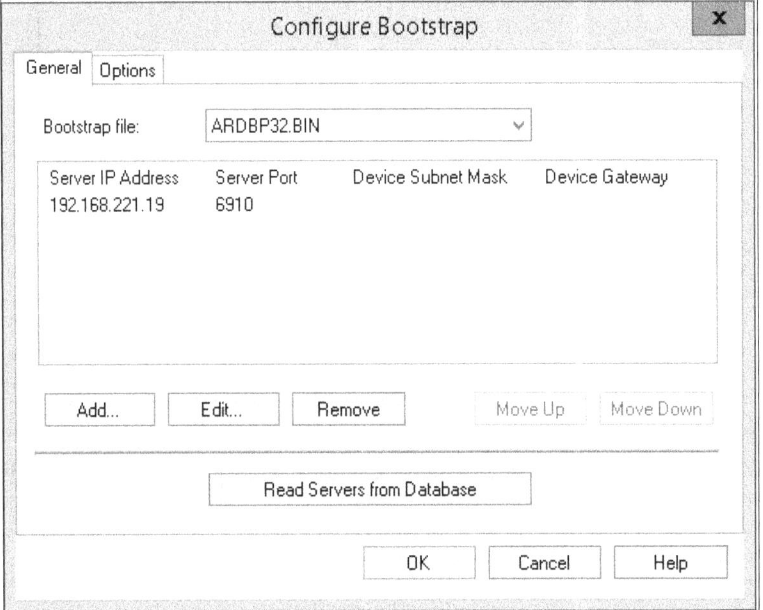


Also, you can load balance the TFTP Bootstrap with the help of NetScaler, and there is a Citrix article that explains how to configure the TFTP load balance for the Bootstrap file step by step.

It is available at the Citrix blog post at `http://blogs.citrix.com/2014/04/01/a-solid-option-for-the-pvs-boot-method-tftp-load-balancing-using-netscaler-10-1/`.

# Configuring Master Target Device

In this section, we will be preparing our master server so that we can create the vDisk from it and later, vDisk can be streamed to the other clients.

In order to prepare the Master Target Device, we have to install the target device on the server/client. The following are the steps:

1. I am going to use the master server that we used for the MCS in the earlier part of this book. Connect your PVS ISO image to the master server, run the `autorun.exe`, and select **Target Device Installation**:

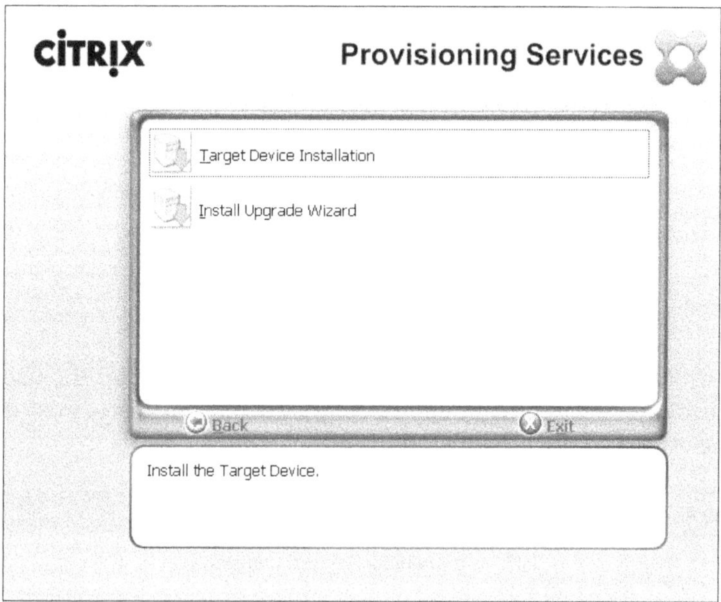

2. It will bring up the introductory window, explaining about the installation we will be doing:

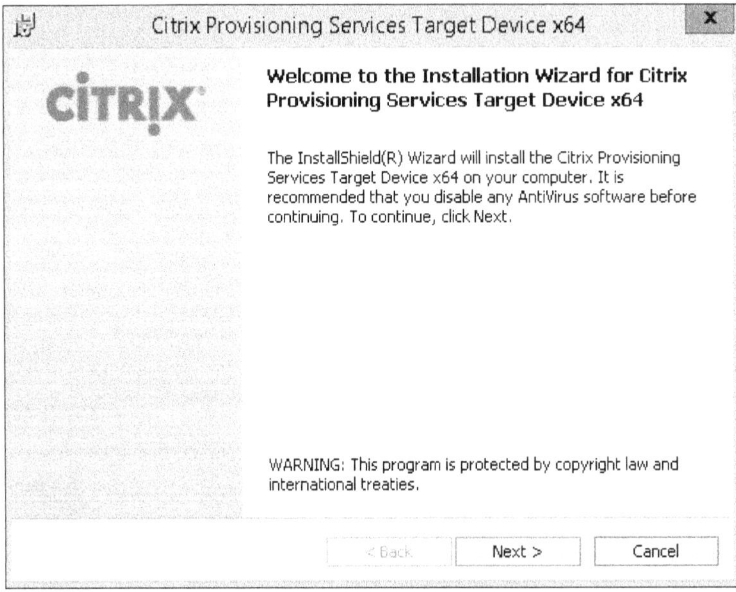


3. Click on **Next** to proceed and accept the agreement, enter the user name and organization details and finally select the install directory. Post this, you will get the option to start the installation:

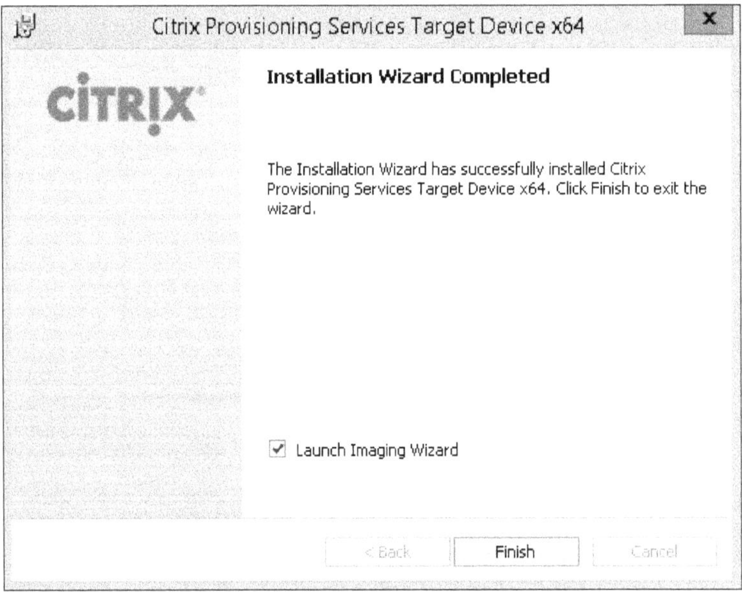

4. It will go through the installation, which will take some time to complete, and once completed, you will see the following screen:

Now your master server is ready for the vDisk creation. Just make sure you have already installed the Citrix virtual delivery agent so that machine booting from vDisk can later be added to the Machine Catalog. In this next section, we will be spending time creating the vDisk.

# Creating a vDisk

In this section, we will creating the master image from the Master Target Device on which we did the installation of the PVS target device. If you can recall, once the installation was completed, it gave us the option to launch the imaging wizard. Following are the steps:

1. When you click on **Finish**, you will get the following window:

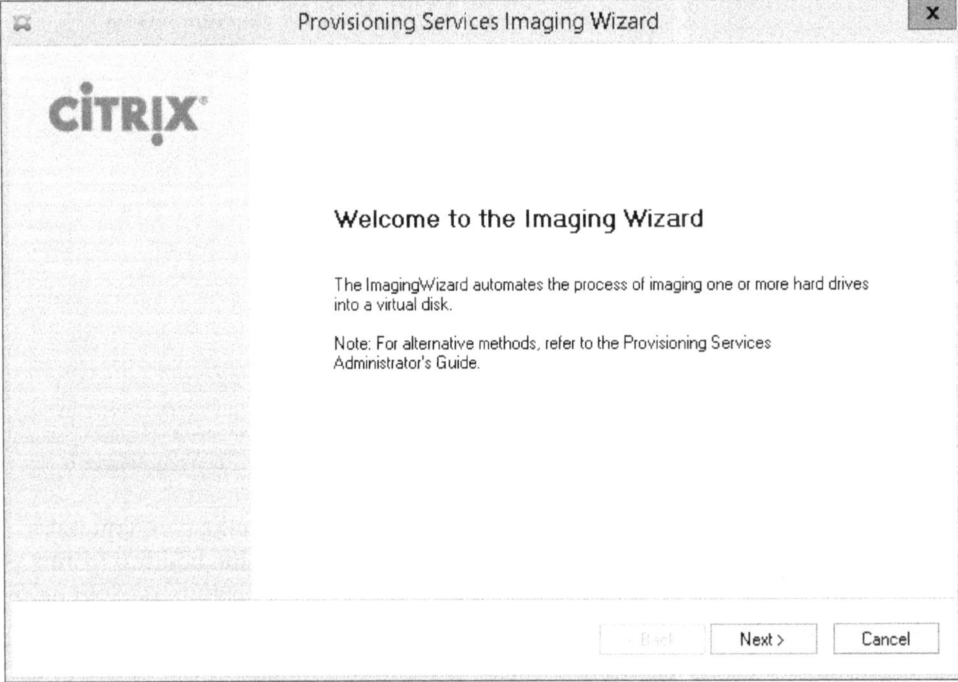

2. Click on **Next** and you will be asked for the information about your Citrix provisioning server. Enter the information and click on **Next**:

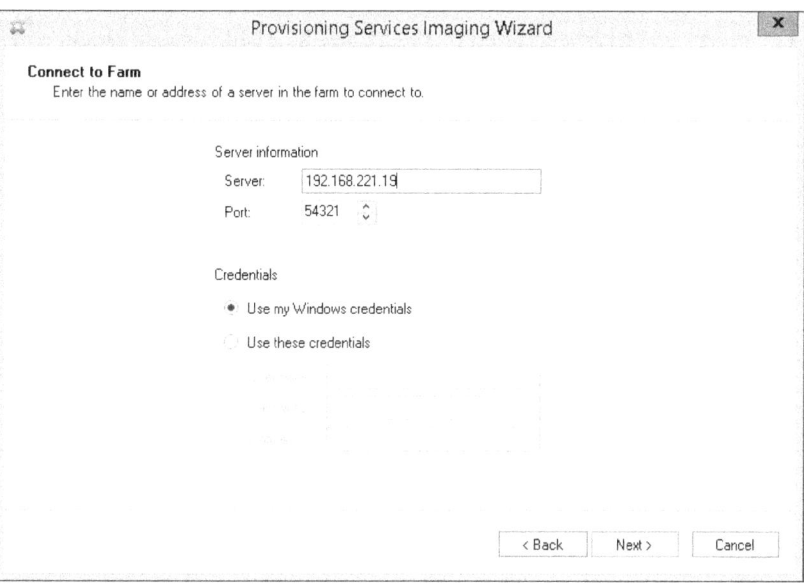


3. In the next window, you will be asked if you want to create a new vDisk or use the existing vDisk. As this is the first image of the PVS farm, I will choose the new vDisk and click on **Next**:

4. On the next screen, name your vDisk and choose the disk type, based on the disk you are using, and select the block size:

> We have selected the block size as 2 MB because block size basically defines the expansion of dynamic and differentiating disk.

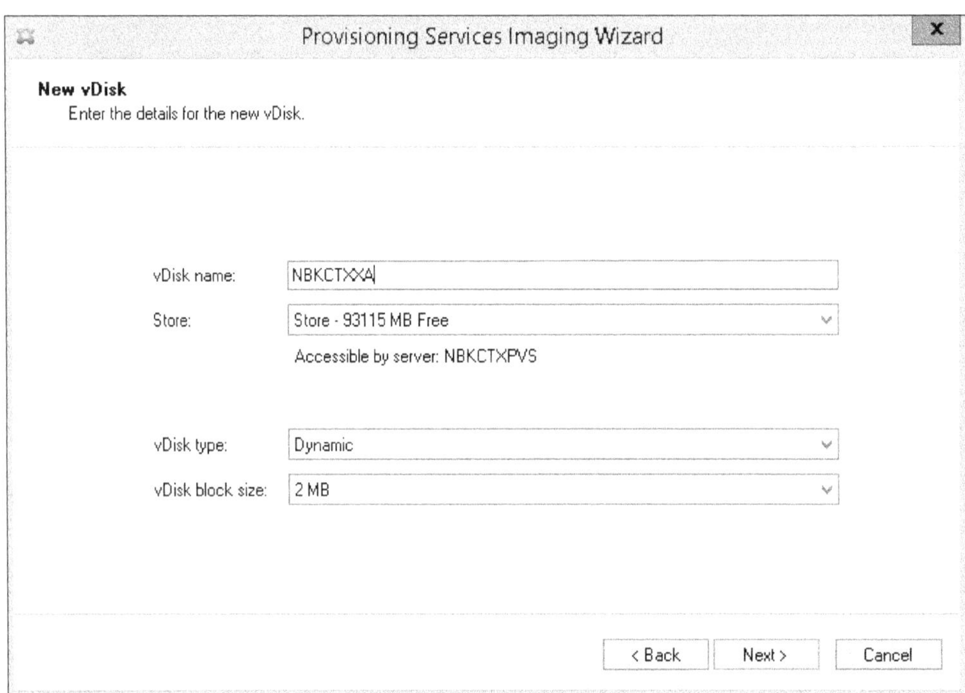

5. On the next screen, choose **Microsoft Volume Licensing** so that once the vDisk will be streamed to the client, it will get activated. In my case, I will use **Key Management Service (KMS)** to license and activate the vDisk:

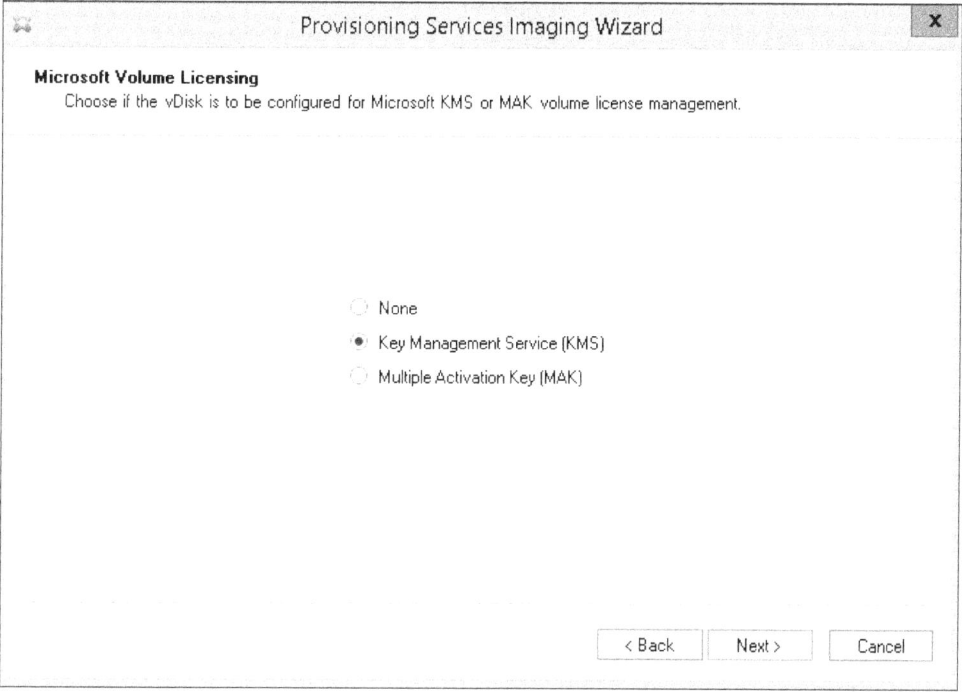

6. The next screen will let you configure your volumes. You can edit them if you want; I will leave the default and click on **Next**:

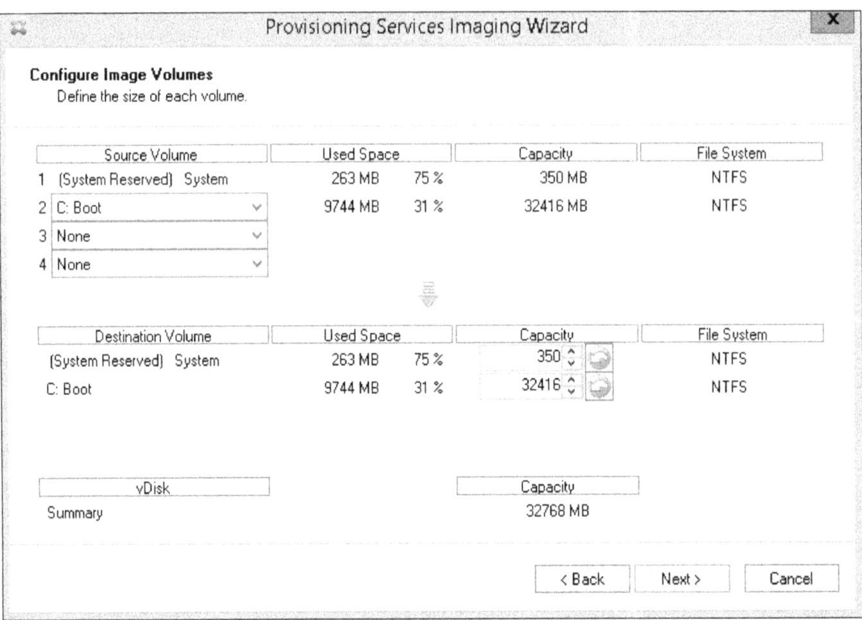


7. You can name the target device here. After that, click on **Next**:

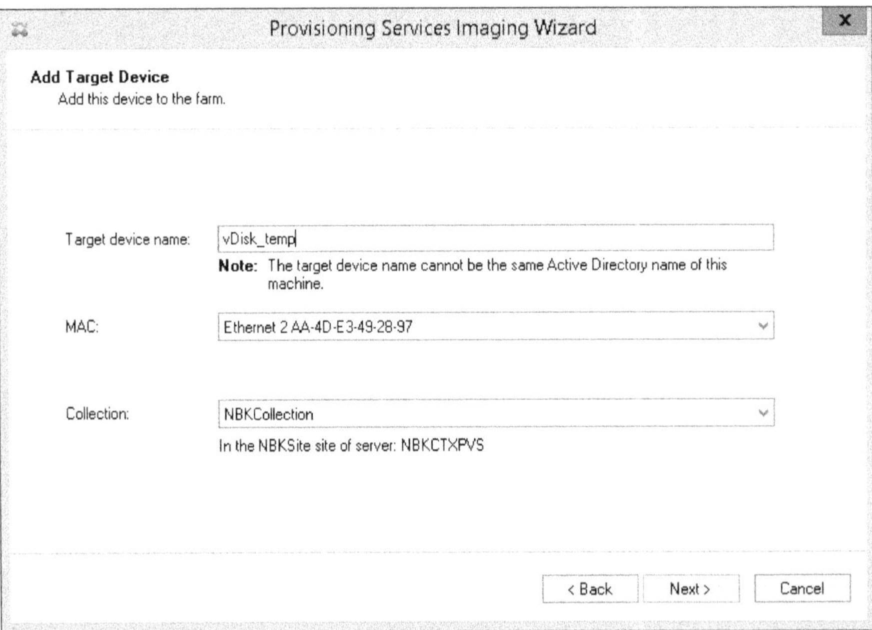

8. The next screen will let you review the configuration options that you have selected. Once you click on **Finish**, it will go through the series of process and some heavy copying of the data, which will create the vDisk on the store where you will store all your vDisk images:

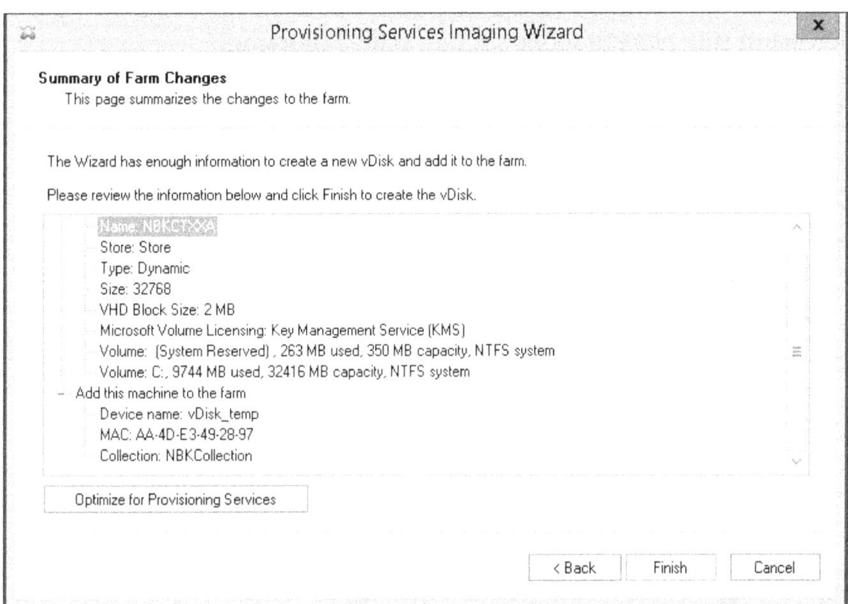

By default, the imaging wizard make changes to Windows settings to improve the performance of the vDisk and you can also change them if you want, based on your environment and organization requirement.

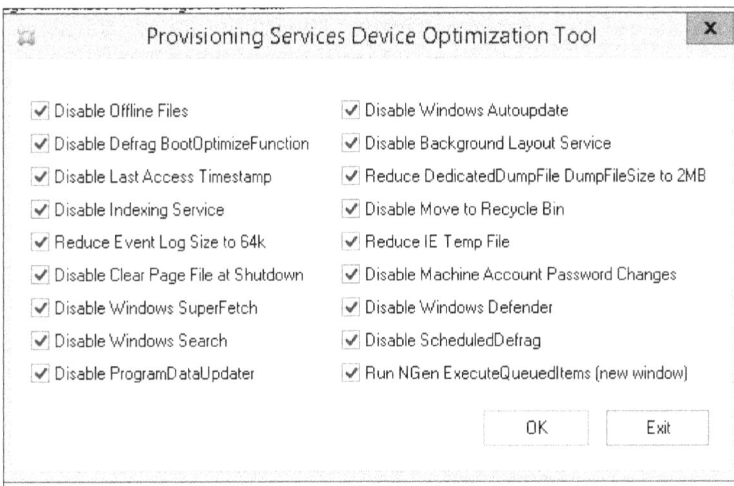

9. After clicking on **Finish** on your master device, before you reboot, make sure you have changed the boot option to network as the first priority. Once the master device is back up, it will boot into the OS and launch the XenConvert tool for the virtual to virtual, copying to create the vDisk.
10. Once done, you can check the vDisk in your PVS console. Inside **Store** in the left-hand side pane, it looks similar to the following:

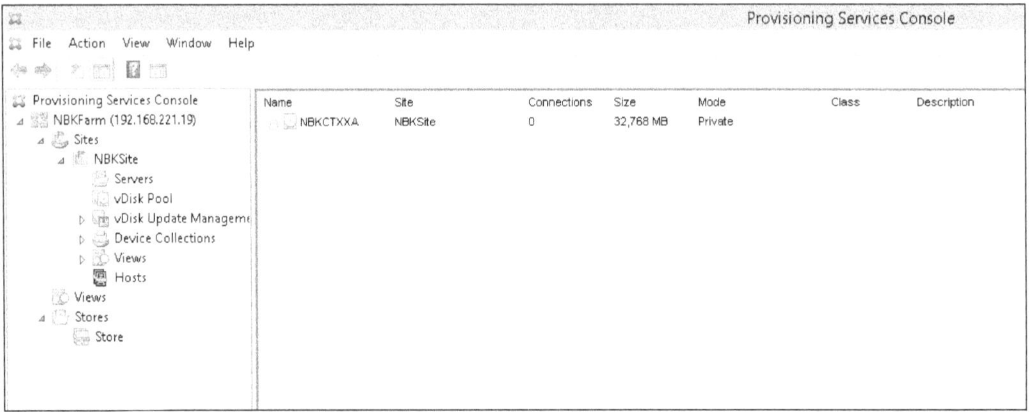


# Assigning a vDisk to a target device

In this section, we will be working on the steps to create the device and then assigning the vDisk to that so that when the device boots up, it gets the vDisk streamed from the Citrix provisioning service.

In order to create the device, we have to make sure that we have the virtual machine created in the hypervisor or the physical machine without hard disk and in the boot option, network should have the top priority. The following are the steps:

1. Once the prerequisites are done, go to the **Provisioning Services Console**, choose **NBKCollection** from **Device Collections**, right-click on it, and select **Create Device...**:

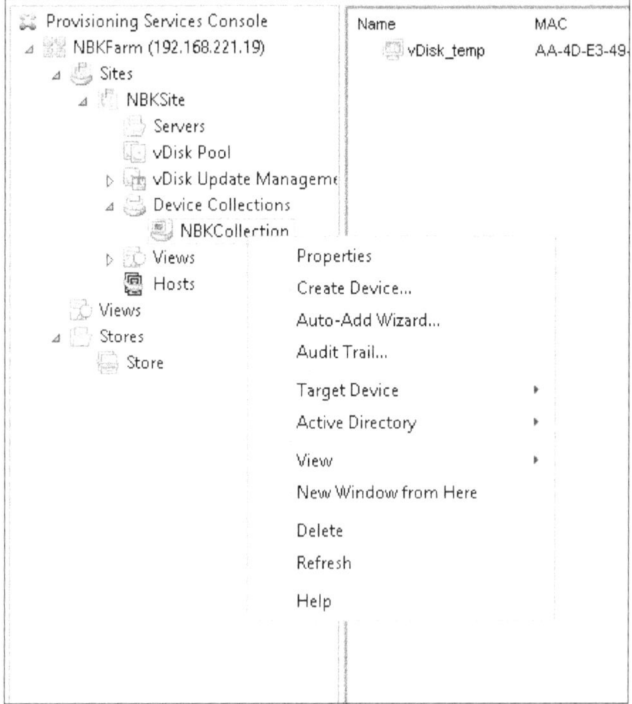


2. It will open **Target Device Properties**, where you have to enter the following details:

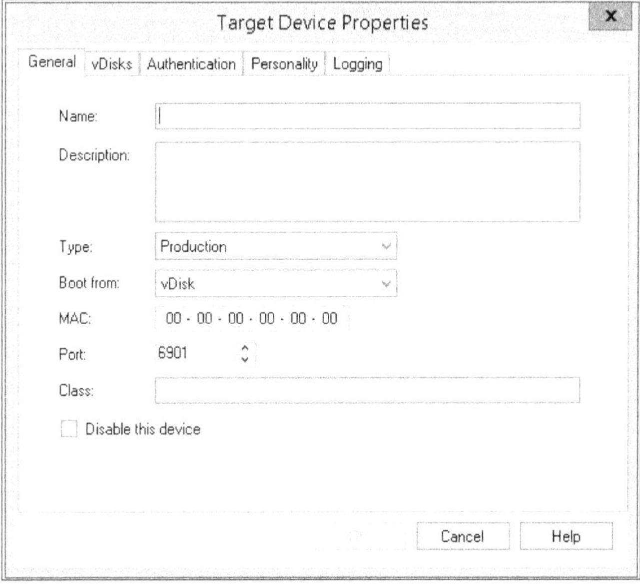

3. Enter **Name**, and **Type** can be production (you can choose other when you are updating your vDisk). Then, enter the **MAC** address of the target device, which you want to boot from vDisk. In the vDisk, you can select the vDisk you want to assign:

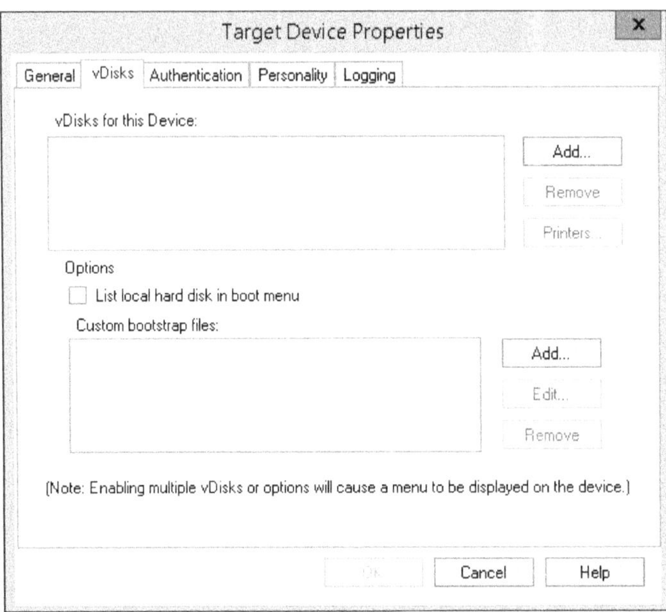


4. Click on **Add...**, and it will show you the store that you have in the PVS farm. You can choose the desired vDisk:

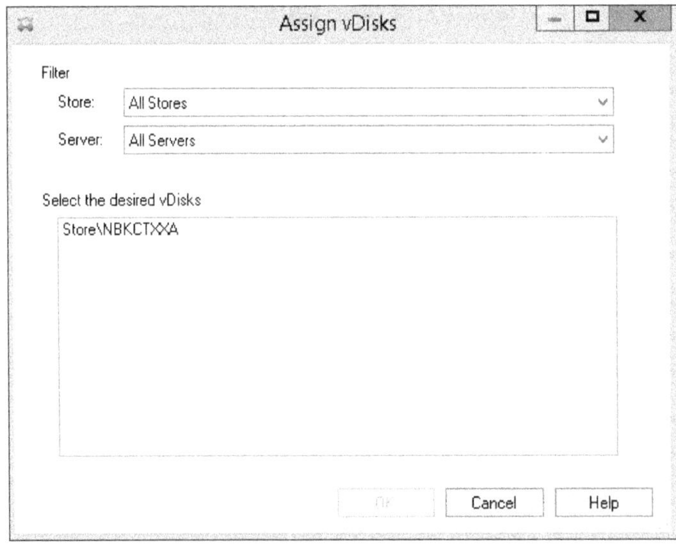

5. After this, you can add authentication as well to make sure users are authenticating to allow the target device to boot. You can enable the logging as well.
6. After creating the device in the PVS, when the device will boot, it will get the IP details and Bootstrap from the DHCP server and later, it will boot from vDisk:

```
Press F12 for boot menu.

Boot device: Network - success.
iPXE (PCI 00:04.0) starting execution...ok
iPXE initialising devices...ok


iPXE 1.0.0+ -- Open Source Network Boot Firmware -- http://ipxe.org
Features: HTTP iSCSI DNS TFTP AoE bzImage ELF MBOOT PXE PXEXT Menu

net0: aa:4d:e3:49:28:97 using rtl8139 on PCI00:04.0 (open)
  [Link:up, TX:0 TXE:0 RX:0 RXE:0]
DHCP (net0 aa:4d:e3:49:28:97)...... ok
net0: 192.168.221.140/255.255.255.0 gw 192.168.221.1
Next server: 192.168.221.19
Filename: ARDBP32.BIN
tftp://192.168.221.19/ARDBP32.BIN... ok
```

# Summary

In this chapter, you spent time learning about the Citrix Provisioning Services and how to implement the Citrix Provisioning Services to have a disk-less environment. You also learnt how it can be used in the XenApp 7.6 infrastructure for the better management of virtual and physical machines, and effective cost management as well when it comes to the cost of the storage.

You learned about the details of the Citrix Provisioning Services architecture, and how to set up Provisioning Service server and configure it, install the Citrix Provisioning Services console, configure the boot from network, configure the Bootstrap for high availability, configure the Master Target Device, create a vDisk, and assign a vDisk to a target device.

In the next chapter, we will test all the components that we implemented so far to make sure that they are working flawlessly and as expected. We will involve some users for the testing purpose, and I am sure you are ready for it!

# 8

# Setting Up NetScaler®

In this chapter, we will be working on setting up the frontend security device to provide secure remote connectivity to the Citrix XenApp 7.6 environment. That device is known as NetScaler Gateway, and we will be spending our time on the following topics:

- An overview of NetScaler Gateway
- Performing the initial configuration of NetScaler
- Configuring NTP
- Configuring high availability for NetScaler
- Creating certificates for NetScaler
- Configuring NetScaler for remote access
- Modifying StoreFront to integrate with NetScaler

## An overview of NetScaler Gateway™

NetScaler is the network appliance and it is available in different types when we talk about the function and features, such as:

- **Application delivery controller (ADC)**: This is capable of doing multiple things, such as load balancing of web servers, SQL servers, SharePoint, and many other known services. It can also do content switching and SSL offloading, act as an application firewall, and connect to Cloud.
- **Gateway**: This is also known as Citrix Access Gateway. This appliance is basically used for securing the remote access for the external users connecting to Citrix XenApp or XenDesktop environment.

# Types of NetScaler® appliance

NetScaler appliance is available in three different types, which can be used based on the requirement of the organization:

- **MPX**: This is the physical version of the NetScaler appliance and is available in different models with different hardware configuration. The starting model, which is MPX 5550, has the Intel CPU installed with 8 GB memory, and is capable of handling 5K concurrent SSL VPN connections and 175k HTTP requests.
- **VPX**: This is the virtual edition of the NetScaler. We can use this edition as a virtual appliance by importing it in the Hypervisor such as VMware ESX, Citrix XenServer, and Microsoft Hyper-v. Again, this comes in the multiple, based on the throughput required, for example, VPX 10, 200, and 1000 (these numbers are based on the throughput in Mbps).
- **SDX**: This is again the hardware version similar to MPX, and the difference between MPX and SDX is that SDX runs the customized version of XenServer and on top, by default, it comes with five instances of NetScaler appliance.

Furthermore, in this chapter, we will configure the NetScaler, so we will use some of the keywords, which are explained here:

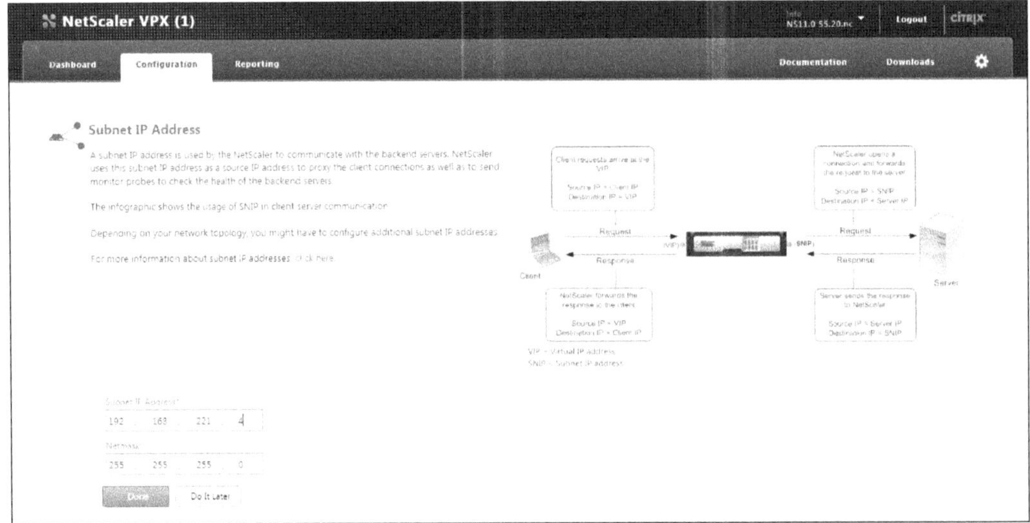


Subnet IP Address configuration

- The very first term is **NSIP**, also known as NetScaler IP, which is used for the management of the NetScaler appliance. We do this configuration at the beginning of the NetScaler configuration, and it is one of the mandatory settings.

- **SNIP** is also known as subnet IP address, which is used to route the traffic to the backend infrastructure.
- **VIP** is Virtual IP address, which we generally create when we want to represent any service, for example, if we want to load balance multiple web servers we need to have a Virtual IP so that users will connect using the virtual IP, and NetScaler will route the different web servers configured in the load balancing based on the load balance rule.

With the help of NetScaler appliance, we can also configure the following features:

- **ICA Proxy**: In this feature, NetScaler allows users to connect to their Citrix session via port `443` and, in the back, NetScaler communicate to the XenApp or XenDesktop servers over the port `1494`.
- **SSL VPN**: With the help of this feature, organizations can set up the browser-based VPN solution and some may term them as a clientless solution for VPN as well.
- **Endpoint analysis**: This feature enables the NetScaler to scan the client machine based on the policy defined. If the client doesn't match with it, NetScaler denies the connection. NetScaler has a number of built scans, which administrator can use, or can create the custom scan based on the registry, OS version, software installed, and others.

I talked about some of the important features, which are used widely, but trust me, NetScaler can do much more than this.

# Performing the initial configuration of NetScaler®

In this section, I will be taking you through the steps on how to configure the NetScaler VPX on Citrix XenServer. In this chapter, we will cover the following topics:

- Installing the NetScaler appliance on XenServer
- Configuring the networking address on NetScaler
- Using NSIP to configure Subnet IP, Hostname, DNS, Time zone, and licensing
- Installing a license on Licenses

# Installing the NetScaler® appliance on XenServer®

In this book, we will be using the latest version of NetScaler, which is 11.0. You can download the same from `http://www.mycitrix.com` from the **Downloads** section, making sure you choose the correct version based on the Hypervisor you will be using. The steps are almost the same in the case of VMware ESX and Hyper-V. Follow these steps:

1. Once you have the NetScaler VPX, go to XenCenter and click on **File** and then on **Import**. This will bring up the import wizard of XenCenter:

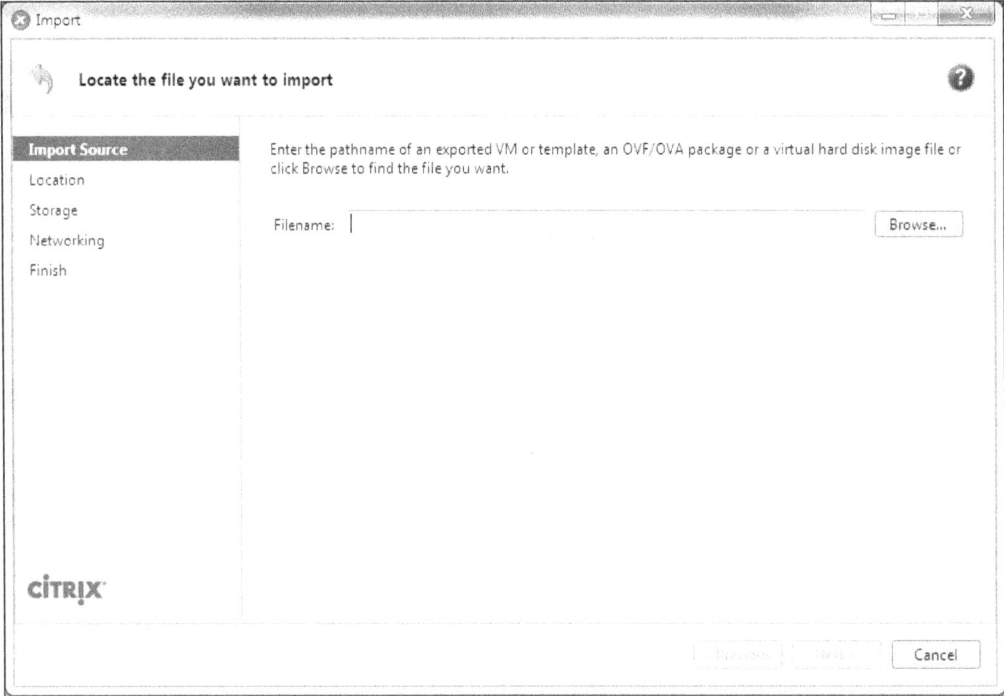

2. Click on **Browse...** and locate the downloaded NetScaler VPX for the XenServer file. The format for XenServer is *.XVA:

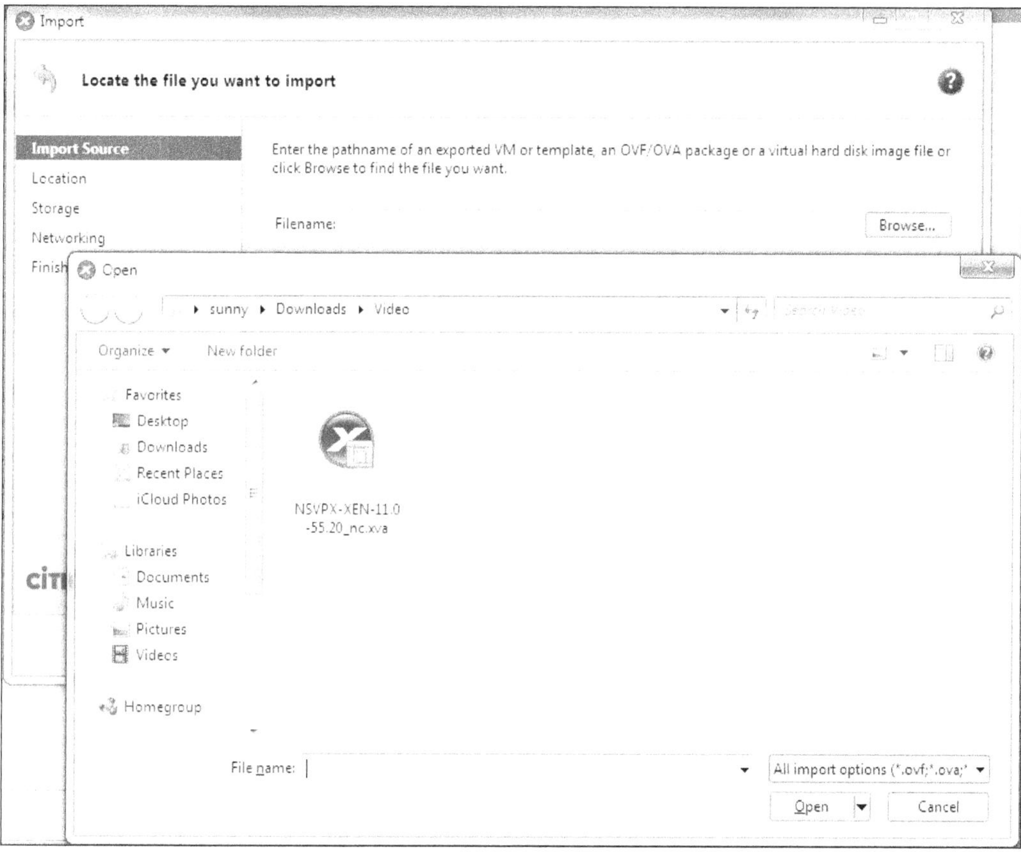

3. Select the file and click on **Open** and then on **Next** to select the pool or XenServer where this appliance will be powered on:

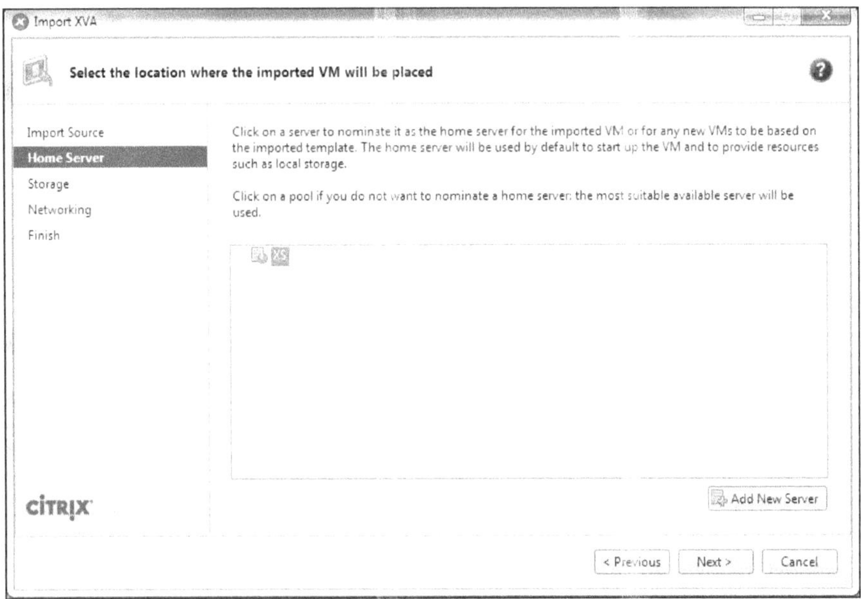


4. Click on **Next** to select the storage where this VM will be stored and then click on **Import**:

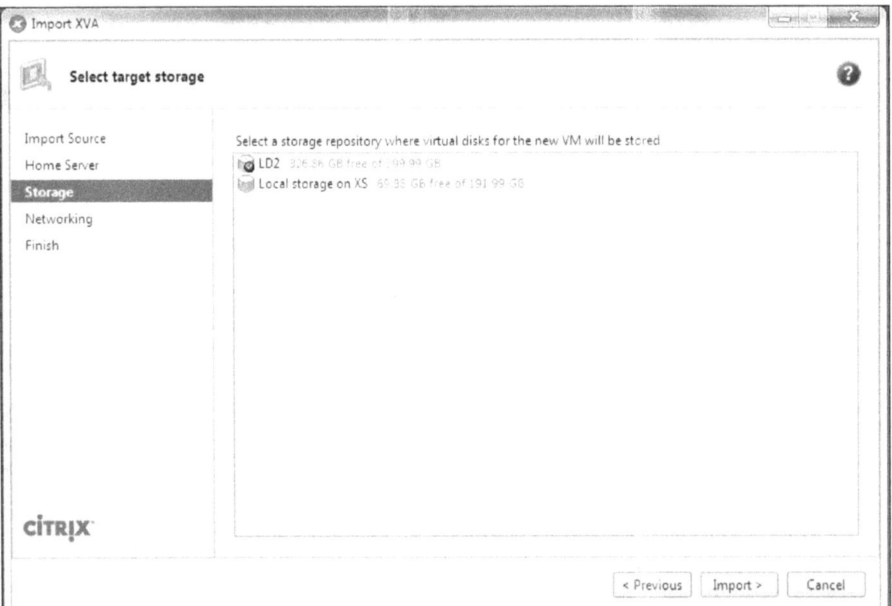

5. It will start uploading the NetScaler appliance into the storage and it will create the VM for it, and you will be asked for the network. Select the network and click on **Next**:

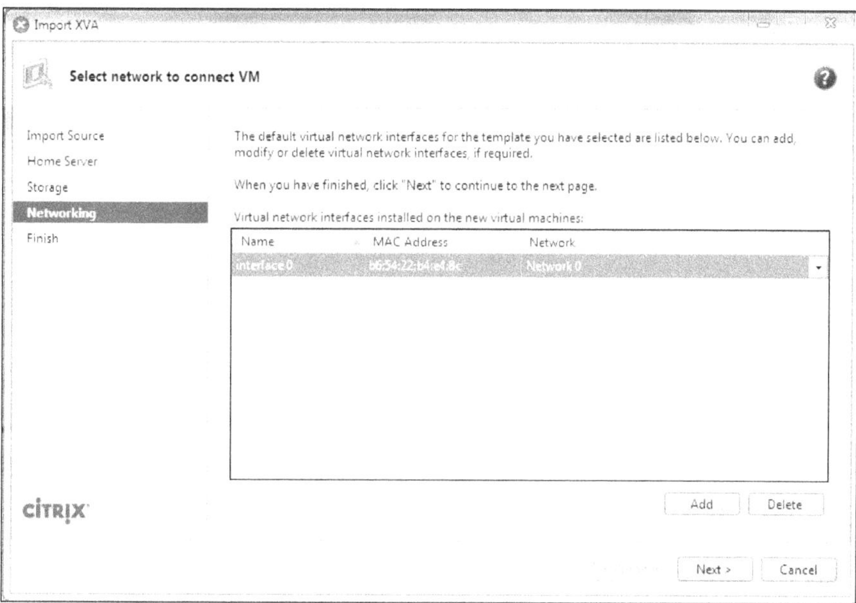


6. On the next screen, you can review the configuration of the appliance. Click on **Finish** to complete the import of the NetScaler appliance:

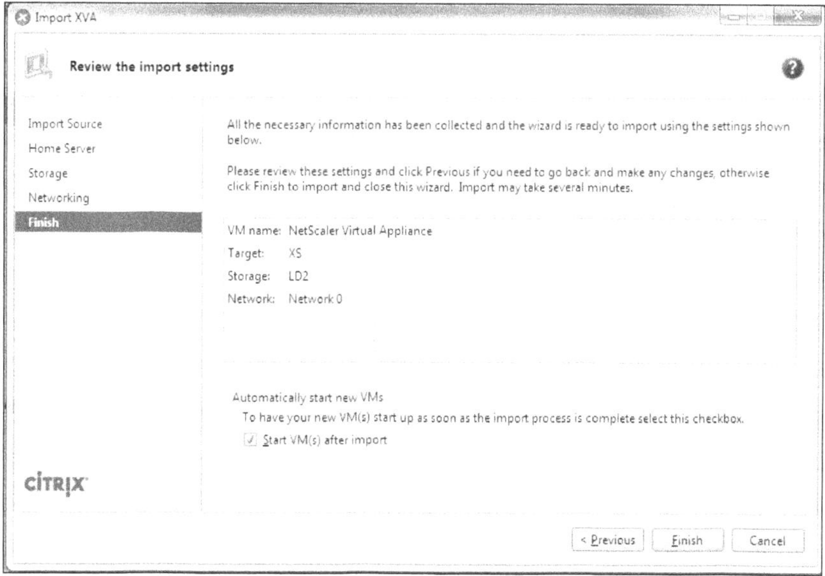

7. It will take a few moments and posts, which you will be able to see in the VM in the XenCenter:

# Configuring the networking address on NetScaler®

Now when we have the NetScaler appliance imported and powered on, we have to make an initial configuration so that we can access the management console of NetScaler, and this initial configuration will be assigning the IP address also known as NetScaler IP. The following are the steps:

1. In order to start the configuration, launch the console of the VM for the appliance, and you will be asked for the NetScaler IP, Subnet mask, and default gateway:

```
2b:1b:00:e1:1f:78:92:cd:6c:c9:18:59:5f:41:a8:d2 root@ns
The key's randomart image is:
+--[ DSA 1024]----+
|  oo.  o+.       |
| ..@ o..         |
|  B.X..          |
|  .*E.           |
|   .o   S        |
|      .   .      |
|     o .         |
|      +          |
|     .           |
+-----------------+
.
sysctl: unknown oid 'machdep.cpu_idle_hlt'
kern.sched.idlespinthresh: 4 -> 32
Start daemons: syslogd Sep 10 04:44:46 <kern.info> ns syslogd: kernel boot file
is /flash/ns-11.0-55.20
inetd cron httpd monit sshd .

!There is no ns.conf in the /nsconfig!

Start Netscaler software
tput: no terminal type specified and no TERM environmental variable.
Enter NetScaler's IPv4 address []:
```

2. Post entering all the information, you have to save the configuration by choosing option **4** from the listed options:

```
tput: no terminal type specified and no TERM environmental variable.
Enter NetScaler's IPv4 address []: 192.168.221.3
Enter Netmask []: 255.255.255.0
Enter Gateway IPv4 address []: 192.168.221.1

------------------------------------------------------------------------
Netscaler Virtual Appliance Initial Network Address Configuration.
This menu allows you to set and modify the initial IPv4 network addresses.
The current value is displayed in brackets ([]).
Selecting the listed number allows the address to be changed.

After the network changes are saved, you may either login as nsroot and
use the Netscaler command line interface, or use a web browser to
http://192.168.221.3 to complete or change the Netscaler configuration.
------------------------------------------------------------------------
    1. NetScaler's IPv4 address [192.168.221.3]
    2. Netmask [255.255.255.0]
    3. Gateway IPv4 address [192.168.221.1]
    4. Save and quit
Select item (1-4) [4]:
.snap/      configdb/  home/      netscaler/ proc/      usr/
bin/        dev/       lib/       nscache/   root/      var/
colorful/   etc/       libexec/   nsconfig/  sbin/
compat/     flash/     mnt/       optional/  tmp/
Select item (1-4) [4]:
```

3. After saving the configuration, your NetScaler appliance will be ready to access via NSIP in the browser and you will see the following confirmation on the console as well:

```
Sep 10 04:52:31 <local0.err> ns nsconfigd: _dispatch(): Feature(s) not licensed
Sep 10 04:52:31 <local0.err> ns nsconfigd: _dispatch(): Feature(s) not licensed
Sep 10 04:52:31 <local0.err> ns nsconfigd: _dispatch(): Certificate with key siz
e greater than RSA512 or DSA512 bits not supported
Sep 10 04:52:32 <local0.err> ns AutoScaleDaemon[1187]: Monitoring daemon started

Sep 10 04:52:32 <local0.err> ns nsumond[1388]: nsumond daemon started
monit monit daemon at 981 awakened
.

 NetScaler initialization is still in progress: please wait
 20 to 30 seconds before attempting to log in.
################################################################################
#                                                                              #
#        WARNING: Access to this system is for authorized users only.         #
#         Disconnect IMMEDIATELY if you are not an authorized user!           #
#                                                                              #
################################################################################


login:  Sep 10 04:53:33 <local0.alert> 192.168.221.3 09/10/2015:04:53:33 GMT  0-
PPE-0 : default EVENT STATECHANGE 74 0 :  Device "self node 192.168.221.3" - Sta
te UP
Sep 10 04:53:36 <daemon.err> ns monit[981]: 'iked' process PPID changed to 1
```

# Using NSIP to configure — Subnet IP, Hostname, DNS, Time zone and licensing

After the initial configuration of IP details in the NetScaler CLI console, we will use NSIP to make the further configuration, and for that, the steps are as follows:

1. We will use NSIP to access the NetScaler management console in the browser, and the default password to log in to the NetScaler management console is:
   - Username: `nsroot`
   - Password: `nsroot`
2. After logging in to the NetScaler management console, you will be able to see the welcome screen where NSIP and Subnet IP will be displayed. The next configuration that we have to make is to configure Subnet IP:

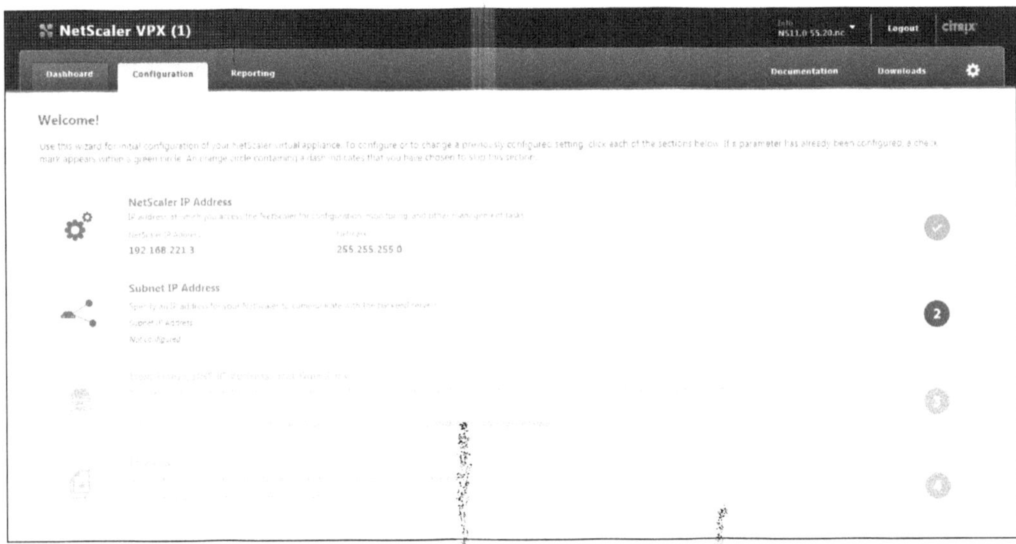


Configuring Subnet IP Address

3. Click on **Subnet IP Address** and enter the IP details. You can also do this configuration later by clicking on **Do It Later**:

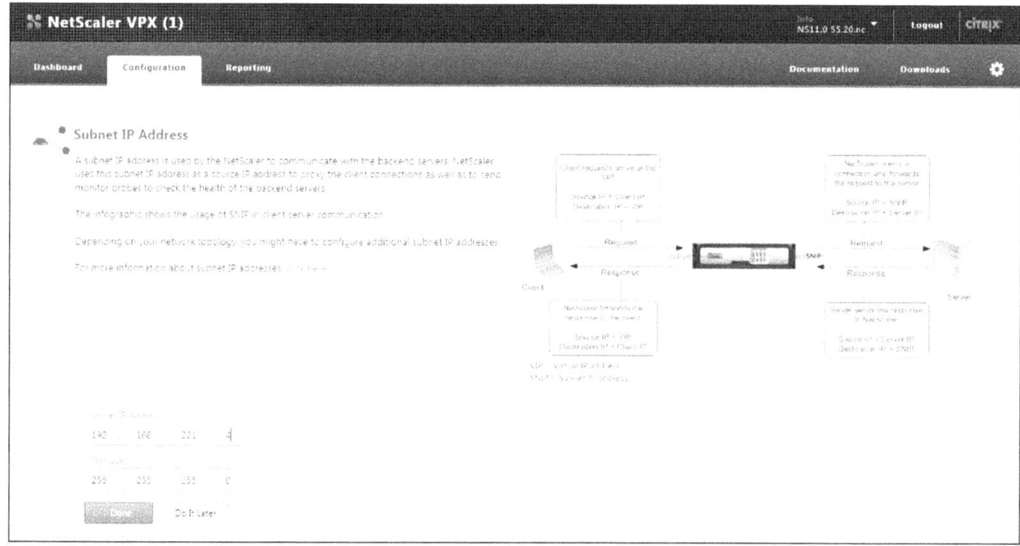


Entering Subnet IP Address details

4. Now click on **Host Name, DNS IP Address, and Time Zone** and enter the details. Then, click on **Done**:

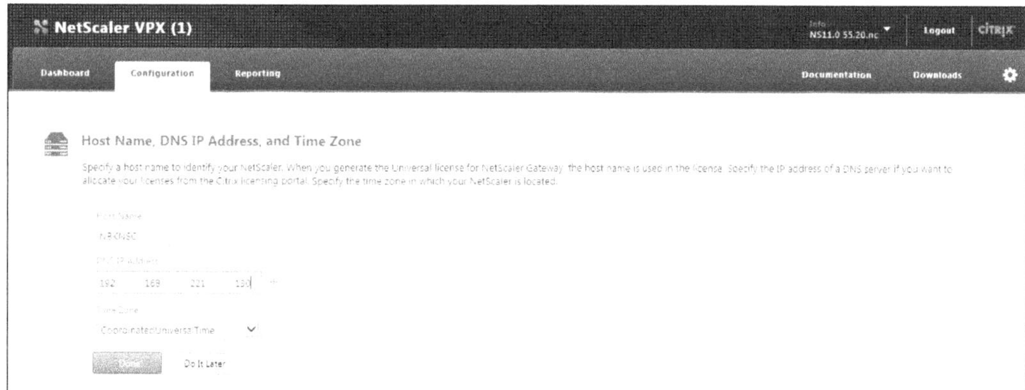


Entering Host Name,DNS IP Address, and Time Zone

5. After clicking on **Done**, it will ask you whether you want to save the configuration and reboot the device. I will click on **Yes**. This will reboot the appliance and it will come back in a few minutes:

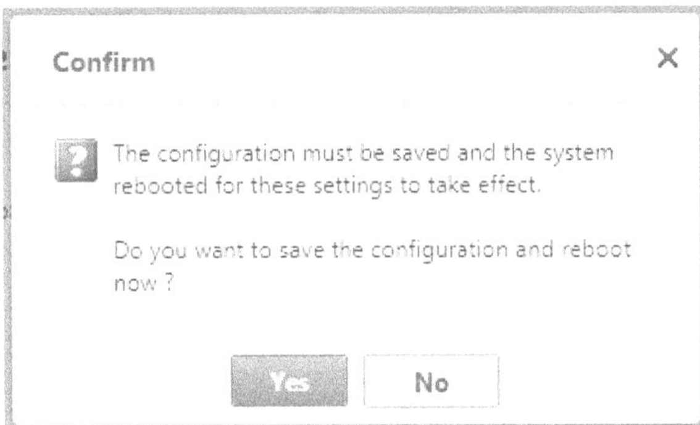

Confirm
The configuration must be saved and the system rebooted for these settings to take effect.
Do you want to save the configuration and reboot now ?
Yes
No


# Installing a license on Licenses

Once we have the appliance accessible again, we have to allocate the license to the NetScaler appliance and for that we need to have the MAC address of the device, and to the get MAC address we have to log in to the console. The following are the steps:

1. You have to log in to the console with the same username and password, which is `nsroot` and `nsroot`, respectively:

```
login: nsroot
Password:
Sep 10 05:54:08 <auth.notice> NBKNSC login: ROOT LOGIN (nsroot) ON ttyv0
Copyright (c) 1992-2013 The FreeBSD Project.
Copyright (c) 1979, 1980, 1983, 1986, 1988, 1989, 1991, 1992, 1993, 1994
        The Regents of the University of California. All rights reserved.
```

2. And then type shell to get into the CLI of NetScaler and execute the `lmutil lmhostid` command. This will give you the MAC address of the NetScaler appliance. Once you have the MAC address, go to `http://www.mycitrix.com` and allocate the license for your NetScaler.

3. Once you have the licensing file, go back to the NetScaler management console. Click on **Licenses**, and it will give you the following screen:

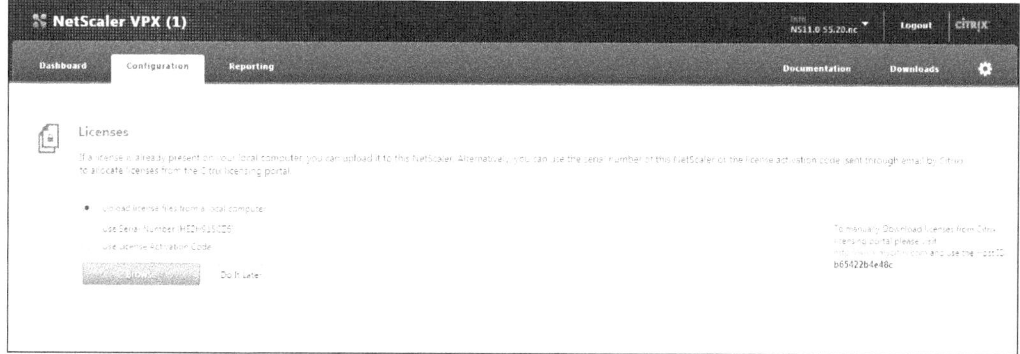


Uploading license files

4. So basically, you have three options to allocate the license. I will chose the first one and will upload the license from the local computer. Browse the license file you have allocated for NetScaler and click on **Open**. This will upload the license file to the appliance and display the following message:

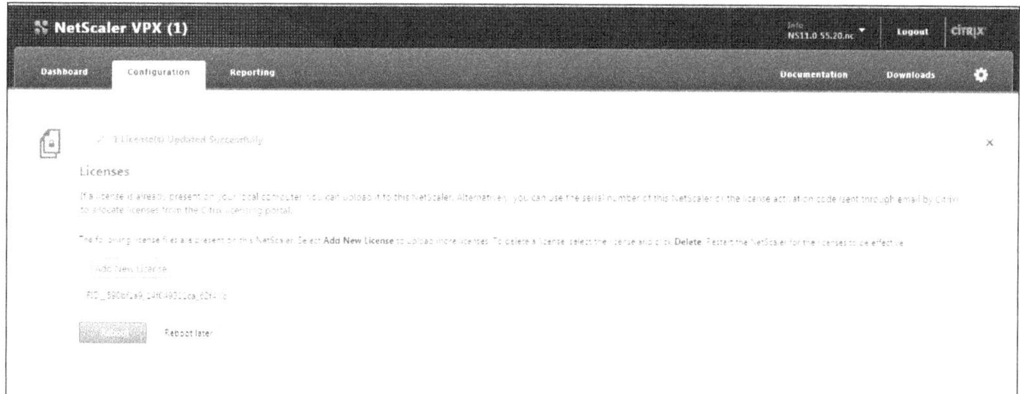


Successful Upload

5.  After the successful uploading of the license file, you have to reboot the NetScaler appliance to save the configuration and reflect the changes, so click on **Reboot**. If your allocation is successful, you will get the following popup:

| Licenses | | | | ×|
|---|---|---|---|---|
| License type | Platinum | | Model ID | 2000 |
| Load Balancing | ✓ | | SSL Offloading | ✓ |
| Content Switching | ✓ | | Cache Redirection | ✓ |
| Global Server Load Balancing | ✓ | | GSLB Proximity | ✓ |
| Authentication, Authorization and Auditing | ✓ | | NetScaler Gateway | ✓ |
| Maximum NetScaler Gateway Users Allowed | 5 | | Maximum ICA Users Allowed | Unlimited |
| Clustering | ✓ | | Web Interface | ✓ |
| Integrated Caching | ✓ | | Front End Optimization | ✓ |
| Rewrite | ✓ | | Responder | ✓ |
| HTTP Compression | ✓ | | Content Filtering | ✓ |
| Application Firewall | ✓ | | Cloud Bridge | ✓ |
| Priority Queuing | ✓ | | Sure Connect | ✓ |
| Surge Protection | ✓ | | DoS Protection | ✓ |
| AppFlow | ✓ | | AppFlow for ICA | ✓ |
| IPv6 Protocol Translation | ✓ | | Dynamic Routing | ✓ |
| BGP Routing | ✓ | | OSPF Routing | ✓ |
| RIP Routing | ✓ | | ISIS Routing | ✓ |
| Content Accelerator | ✓ | | AppQoE | ✓ |
| NetScaler Push | ✓ | | Web Logging | ✓ |
| vPath | ✓ | | RISE | ✓ |
| Callhome | ✓ | | Large Scale NAT | ✓ |

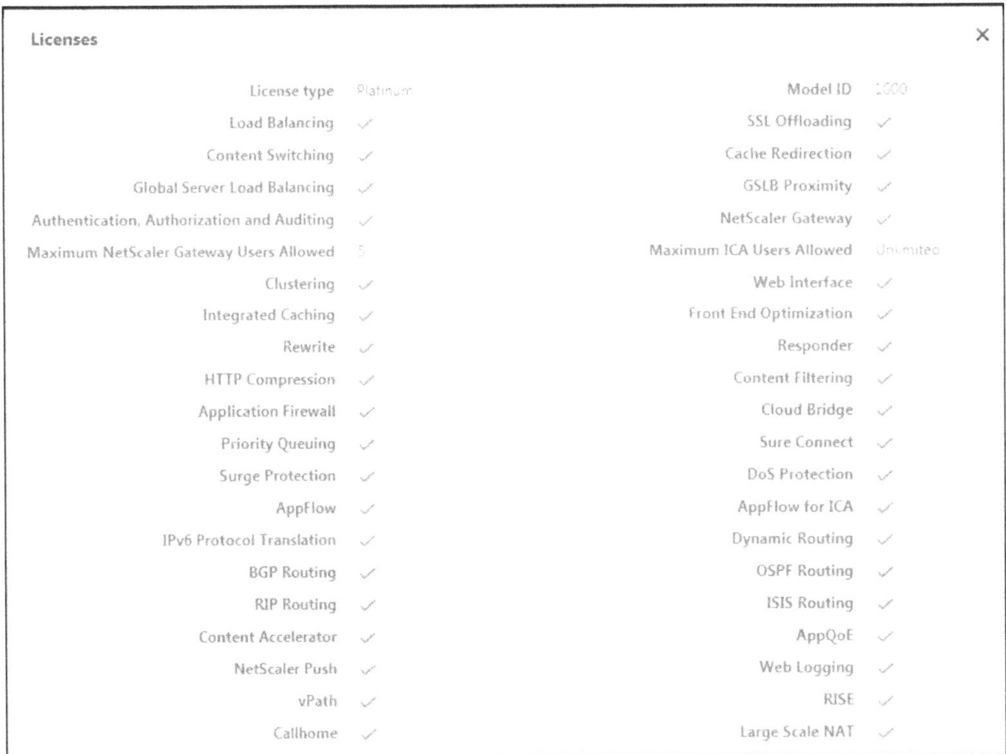

# Configuring NTP

This is going to be a quick configuration of the NTP server to synchronize the clock on the gateway. In order to do that, follow these steps:

1.  Click on the **Configuration** tab and expand **System**:

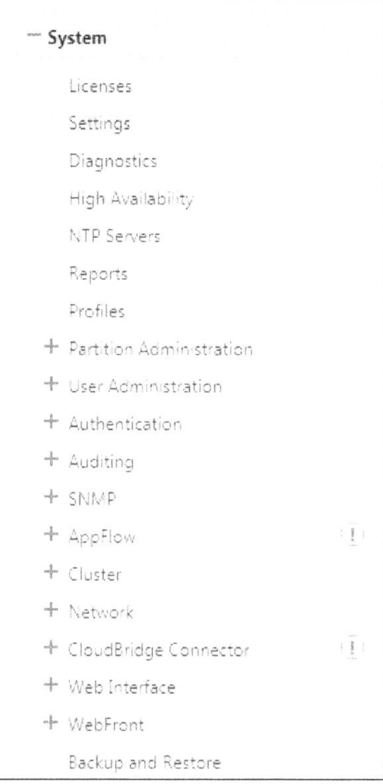


2. Select **NTP Servers** and click on **Add**. You will get the following form in which you can enter the information about your NTP server and poll interval. Once done, click on **Create**:

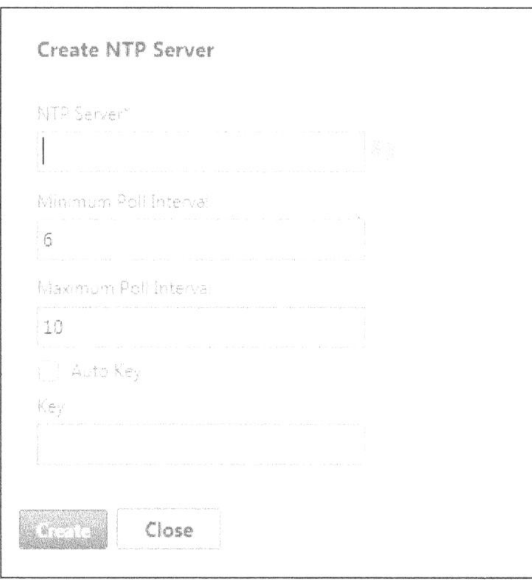

3. Once created, you will see them in the **NTP Servers** list:

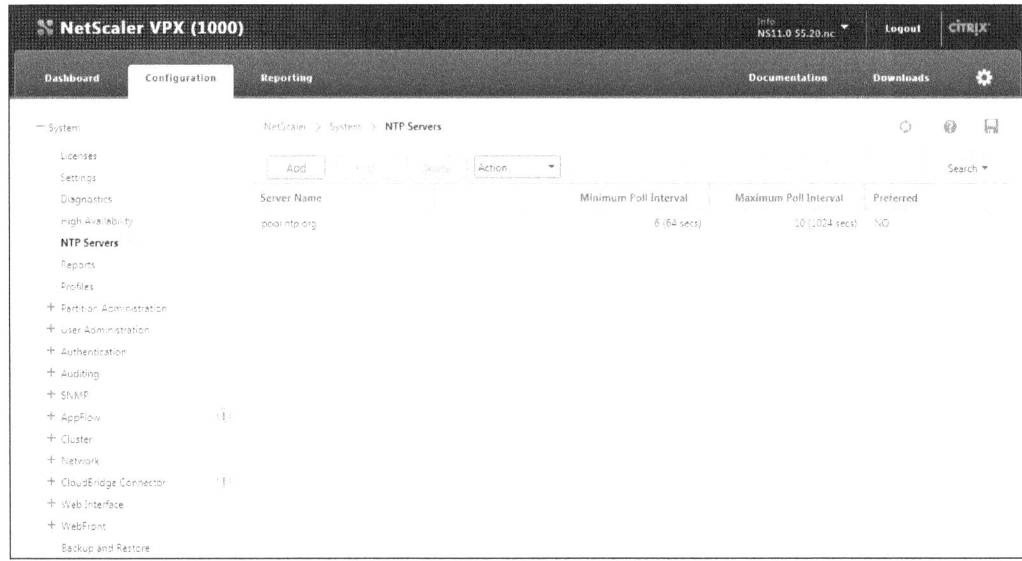


NTP Servers list

4. Now click on the **Action** dropdown and then on **Configure NTP Synchronization**. Enable the synchronization and click on **OK**:

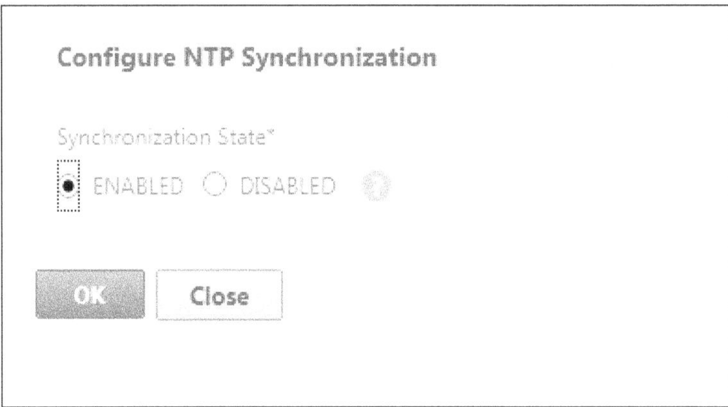

5. Once enabled, you system time will change as per the NTP server and you can verify that by going to the **System** view:

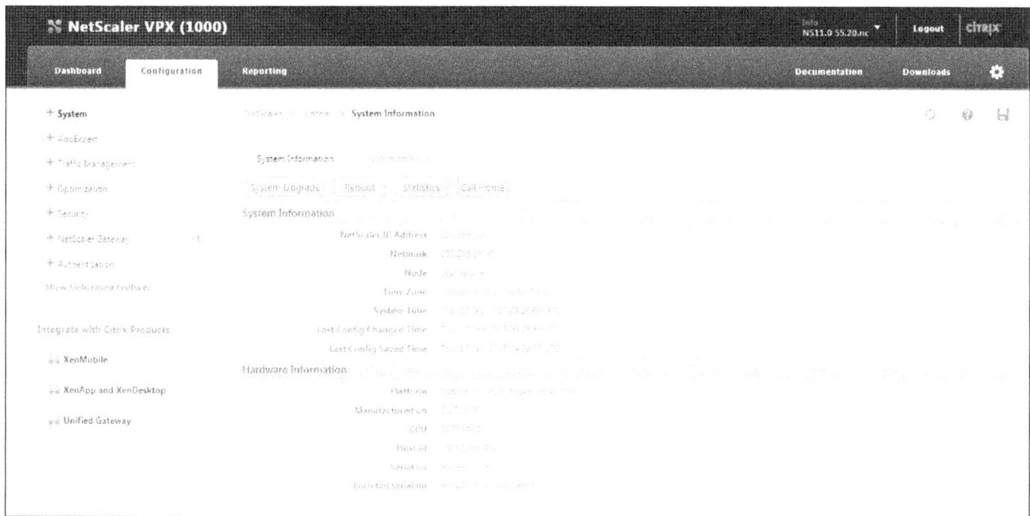


System information

# Configuring high availability for NetScaler®

We will enable this so that in case of multiple NetScaler appliances we can remove the single point of failure. This will sync the files and make sure that all your configured services on the NetScaler appliance are always running.

In order to do this, you have to repeat the same steps that we did in this chapter before so that you can prepare one more NetScaler, which will be added to the high availability. Make sure the new appliance has NSIP and licensing configured on it.

1. Once you have the new appliance ready, go to the previous appliance and in the **Configuration** tab, expand the **System** node and select **High Availability**:

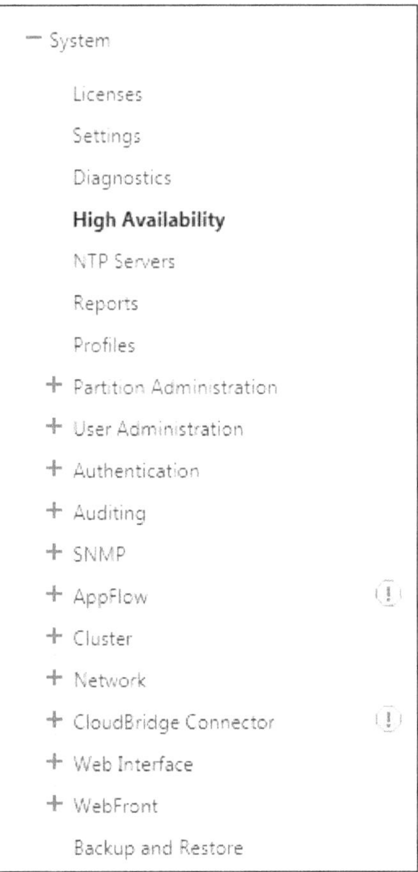


2. On the right-hand side, you will be able to see a node that is the current appliance you are connected to. Now you have to add the newly-configured appliance here and for that, click on **Add**:

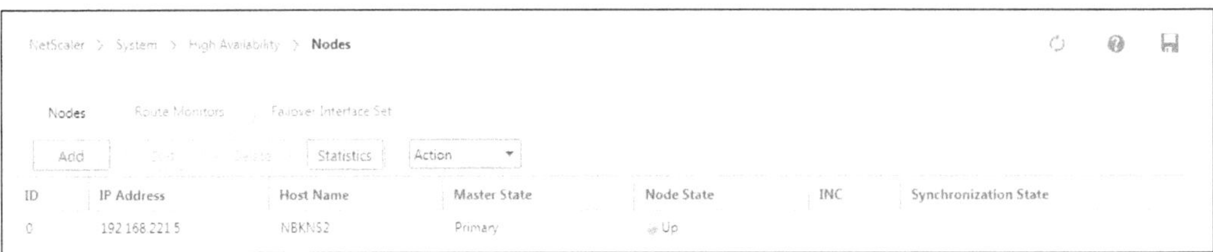

3. The next screen will be where you have to enter the details about your secondary node, such as NSIP, and username and password:

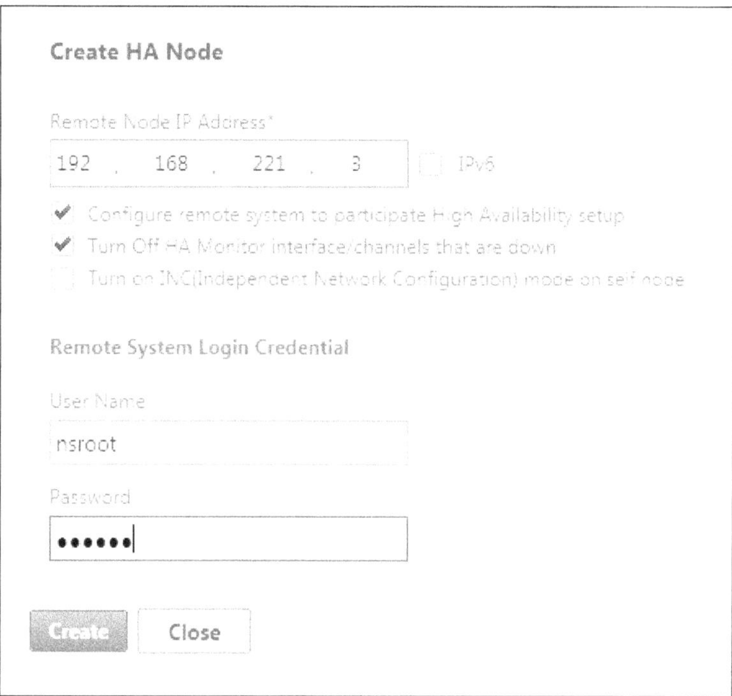


4. After filling up the details required, you have to click on **Create**. This will add the new node as a secondary node in **High Availability** and will take some time to synchronize with the primary node. Once done, you will see this:

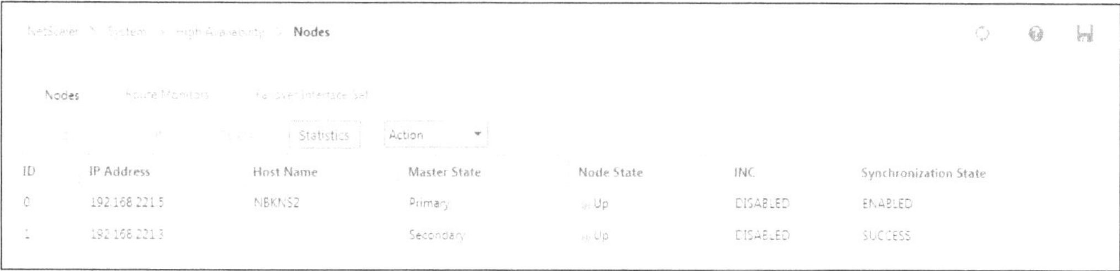

Nodes
Nodes
Statistics
Action
ID
IP Address
Host Name
Master State
Node State
INC
Synchronization State
0
192.168.221.5
NBKNS2
Primary
Up
DISABLED
ENABLED
1
192.168.221.3
Secondary
Up
DISABLED
SUCCESS

5. Now we have to edit the secondary node, which is the fail safe. This is generally done to make sure one node is running even when both the node is impacted due to some issue. In order to do that, you have to edit the primary node and check mark the box which says **Fail-safe Mode** and click on **OK**:

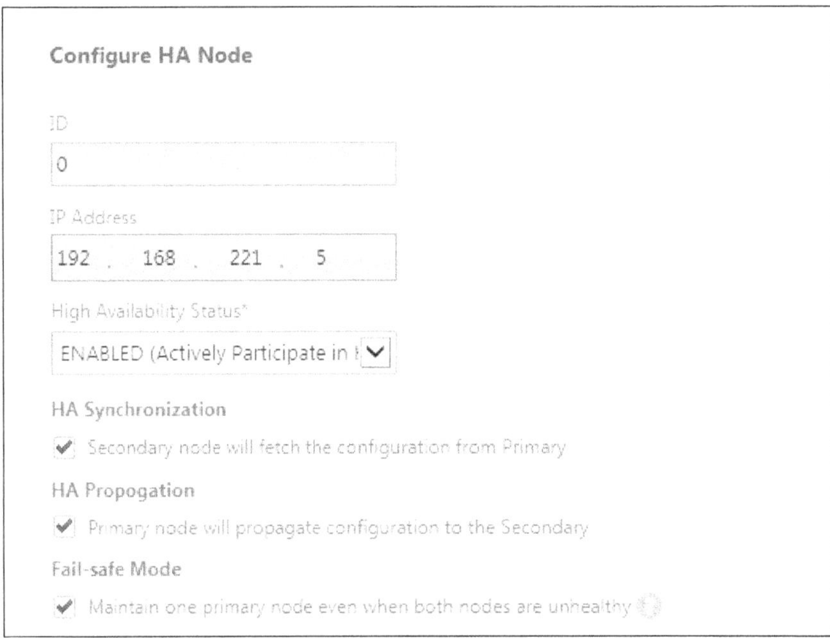


You can verify the same by connecting to the console of the appliance by executing the `SH HA Node` command. This command will list all the services running and the information about the nodes.

# Creating certificates for NetScaler®

In this section, we will be working on how to create a certificate for NetScaler. Later, that certificate can be used for the StoreFront services. The following are the steps:

1. In order to create the certificate, go to the NetScaler management console and expand **Traffic Management** and click on **SSL**:

2. From **SSL Keys**, click on **Create RSA Key**:

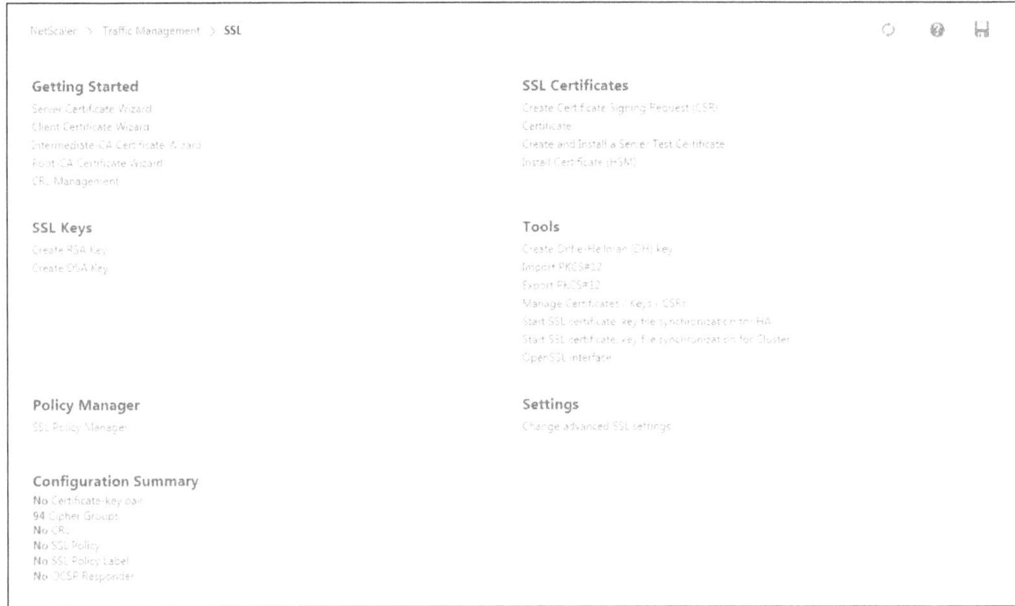


3. It will give you a form to fill up. Enter the details like this:
    - Request file name: `StoreFront.key`
    - Key size: `2048`
    - Public exponent value: `F4`
    - Key Format
    - PEM Encoding Algorithm
    - PEM Passphrase and Confirm PEM Passphrase
4. And after this, click on **Create**. The next step will be to create a certificate signing request. Enter the following information:
    - Request file name: `StoreFrontCert.txt`
    - Key File name: Browse the key file you created
    - PEM Passphrase (For Encrypted Key): Enter the password which was created in the last step
    - Distinguished name: In this section, you have to mention the details of the location, common name, organization name, and password

5. After giving all the details, click on **Create**. It will show you that the request file has been created. Click on **View**, and it will show you the text:

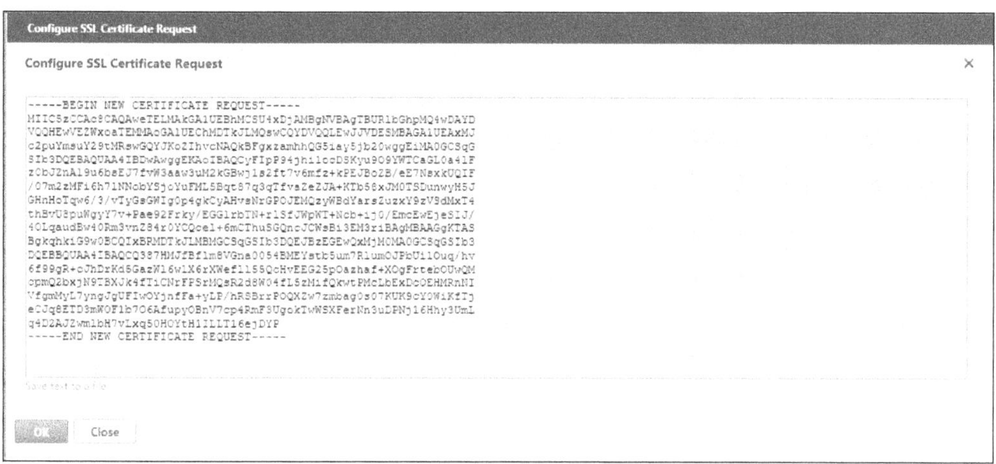


6. Now you can go to the certificate authority and get the new certificate issued with the help of the request file.
7. Once you have the certificate file issued from the certificate authority, go back to the NetScaler management console and in the **Configuration** tab, expand **Traffic Management** and then **SSL** and finally, click on **Certificates**:

8. From the right-hand side, click on **Install** and fill in the following information:

9. Click on **Install** to complete the certificate installation.

# Configuring NetScaler® for remote access

Now that we have configured the initial configuration and HA, and installed the certificate, our NetScaler appliance is ready to host the services. I will take you through the steps to create the Gateway to provide secure remote access to the users coming in from outside the organization. The following are the steps:

1. In order to start the steps, log in to the NetScaler management console and, in the **Configuration** tab, click on **XenApp and XenDesktop** under **Integrate with Citrix Products**:

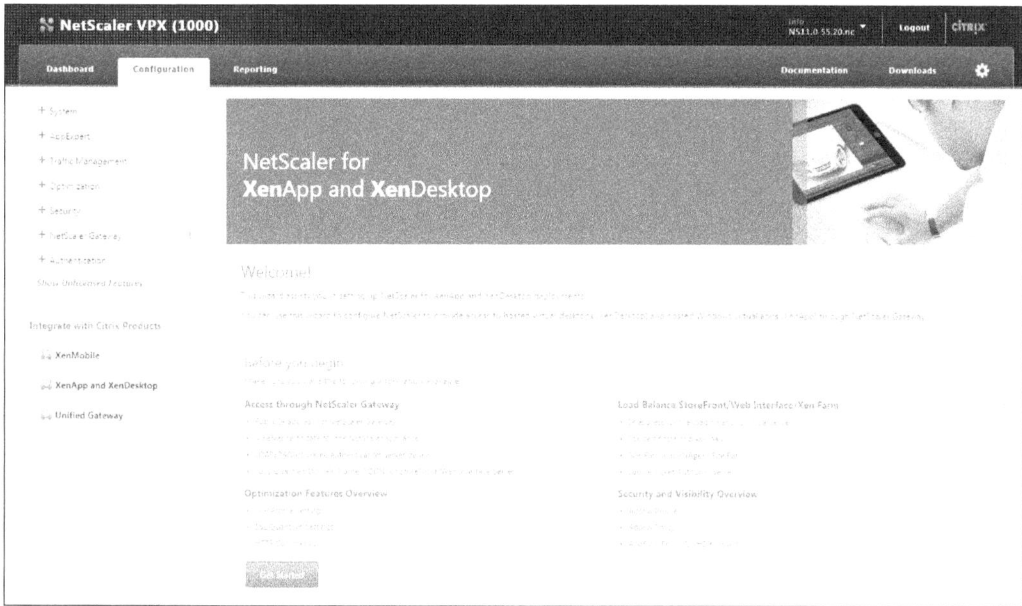


2. Click on **Get Started**, and you will asked whether you want to create the Gateway for Web Interface or StoreFront. Here, in this chapter, we are creating the Gateway for StoreFront:

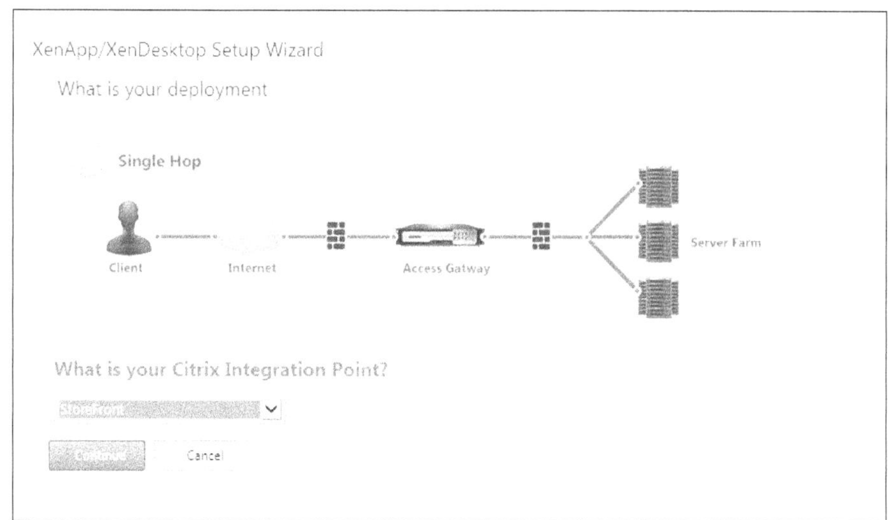

3. Click on **Continue** and enter the details as shown here:

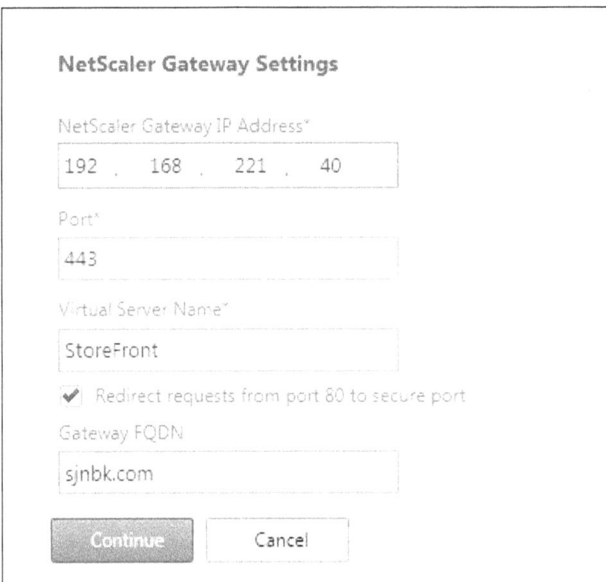

> Clicking on the redirect request from port `80` will redirect all the traffic from `80` to `443`, for example, if a user is accessing the StoreFront Gateway URL via port `80`, NetScaler will automatically redirect to `443`.

4. The next screen will ask you to import the certificate. You can simply choose the certificate that you installed in the beginning of this chapter.

5. Next, you have to configure the authentication policy which will authenticate the users on the Gateway portal itself. The following is the form that you have to fill in with the details of your environment:

6. Click on **Continue** to save the Authentication LDAP policy. Now, you will be asked for the details of your StoreFront server in which you have to mention these:
    - StoreFront server FQDN
    - Site path
    - Single sign-on domain
    - Name of the store

- STA name: Delivery controller server
- StoreFront server IP
- Protocol via which it can be accessed and the port:

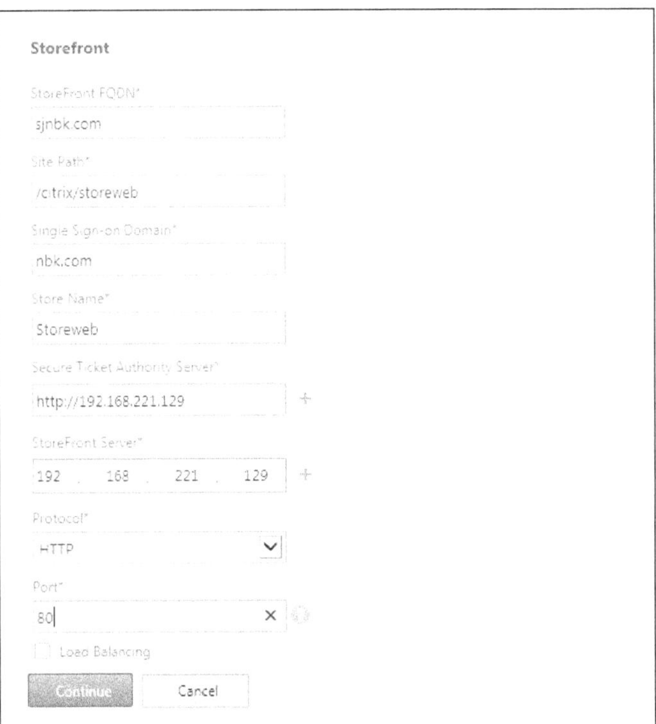


7. Click on **Continue** to save the configuration. You can also configure the load balancing as in the production environment, you will have more than one StoreFront server to equally distribute the traffic. You should use the NetScaler appliance to load balance your StoreFront server.
8. In the last step, you have to point the farm as well as configure StoreFront. We will choose the XenDesktop and give the details of the Delivery Controller server and then click on **Done**. With this, you have secured the remote access for the users connecting from external access:

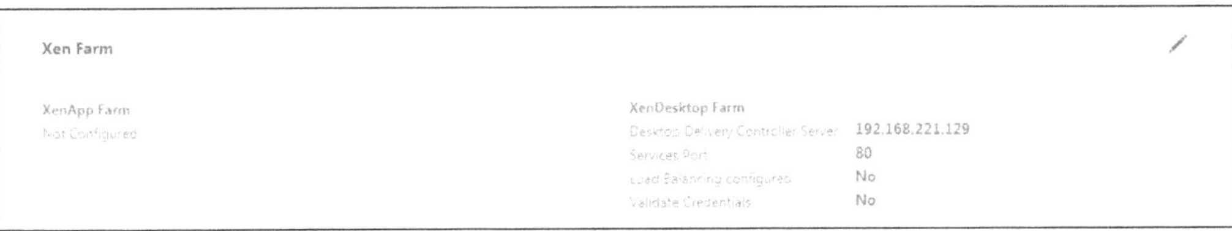

# Modifying StoreFront™ to integrate with NetScaler®

Now that we have configured the Gateway on the NetScaler, we now have to integrate that Gateway URL to our StoreFront so that when your users go to connect to the Gateway URL, they get logged in successfully:

1. In order to do that, go back to your StoreFront server and launch the StoreFront console. The very first thing that we have to do is to enable **Pass-through from NetScaler Gateway** authenticate mode in NetScaler Gateway in the **Authentication** node:

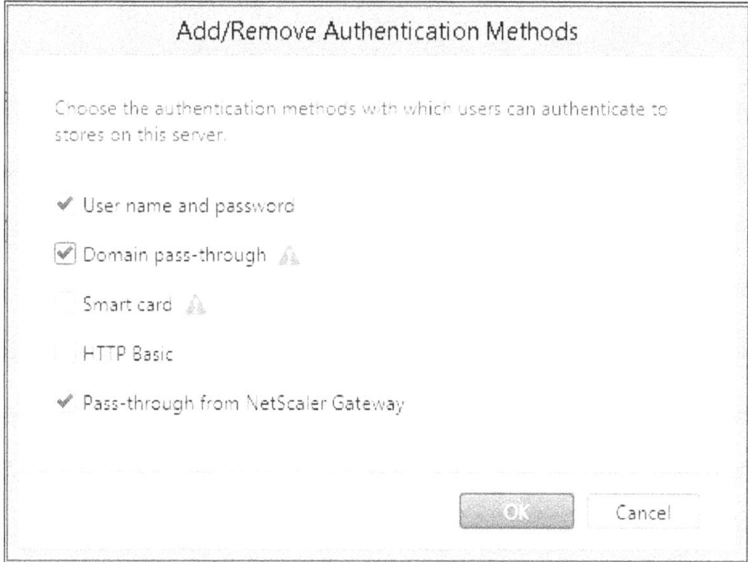


2. Now select the **NetScaler Gateway** node in the StoreFront console and from the right-hand side pane, click on **Add NetScaler Gateway Appliance**:

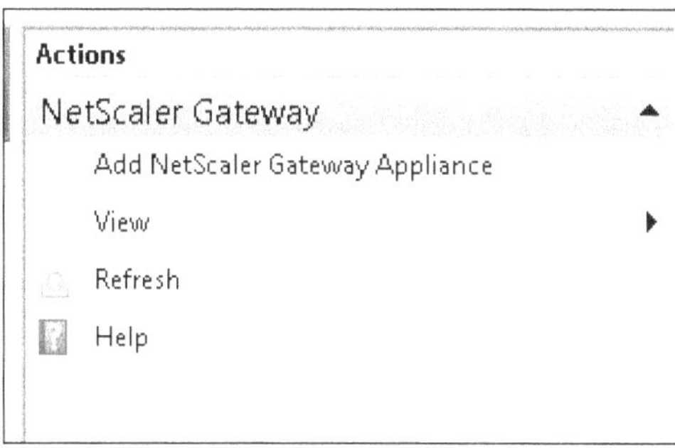

3. It will open a wizard where you have to enter the details of the Gateway, such as the name of the Gateway, its URL, version of the appliance, the Subnet IP address (optional), logon type, and callback URL which typically resolves the Virtual IP that you configured in the NetScaler Gateway:

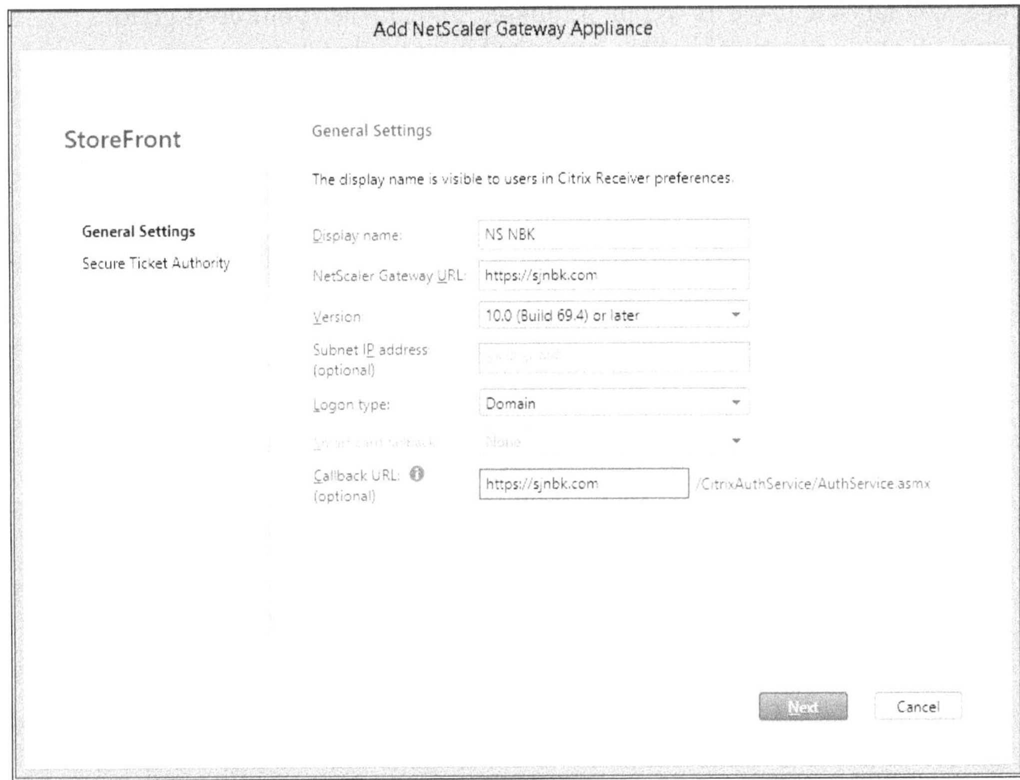


4. Click on **Next**, and you will be asked for **Secure Ticket Authority** (**STA**). Here, you have to point it to the Delivery Controller over the port `443`:

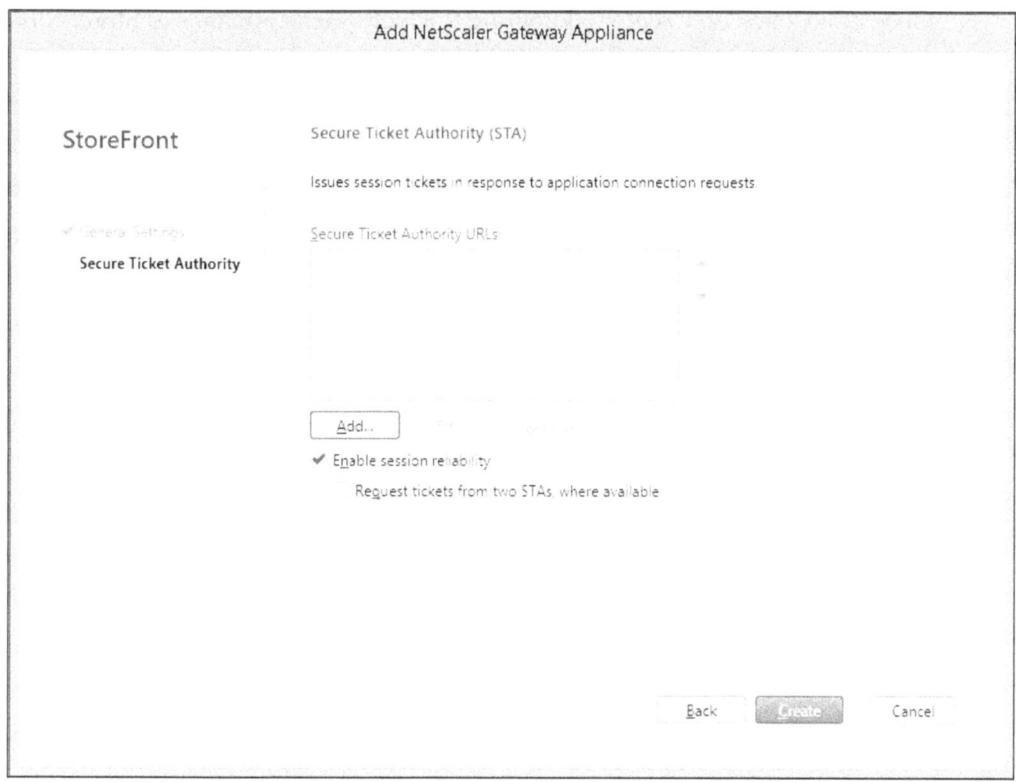


5. Click on **Add...** to add the STA server:

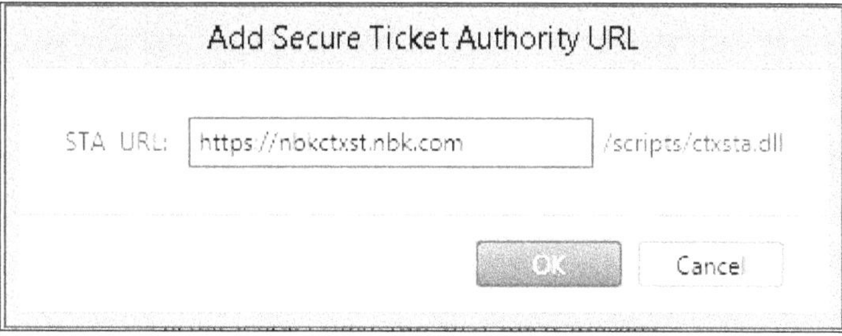

6. Once done, click on **Create** to integrate the NetScaler appliance to StoreFront. You can see the configured appliance here:

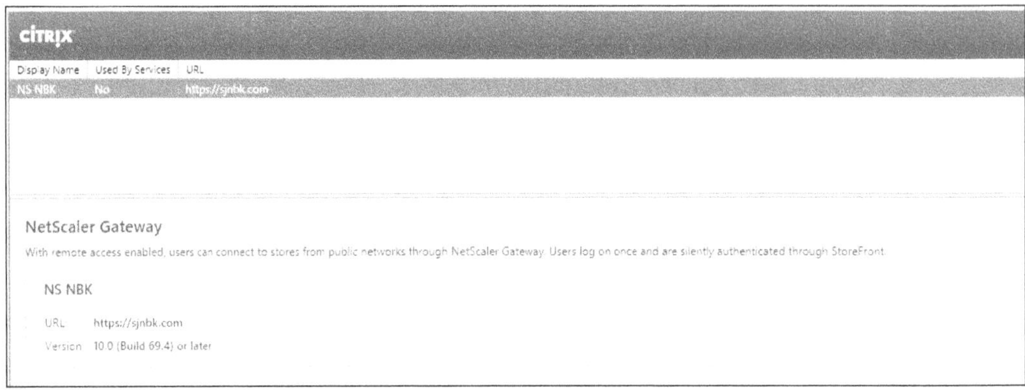


7. Now we have to enable the remote access for the Store as well. This can be done by going to the **Store** node from the right-hand side pane. Choose **Enable Remote Access** from the left pane:

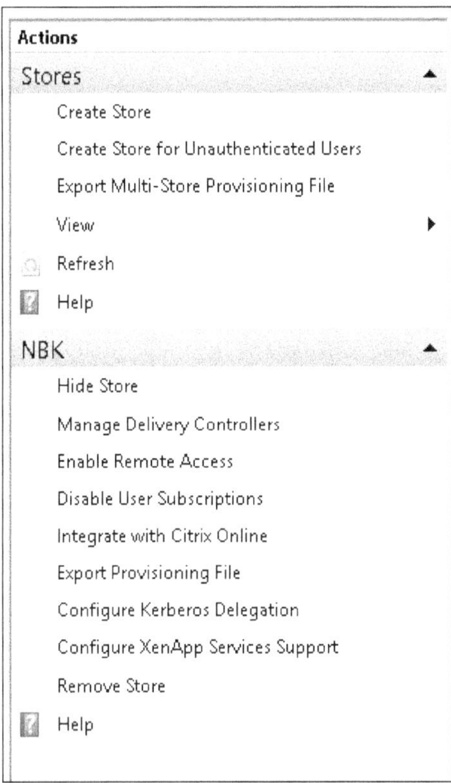

8. It will give you the **Enable Remote Access** wizard where we will select **No VPN tunnel** and the configured NetScaler appliance. We will then click on **OK**:

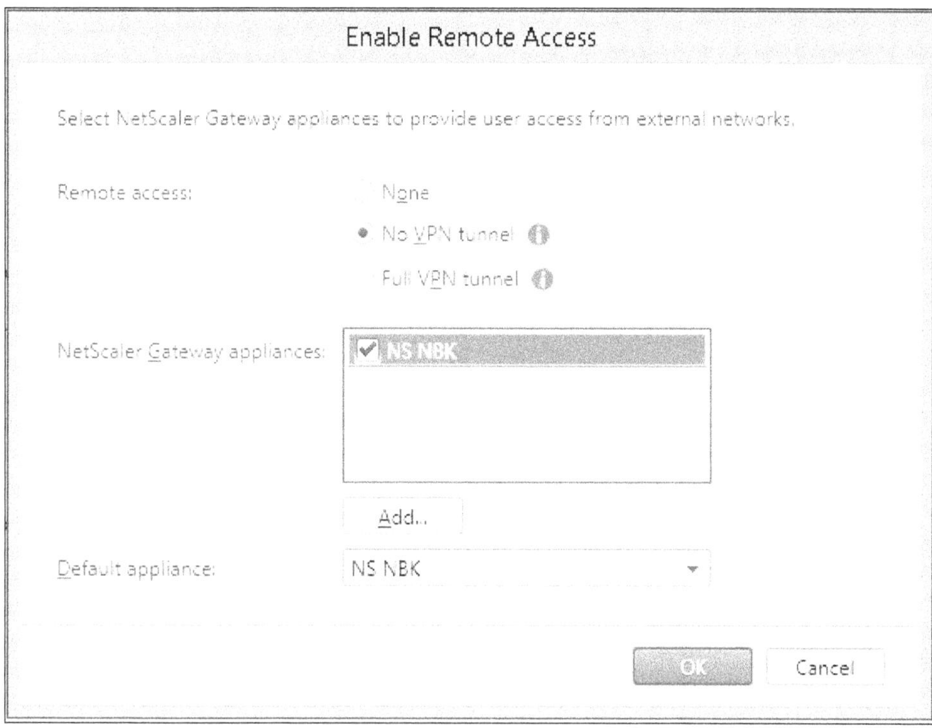


After this, you will see that your store access has now changed to internal and external networks. Now you can share the URL with users, and they can securely access the XenApp site.

# Summary

In this chapter, you spent time on getting to know about the NetScaler appliance and configuring the appliance for the Citrix Gateway purpose so that when users are connecting to the XenApp site, they can access resources securely. You learned what NetScaler Gateway is. You also learned how to perform the initial configuration of NetScaler, configure NTP, configure high availability for NetScaler, create certificates for it, configure NetScaler for remote access, and modify StoreFront to integrate with NetScaler.

# Index

## A



## B



## C



## D

# X

Thank you for buying

**Mastering XenApp®**

# About Packt Publishing

Packt, pronounced 'packed', published its first book, *Mastering phpMyAdmin for Effective MySQL Management*, in April 2004, and subsequently continued to specialize in publishing highly focused books on specific technologies and solutions.

Our books and publications share the experiences of your fellow IT professionals in adapting and customizing today's systems, applications, and frameworks. Our solution-based books give you the knowledge and power to customize the software and technologies you're using to get the job done. Packt books are more specific and less general than the IT books you have seen in the past. Our unique business model allows us to bring you more focused information, giving you more of what you need to know, and less of what you don't.

Packt is a modern yet unique publishing company that focuses on producing quality, cutting-edge books for communities of developers, administrators, and newbies alike. For more information, please visit our website at `www.packtpub.com`.

# About Packt Enterprise

In 2010, Packt launched two new brands, Packt Enterprise and Packt Open Source, in order to continue its focus on specialization. This book is part of the Packt Enterprise brand, home to books published on enterprise software - software created by major vendors, including (but not limited to) IBM, Microsoft, and Oracle, often for use in other corporations. Its titles will offer information relevant to a range of users of this software, including administrators, developers, architects, and end users.

# Writing for Packt

We welcome all inquiries from people who are interested in authoring. Book proposals should be sent to `author@packtpub.com`. If your book idea is still at an early stage and you would like to discuss it first before writing a formal book proposal, then please contact us; one of our commissioning editors will get in touch with you.

We're not just looking for published authors; if you have strong technical skills but no writing experience, our experienced editors can help you develop a writing career, or simply get some additional reward for your expertise.

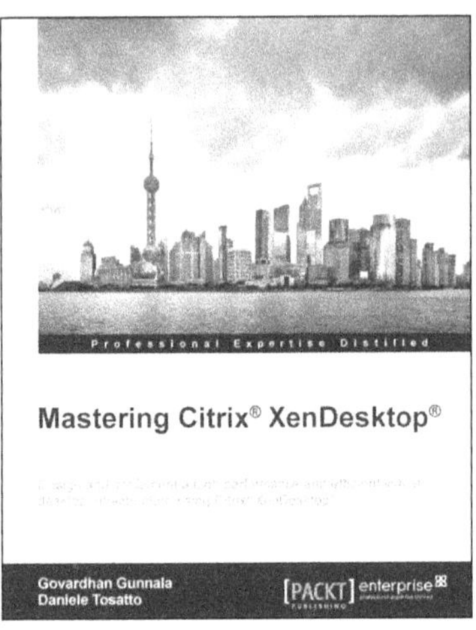

## Mastering Citrix® XenDesktop®

ISBN: 978-1-78439-397-7 Paperback: 484 pages

Design and implement a high performance and efficient virtual desktop infrastructure using Citrix® XenDesktop®

1. Design, deploy, configure, optimize, troubleshoot, and maintain XenDesktop for enterprise environments and to meet emerging high-end business requirements.
2. Configure Citrix XenDesktop to deliver a rich virtual desktop experience to end users.
3. A comprehensive, practical guide to monitoring a XenDesktop environment and automating XenDesktop tasks using PowerShell.

---

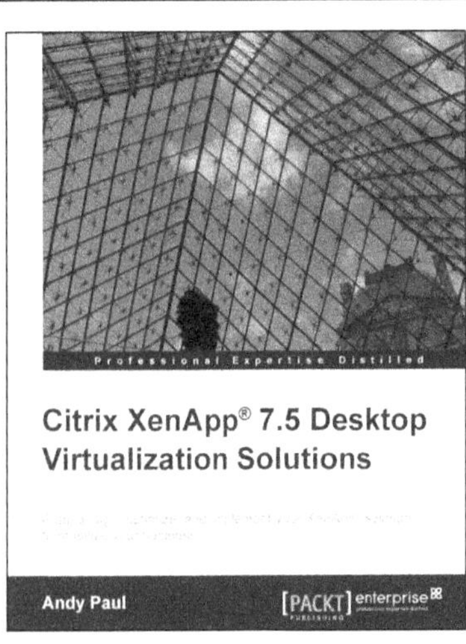

## Citrix XenApp® 7.5 Desktop Virtualization Solutions

ISBN: 978-1-84968-968-7 Paperback: 328 pages

Plan, design, optimize, and implement your XenApp® solution to mobilize your business

1. Optimize your XenApp solution for the best end user experience.
2. Design a robust infrastructure for application and desktop delivery.
3. Easy to follow guide that will help you to utilize the capabilities of the Citrix XenApp environment.

Please check **www.PacktPub.com** for information on our titles

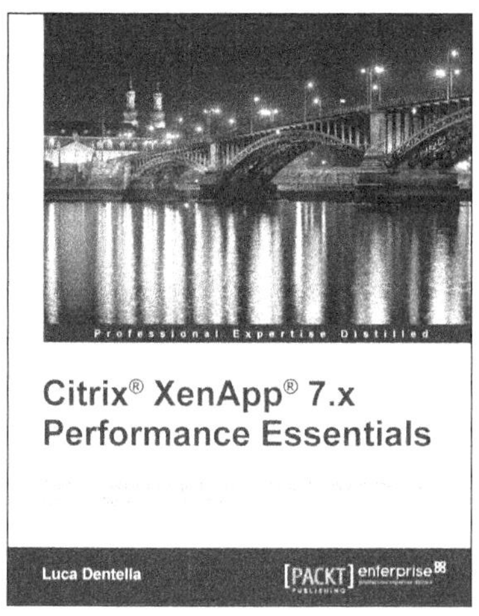


## Citrix® XenApp® 7.x Performance Essentials

ISBN: 978-1-78217-611-4 Paperback: 120 pages

Tune and optimize the performance of your farms with the new improved XenApp® architecture

1. Monitor your infrastructure using the new tools, and learn how to optimize the end-user experience.
2. Discover the new FlexCast Management Architecture of XenApp 7.5 and its components.
3. Explore the new features designed for mobile and remote users.

---

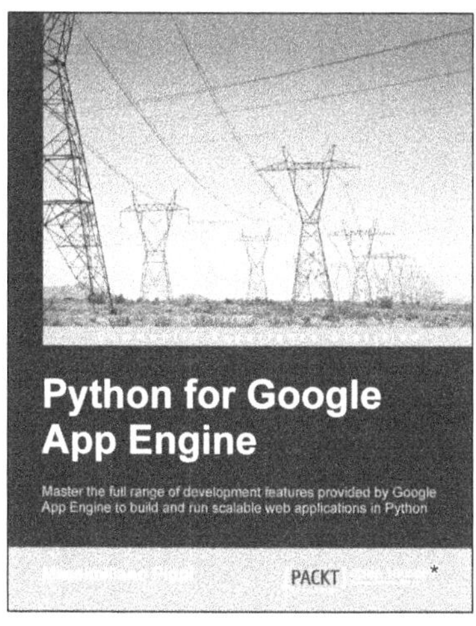


## Python for Google App Engine

ISBN: 978-1-78439-819-4 Paperback: 198 pages

Master the full range of development features provided by Google App Engine to build and run scalable web applications in Python

1. Use the power of Python to build full-fledged, scalable web applications running on Google's infrastructure.
2. Learn how to use Google Cloud Platform tools and services adding features and enriching your Python web applications.
3. Build a real-world web application in no time with this comprehensive step-by-step guide.

www.ingramcontent.com/pod-product-compliance
Lightning Source LLC
Chambersburg PA
CBHW061404210326
41598CB00035B/6097

* 9 7 8 1 7 8 5 2 8 4 8 6 1 *